Packed full of amazing insights, case studies and practical examples for implementing agile transformation across any organization.
Duncan Hammond, VP, Transformation, Warner Music

'Agile' and 'transformation' aren't just pretty words to say. They're the new way of operating business, and you can't afford to be left behind. You couldn't ask for a better expert guide on the journey than Neil Perkin.
Scott Brinker, VP, Platform Ecosystem, HubSpot; author of *Hacking Marketing*

An inspiring and practical guide to the why, what and how of transforming businesses to meet the challenges and opportunities of digital disruption. Neil Perkin's clear and succinct writing provides an accessible and comprehensive road map for leaders to drive customer focused digital innovation.
Judy Gibbon, Chairman, Wonderbly

Agile Transformation

*Structures, processes and mindsets
for the digital age*

SECOND EDITION

Neil Perkin

First edition published in Great Britain and the United States in 2020 by Kogan Page Limited
Second edition published in 2023

2nd Floor, 45 Gee Street
London
EC1V 3RS
United Kingdom

122 W 27th St, 10th Floor
New York, NY 10001
USA

4737/23 Ansari Road
Daryaganj
New Delhi 110002
India

www.koganpage.com

ISBNs

Hardback   978 1 3986 0880 1
Paperback   978 1 3986 0878 8
Ebook   978 1 3986 0879 5

British Library Cataloguing-in-Publication Data

A CIP record for this book is available from the British Library.

Library of Congress Cataloging-in-Publication Data
Names: Perkin, Neil, author.
Title: Agile transformation: structures, processes and mindsets for the
  digital age / Neil Perkin.
Description: Second edition. | London; New York, NY: Kogan Page, 2023. |
  Includes bibliographical references and index.
Identifiers: LCCN 2022055526 (print) | LCCN 2022055527 (ebook) | ISBN
  9781398608788 (paperback) | ISBN 9781398608801 (hardback) | ISBN
  9781398608795 (ebook)
Subjects: LCSH: Organizational change. | Strategic planning. | Business
  Enterprises–Technological innovations.
Classification: LCC HD58.8 .P467 2023 (print) | LCC HD58.8 (ebook) | DDC
  658.4/06–dc23/eng/20221118
LC record available at https://lccn.loc.gov/2022055526
LC ebook record available at https://lccn.loc.gov/2022055527

Typeset by Integra Software Services, Pondicherry
Print production managed by Jellyfish
Printed and bound by CPI Group (UK) Ltd, Croydon, CR0 4YY

CONTENTS

01

A new operating system for a new operating environment

Why this book, and why now?

Writing my first book on digital transformation[1] was something of a cathartic exercise for me, having worked for many years to help corporates of all types become more native to the digital empowered world in the way that they think and operate. At the time there was plenty of material that talked about the 'why' of transformation, but precious little that talked about the 'how'. The book was designed to fill this gap. And thankfully it seems to have struck a chord.

The work that I've undertaken since that first book came about, working with a broad range of large global businesses, has served to validate a lot of the approaches that I set out in that book but it has also opened the opportunity to go deeper into some of the fundamental areas of change and opportunity. I fully expect this book to also be a means to catharsis as, whilst the business environment has fundamentally changed forever, many companies still haven't truly adapted to face this challenge.

Digital technologies have impacted in countless ways to create a climate of rapidly changing competitive and consumer dynamics, heightened unpredictability and disruptive new market entrants, and yet many businesses remain stuck. Stuck in outdated modes of working that keep them from moving fast. Stuck with structures that originated in a different era and that actively hinder agility and horizontal collaboration. Stuck with processes that make bold innovation difficult if not impossible. Stuck with cultures that reward conformity and status rather than entrepreneurialism and originality. Stuck with approaches that celebrate efficiency over learning.

After several years of corporate focus on digital transformation many organizations still pursue rigid, linear change management programmes that are doomed to fail. Many still prioritize chasing shiny technology over empowering their people to drive lasting change. Many pay lip service to new ways of operating without ever really changing the fabric of how the organization works or building the culture that can genuinely support change.

More recently the potential of agile working and principles to generate business value far beyond technology teams has been recognized by some enlightened companies as a route to greater organizational agility. And yet in so many cases these principles remain poorly understood, undervalued, or badly applied. In some organizations the word 'agile' has become overused and abused to the point where it is no longer helpful, and where it fails to represent the true potential of what is possible. Many businesses are playing at the edges, or scratching the surface, or still failing to grasp the scale of change that is really needed.

If we are to truly reshape organizations for the new world we need to take a more sophisticated, adaptive approach to transformation. We need to rethink embedded assumptions about structures, processes and leadership that were born of a legacy, industrialized world. We need to understand how we can scale agile principles and culture appropriately to support lasting change. We need to take a far more sophisticated approach to the application of different ways of working, both new and old. There is a need to build on what has come before, to go beyond most interpretations of 'digital transformation' and to go deeper into fundamental aspects of organizational structure, process, culture and leadership to help define what organizational agility really means and help leaders of all kinds to build a practical roadmap for lasting change. There is a wider need to reimagine what the organization is, how it operates, and how it is led.

This book is about helping businesses to become unstuck. It is about generating an entirely new level of organizational agility. It is about transforming business to become truly fit for purpose for a very different world.

The new operating environment

The narrative is, by now, familiar. It is expressed in conference talks that speak of the 'Uberization' of entire industries, or in catchy soundbites like: 'the pace of change has never been this fast, yet it will never be this slow again'.[2] It is captured in visualizations like the one famously created by Nicholas Felton for the *New York Times* that shows how technology adoption is spreading faster than ever (the telephone took decades to reach a penetration of 50 per cent of US households yet the mobile phone took less than five years).[3] It is supported by studies such as that conducted by strategy and innovation consultancy Innosight (based on work originally done by Professor Richard Foster at Yale University) that showed that the average tenure of companies on the S&P 500 reduced from 33 years in 1964 to just 24 years in 2016 and is forecast to shrink to just 12 years by 2027.[4]

Just about every business is faced with an operating environment that is riven with heightened unpredictability and rapidly changing consumer, competitive and market contexts. And yet most businesses have grown up in a very different world. A world of greater stability in which contexts changed more slowly and allowed for greater time to sense and respond. A world where advantage came from leveraging scale and locked-down, hierarchically driven efficiency. A world characterized by rigidity in process and structure. A world of top-down leadership where all the answers flowed from the top of the organization downwards.

This new operating environment requires a very different organizational response. More than that, it requires a very different type of organization. Current structures and the dominant ways of thinking are the legacy of a very different environment, and are no longer fit for purpose for the modern world. Businesses of all types have an urgent need to transform to become far more adaptive and responsive to rapid change. They need to innovate not just episodically, but continuously. They need to optimize for the present whilst also designing and creating for the future and they need to do this continuously. They need leadership and cultures that support moving fast, greater experimentation and a wholly different way of operating.

This is beyond setting up an innovation lab or a few agile teams. It is beyond sending the board for a trip to Silicon Valley. It is beyond investing in a big piece of new technology.

This is about agile transformation of the entire organization.

Avoiding the Wile E Coyote effect

One of the challenges inherent in digital disruption is that by the time it becomes widely evident that your business is being disrupted it is often already too late to do anything meaningful about it. Analyst Benedict Evans has described this as the 'Wile E Coyote effect' – the problem of lagging indicators and how headline metrics that companies often focus on tend to be the last ones to start slowing down. This can ultimately mean that at the point when it is most critical for an incumbent to innovate, everything can still look pretty good for that business and the leadership sees no reason to change trajectory. This is, however, precisely the time when a new technology or model enters the market and starts to rapidly erode the dominance of the existing model. Hence the Wile E Coyote effect:

> you've run off the cliff, but you're not falling, and everything seems fine. But by the time you start falling, it's too late[5]

Ben points at ex-Apple executive Michael Mace's analysis of BlackBerry, written just at the point of their collapse. Mace noted at the time that BlackBerry's market was saturating, they had seemingly lost the ability to create great products, and were drifting into a situation where they could not afford the investments needed to succeed in the future (a line that is easily crossed and very difficult to rectify).[6] The history of failed computer platforms, he says, tells us that the early symptoms of decline are typically very subtle and easily rationalized away by executives. Like Wile E Coyote, by the time the symptoms become obvious, you're hanging in mid-air with nothing beneath you:

> Nokia and BlackBerry were skating to where the puck was going to be, and felt nice and fast and in control, while Apple and Google were melting the ice rink and switching the game to water-skiing.[7]

In Ernest Hemingway's 1926 novel *The Sun Also Rises* the character Mike Campbell is asked about his money troubles:

> 'How did you go bankrupt?' Bill asked.
> 'Two ways,' Mike said. 'Gradually and then suddenly.'[8]

The point is that disruption is the same. When it begins you don't necessarily notice it because all your leading indicators are still pointing in the same direction, but then it can happen very quickly.

FIGURE 1.1 BlackBerry sales (US $ millions)[9]

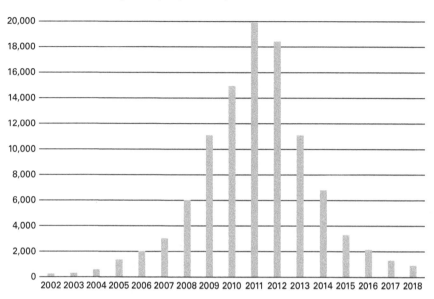

Tracking simple measures such as revenue over time can hide the real picture of what is about to happen. Mace, for example, writes about how the key symptoms to watch are small declines in two key metrics: the rate of growth of sales, and gross profit per unit sold (gross margins). As products move through the traditional diffusion curve from early adopters, through early and late majority to late adopters, pricing incentives may well be used to help boost sales and growth.

In the early stages as the product moves from innovators to early adopters, for example, we may introduce a pricing incentive to accelerate growth. Then as we reach the transition from early adopters to early majority we may cut prices in order to enter the mainstream. As the technology matures and the middle portion of this curve gets consumed the company may introduce another price incentive, perhaps to hit short-term sales targets, and this may still act to boost sales and so lead to the belief that the product is truly hitting the mainstream. Yet without realizing it (and bearing in mind that the market for any given product is finite), rather than reaching the real mainstream market you are instead consuming the late adopters. This, in effect means that you can then fall off the cliff:

> Companies tend to assume that because the adoption curve is drawn as a smooth-sided bell, your demand will tail off at the end as gradually as it built up in the beginning. But that isn't how it works.[10]

It may take a good deal of time and effort in the early stages to build up momentum, but as the technology or product matures and you begin to saturate your market the momentum you have built up through well-optimized brand, marketing and distribution means that you 'gulp' through the late adopters rapidly and sales continue to grow until they suddenly drop. Hence the Wile E Coyote effect.

In this scenario, gross margin has declined over time but sales may still improve until they drop very quickly. The key then, is to track a broader set of metrics to enable a more rounded picture, and to be adept at recognizing those early signals and be prepared to reorient the organization towards experimentation rather than simply efficiency.

CASE STUDY
Kodak and Fujifilm

Kodak is one of those totem exemplars of digital disruption, often characterized as a business whose leaders ignored or failed to recognize the impending developments in (and implications of) digital technology. Yet the reality is far more nuanced and enlightening.

Famously, it was Steven Sasson, an engineer who worked for Kodak, who invented digital photography and made the first digital camera in 1975. Management were, it seems, initially sceptical about the early prototype. But as Willy Shih a former Kodak staffer noted, when the technology began to develop further and gain scale Kodak management were very aware of the encroachment of digital and continuously tracked the rate at which digital was replacing film.[11] The disruption, however, brought challenges on multiple fronts which, rather than catalysing change, contributed to inertia. Most notably:

- Making film was an enormously complex manufacturing process meaning that barriers to entry were high, competition limited. In short, it was characterized by scarcity.

- Digital imaging on the other hand, based on general-purpose semiconductor technology that had its own scale and learning curves but also broad applicability, had commoditized the market and had far fewer barriers to entry.

- The technology was well outside Kodak's core capability, making it difficult to compete and to offer something distinctive.

- The modularity of digital cameras meant that you no longer needed highly specialized skills and experience. Modularization commoditizes – any engineer could put one together with component parts.

- A large incumbent business like Kodak had invested over time in manufacturing and distribution efficiencies and benefited from economies of scale – when sales and production decline, those benefits matter less, and many of the gains that you could once capitalize on work against you as volumes decline.

- The problem of declining scale and securing sufficient shelf space through its retail distribution network was exacerbated since, in Kodak's case, the cause wasn't new competitors – the entire category was disappearing.

- Management didn't talk about the issues publicly for fear of making it a self-fulfilling prophecy but Kodak was caught – it couldn't abandon billions of dollars of profits when it didn't have any new products to capture demand.

- Kodak's entire ecosystem that had been built over decades was one that only supported film-based photography (retail partners made large profits from photo finishing, for example, which brought customers in-store multiple times). As these advantages reduced, management underappreciated the rapidity of the decline in photo printing, and retailers became less loyal to the Kodak brand.

- Kodak did actually have a separate division (unconstrained by legacy approaches) that was established to explore and develop the digital opportunity. This did see some success, achieving a good share position in digital cameras, only then to be consumed in the tsunami of smartphones with built-in cameras.

- Kodak experienced great difficulty in managing the complex (and emotionally charged) people issues surrounding a business in decline – thousands of staff who knew that they were managing decline but struggling with transferable skills, managers fighting for control of diminishing resources, or feeling entitled to be reassigned, which fuelled internal politics and strife.

Kodak faced huge challenges on multiple fronts – competitive, category, operational and ecosystem – but it is too simplistic to say that its downturn to eventual bankruptcy protection was solely down to its inability to recognize that digital was coming. Yes, Kodak failed to look ahead and anticipate the level and type of impact that the next wave of technology (and its application) would have. But along the way, there was a litany of compounding factors that made change difficult, and which are instructive for any legacy business.

Large businesses need to retain the capacity for bold thinking and a willingness to reinvent, even if that means that you will be misunderstood. As Jeff Bezos of Amazon once said:

A big piece of the story we tell ourselves about who we are, is that we are willing to invent. We are willing to think long-term. We start with the customer and work backwards. And, very importantly, we are willing to be misunderstood for very long periods of time. I believe if you don't have that set of things in your corporate culture, then you can't do large-scale invention.[12]

Kodak is the classic case study of a large business getting stuck. In his account of the decline, Willy Shih says that, in hindsight, one approach that Kodak might have taken would be to refocus the business to compete on capabilities rather than on the markets it was in.[13] This kind of thinking is helpful in that it might allow the business to apply its skills and knowledge in different ways to explore new value, but also to challenge the kind of toxic assumptions that Kodak fell victim to.

The story of how Fujifilm responded to exactly the same challenges that Kodak faced is a stark contrast to this. Like Kodak, digital technology presented an existential threat to Fujifilm's core business and advantage. Under Shigetaka Komori and Kenji Sukeno, the leadership team recognized early on that demand for conventional film was going to disappear within a decade and so they focused on how the company might apply its technical expertise that had been garnered over decades in completely new ways. They began with an inventory check of Fujifilm's technological expertise and considered multiple options for how they might reapply and leverage that capability before deciding to build two separate but connected businesses in life sciences and cosmetics.

Moving into beauty products was no small leap for the company but management realized that their knowledge of collagen, the material that is used to stop film from deteriorating and fading, could be used to create an anti-aging skincare product line that they called Astalift. With pharmaceuticals, they realized that alongside realigning their technical expertise they would need to acquire an entirely new customer base and so they acquired Toyama Chemical, a poorly performing mid-sized drugs manufacturer, to help accelerate their capability. They then built on this acquisition by improving the efficiency of the plants and launching new drugs to combat influenza and Ebola. Alongside beauty and pharma, the company also started producing computer storage devices and printing hardware.

This radical diversification helped to not only cushion the impact of falling film sales but maintained their profitability. The transition was not without its difficulties. Along the way they cut costs by over US $500 million, shut down manufacturing facilities and had to sacrifice 5,000 jobs.

Healthcare and cosmetics are now Fujifilm's most profitable divisions, yet the company hasn't forgotten its heritage, nor the photography culture that came with it, and it still produces film even though it contributes less than 1 per cent of the company's profits. In 2012, the year that Kodak filed for Chapter 11 bankruptcy protection, Fujifilm's diversified revenues were more than US $21.4 billion. That same year the company re-launched the Instax mini camera, recognizing that not everything is digital, and now sells millions of Instax cameras worldwide.

A key task of the leadership was bringing their people on the journey with them and encouraging a more open and transparent approach to creating value rather than the closed, protective approach that had characterized filmmaking. They realized that they needed to become far more attuned to the needs of their potential customers and how they might solve their problems. Fujifilm have built three open innovation hubs to support this continuing diversification and creation of new value. As company president Kenji Sukeno said more recently of the story that he told to people in the business:

> What I suggested was that we open Fujifilm's technical capability to the world, so that the world can look at it and then come to us saying, 'If we combine Fujifilm's technology and our technology, we can come up with this particular solution'. This is what I suggested to them.[14]

Fujifilm's story provides an excellent counterpoint to that of Kodak. Fujifilm was willing to think big, to be bold about setting a new direction and then invest in taking the company firmly in that direction. Kodak got stuck. Fujifilm didn't.

The nuance of radical change

Many things around us are changing quite profoundly, and faster than ever before. But not everything changes. In order to make smarter decisions about the response to change and avoid becoming overly distracted or tactical in chasing the latest new shiny technology with questionable value, we need to understand both what is changing and what is not.

As Jeff Bezos once said:

> I very frequently get the question: 'What's going to change in the next 10 years?' And that is a very interesting question; it's a very common one. I almost never get the question: 'What's not going to change in the next 10 years?' And I submit to you that that second question is actually the more important of the two – because you can build a business strategy around the things that are stable in time.[15]

Bezos talks about how fundamental customer needs like access to a great product range, good value, cheap prices and fast delivery remain constant. Fundamental needs change slowly, if at all. So that affords the opportunity to invest energy and focus in areas that you know will pay dividends over the long term. Essential elements like these should be the guiding North Star for any business.

Yet the way in which we may deliver to these fundamental needs has been affected by rapid and dramatic change, so let's be clear about what these changes are and what they mean.

CAPABILITY ACCESS

The democratization and widespread availability of new and potentially transformational enterprise and automation services means that even the smallest startup now has access to scaled capability that was once only the domain of large, well-funded businesses. Barriers to entry have been vastly reduced. For example, with the right approach any business regardless of scale can access some of the best digital infrastructure technology, analytics tools and open-source machine learning capability currently available (simple examples include the suite of services available via Amazon Web Services and Google Tensorflow).

This radical democratization and proliferation of digital technology infrastructure enables early-stage businesses to combine the nimbleness and adaptability of a smaller company with the scaled capabilities of a much larger one. The impact has been compounded as the adoption rate for each wave of new infrastructure technologies has become ever faster, and this has been amplified by increasing economic liberalization and globalization. Economic activity can now be effectively coordinated at global scale in far more cost-efficient ways enabling more rapid scaling within and across markets.

ACCESS TO KNOWLEDGE AND EXPERTISE

The democratization of information has fundamentally changed the value dynamic. The value of specialist expertise has not diminished but when we can find the answer to pretty much any question on Google, and harness internal and external expertise more easily than ever (and even access some of the best teaching online for free, like courses from Stanford University), advantage shifts from being focused on the stocks of knowledge that we have built up in the business over time to being more about the flow of ideas and knowledge, how we apply it, and what we choose to do with it.

The democratization of information has led to far more empowered consumers, changing the dynamic between company and customer forever. Greater transparency in pricing, brand provenance, company culture and peer review has led to new margin and reputation pressures and broken down the information asymmetry between organizations, their customers and employees.

DATA

An elemental part of this shift in the information dynamic is, of course, the ability to access, filter and utilize the wealth of data that are now being continually generated. This is clearly not new news but businesses need to get better at extracting value from data by structuring good quality data, interpreting patterns and meaning, and originating processes that can execute against actionable insights quickly. And we've yet to scratch the surface of how machine learning will take this to a completely different level. Gartner's model for maturity in data analytics represents this as a progression of value from basic descriptive analytics (what happened) to diagnostic analytics (in which we understand why it happened), to predictive analytics (where we can predict what will happen), and eventually to prescriptive analytics (understanding how we can actually make it happen).

NETWORKED VALUE AND CONNECTIVITY

With the explosion in the connection of things and people, network dynamics have changed some fundamental ways in which we think about value creation. This is writ large in a diverse set of impacts from the development of platform business models and ecosystems that have changed competitive dynamics considerably in some sectors, an exponential growth in the flow of data through APIs, the operational efficiency gains that can be derived from connected machines, the rapidity in which ideas and content can spread through networks, the eroding of traditional barriers like geographical borders and market boundaries, and the ease with which collaboration can happen.

LOWERING TRANSACTION COSTS

Digital has completely changed the cost dynamic in many areas of value chains, reducing key elements of some chains to zero marginal cost and enabling dramatic changes in efficiency and new entrants to compete at relative scale from a small base. The concept of value chains, originated by Michael Porter in the 1980s, has long been a way to express the set of activities undertaken by a business to deliver value to market in the form of a product or service. Competitive advantage comes from the sum or the average of its transaction costs across the string of components that make up the value chain, and the ability of the company to lower transaction costs through standardization and improvements in efficiency. New digital infrastructures and technologies have enabled dramatic changes in cost efficiency and differentiation to the extent that it has resulted in the rewiring of entire value chains, not only changing competitive dynamics but opening up markets to wholly new types of competitors. Growing automation will continue to generate significant opportunity in this way.

THE SHIFT FROM PRODUCTS TO SERVICES

As connection between people, objects and machines becomes ubiquitous, and digital technologies are integrated into an ever-increasing number of products in new and ingenious ways, more and more products are becoming services – characterized by connection, continual iteration and improvement, enhanced propositions and deepening relationships over time. So we have the Tesla car that improves its performance over time as its software continually updates. We have digitally connected thermostats and door locks that enable you to control your home remotely. And we have connected toothbrushes that as well as telling you how to brush better give you discounts on dental insurance when you do. In a relatively short space of time we have had a proliferation of 'as a service' offerings in everything from software, manufacturing, shopping, transportation, content, health and education.

For organizations this presents both opportunity in the form of the advantage that can come from exceptional customer experience combined with dramatically lowered transaction costs, but also significant challenge for businesses not well practised in service design and innovation. Now product/service improvement is continuous rather than episodic. Fixes and enhancements are continuous and frequent, requiring a different rhythm to the business. The role of data, analytics, customer experience and content become a key differentiator, but this also runs alongside continually increasing customer expectation, the need for ongoing adaptability and greater responsiveness in direct-to-consumer relationships and supply chain, shortened cycles and more transient advantage, new aggregation possibilities, and greater risk shifting to the value generation rather than consumption side.

A succession of industries from retail, entertainment and media to now banking, insurance, education, automotive, logistics, and even consumer packaged goods are being disrupted by new market entrants, new customer relationship dynamics, and nimble, digitally focused propositions. For incumbents the danger of being disintermediated (where market intermediaries are usurped or replaced) or 'unbundled' (where a multiplicity of smaller, nimble competitors attacks a product or service portfolio) has never been greater.

For many, the threat of 'horizontal innovation', or the rapid entrance and scaling of new, digital-native players into the market looms large, making it hard to see where your next competitor is going to come from. The potential for technologically adept and nimble young and not so young (Amazon was launched in 1994) businesses reconfiguring a market through software and then reapplying their capabilities horizontally by moving into entirely new markets is very real. The development of new digital infrastructure and highly adaptive ways of working enables them to move fast and scale fast.

SCALING DYNAMICS

Digital networks have brought with them a dramatic shift in scalability that gives individual people access to a global market, small teams the ability to originate and scale transformational ideas, and businesses with finite resources to have disproportionate impact. Pre-digital, for example, it would potentially have taken decades for a business to expand to a global scale yet in a little over six years Netflix was able to complete an international expansion that has taken them into no fewer than 190 countries worldwide.[16] At the same time ease of access to global markets, global talent and capability has transformed approaches to outsourcing and talent networks enabling far greater scalability and flexibility in resourcing.

Ray Kurzweil used the phrase the 'second half of the chessboard' to describe how exponentially growing factors can significantly impact business strategy. The 'wheat and chessboard problem' is a mathematical problem based on identifying the total number of grains of wheat that you would end up with if you were to place one grain of wheat on the first square and double it every subsequent square on the board. The story is often told of how the inventor of chess (who some say was an ancient Indian minister) requested that his ruler give him wheat according to this rule as a reward for his invention. The ruler scoffed at this apparent meagre reward, until his court treasurers came to him and said that there was not enough wheat in the kingdom to fulfil the request. This is because the number of grains rises exponentially. For the first half of the board the total number is large but manageable, at 4,294,967,295 grains, or around 279 tonnes of wheat. The numbers in the second half rapidly become too vast to manage. And by the time you'd finished the entire chessboard would have 18,446,744,073,709,551,615 grains of wheat, equivalent to about 1,199,000,000,000 metric tonnes. To give some context, that is over one and a half thousand times as big as the total global wheat production in a year.[17]

Not everything that digital enables becomes exponential, of course, but network effects and compounding loops have the potential to bring very different scaling dynamics to bear in critical areas.

CUSTOMER EXPECTATION

Whilst some areas of consumer behaviour are changing rapidly, more fundamental needs are arguably not. But customer expectation is changing fast and changing all the time. Services like Lemonade Insurance, Monzo, Revolut, Netflix, Uber and Amazon set a new bar for customer experience that raises customer expectation (not only in category but more broadly across sectors) for how easy to use and convenient services should really be.

In spite of the promise of technology to simplify, the reality is that technology also creates growing interdependencies and challenges with competing ecosystems that can result in poor interoperability and unnecessary friction. In spite of there being more insight and data available than ever into customers' needs, wants and frustrations, many customer journeys are broken and many interactions designed around the needs of the business rather than the end-user.

This continuously rising benchmark for customer experience creates a significant challenge to businesses that are not able to operate in adaptive, customer-centric ways, but also significant advantage for those that can deliver well and use raised expectation as a catalyst for innovation. Jeff Bezos (in his 2018 annual letter to shareholders) said:

> One thing I love about customers is that they are divinely discontent. Their expectations are never static – they go up. It's human nature.[18]

Bezos describes how the cycle of improvement required to serve customer appetite for better solutions is happening faster than ever, but the phrase 'divinely discontent' demonstrates how the real opportunity is to use continually rising customer expectation to challenge your teams to do it better or do it differently.

As we'll go on to discuss, digital is, of course, exceptionally adept at rewriting the rules of competitive advantage but when rapid disruption can come from anywhere, markets and environments are becoming increasingly unpredictable, and disintermediation is happening quicker than ever before, we need to reimagine our response and reorientate our organizations towards a new and consistently higher level of organizational agility.

Why companies become resistant to change

Why do businesses become inflexible over time? In their study relating to a dynamic theory of organizational rigidity researchers Arijit Mukherjee and Luis Vasconcelos found that the way that a company responds to adverse challenges can contribute to companies becoming increasingly rigid over time.[19] Despite many organizations' efforts to encourage their teams to adapt to localized or new information, when the company suffers a negative shock of some kind (such as rapid changes in market conditions, failed products or a drop in revenues) a typical response is to attempt to get back on track by implementing standardized procedures that 'ignore local infor-mation but yield satisfactory (though suboptimal) performance'. The study concludes that adopting these standardized processes may help the company to survive the shock in the short term, but it generates inefficiencies in the future. As the researchers say:

> Although the firm may recover, it becomes more vulnerable to future shocks, and consequently, more reliant on the standardized work procedures.[20]

Standardization of procedures is essential for businesses to scale but when new and significant contexts emerge, an agile business needs to recognize to adapt processes to new local information. Failure to do so simply serves to make companies more fragile over time and susceptible to the kind of disruption which can come from overly rigid and entrenched approaches.

Resistance to change can also be amplified by the social constructs and behaviours that emerge around how the company has dealt with challenge and opportunity over time. These previous experiences can create an expectation around behaviours and approaches which can prove hard to change. As the relationships between people and stakeholders in the organization mature around existing models, technologies or ways in which the organization has solved problems in the past, it can prove increasingly difficult to unpack these informal social structures. Relationship status can be a powerful driver of inertia within businesses. Stakeholders naturally want to protect their status within the organization and when something happens which requires a modification to that status people can become resistant to change and the environment can become increasingly political.

Instead, businesses need to become what Nassim Nicholas Taleb would call 'Antifragile'. In his book on the topic Taleb delineates between robustness, resilience and antifragility.[21] Rigidity can cause a business to become to increasingly fragile over time, meaning that it is more likely to break in the face of any kind of negative shock. If a company is robust, then it is more likely to be able to resist and push back against known challenges and stresses but it is not doing so through adaptation. If a company is resilient, it may be able to better absorb the impact of adverse occurrences, but it still attempts to re-establish itself as close as possible to its original state. As Taleb describes, however, an antifragile system is one that *improves* as a result of failures and significant challenges. This is the difference between a rigid organization which retrenches and is resistant to change, and an agile or antifragile one which rapidly adapts to new contexts and thrives within a fast-changing environment.

The future of disruption: solving the big problems

As the sources of disruption broaden, so the types of disruption are evolving too. With new waves of technological capability and application such as machine learning, the 'internet of things' and predictive analytics becoming increasingly democratized and widespread, they are enabling a new generation of challenges to be addressed. We are, as renowned analyst Ben Evans of venture capitalist firm Andreessen Horowitz has eloquently described it, reaching 'the end of the beginning' of digital disruption.[22]

Evans has pointed out that three-quarters of the people in the world are now digitally connected and the rest will follow, meaning that the 'access story' of the internet age is approaching its end but instead the 'use story' is just beginning. The first 20 years of the internet has largely been about comparatively easier, albeit disruptive, jobs that digital has enabled us to do based on aggregation, information arbitrage, comparison and new routes to market. As connection between people and things becomes truly ubiquitous the nature of disruption moves from reimagining the easier, more obvious areas towards harder and larger markets, opportunities and problem areas.

So rather than it being about transport information, ticketing and services it becomes about self-driving cars and infrastructure. Rather than it being about financial services, transactions and payments it becomes about cryptocurrency and the nature of money itself. Rather than it being about e-commerce and digital sales it becomes about logistics, consumer enablement and a much larger slice of total consumer spending. As Evans says:

> Tech is building different kinds of businesses, and so will take different shares of that opportunity, but more importantly change what those industries look like. Tesla isn't interesting because of what it does to gasoline, but because of what it does to the car. Netflix changes TV, but so does Twitch.[23]

As connected, electric vehicles become the norm, for example, they can repair themselves, recharge and even improve performance remotely, removing the need for petrol stations, car maintenance and parts.

The point is that digital disruption will not stop. The next wave will remake industries and markets all over again as digital solves these larger problems and results in even bigger change. Just as the first wave of disruption and innovation was catalysed by the open, decentralized, permissionless and networked nature of the internet, so technologies such as machine learning and crypto will provide new permissionless layers that will support fundamentally new ways to create value.

The changing nature of advantage

Given the evolving nature of digital disruption and the continuing heightened unpredictability that it brings, it has never been more important for organizational strategy and capability to be adaptive to changing contexts. Yet still much corporate strategy remains unchanged and inflexible.

In 2014 Boston Consulting revisited their renowned growth share matrix, which famously maps a portfolio of products or services on a two-by-two matrix against growth and share, generating the categorizations of 'Cash Cows', 'Problem Children' (or question marks), 'Stars' and 'Dogs'.[24] This matrix has been a centrepiece of business school teaching since BCG founder Bruce Henderson originated it over 40 years ago, as a way to understand how companies could make sensible investment decisions based on sustainable returns, cost-efficiencies and growth potential that could lead to sustainable advantage.

The updated research mapped every US listed company to a quadrant on the matrix and found some fundamental ways in which it had changed. Comparing two five-year periods from 2008 to 2012 and 1988 to 1992, BCG found that companies in 75 per cent of industries were circulating far faster through the quadrants, and that the share of total profits that were captured by cash cows had declined by 25 per cent over 30 years. Cash cows were fewer, and their lifespan had dropped (by up to 55 per cent in some industries).

As rates of change have increased, the time between innovation and adoption has declined and margin volatility has gone up meaning that businesses need to constantly renew their advantage and improve the responsiveness and speed with which they shift resources amongst products, services and business units. The ability to rapidly adapt to and shape changing contexts has become a new driver of advantage. BCG's recommendation out of the research was for much greater focus on systematic (rather than episodic) experimentation to originate and rapidly develop a succession of promising new propositions.

This focus on constant renewal has been expressed by Columbia Business School professor Rita Gunther McGrath (in *The End of Competitive Advantage*[25]) as the shift from exploiting long-term, sustainable advantage to the ability to generate a series of transient competitive advantages that combine to maintain long-term positional and competitive benefit. Her analysis, based on looking at companies with a significant market capitalization that had outperformed over a 10-year period, revealed some specific characteristics that had enabled the standout businesses to exceed their competitors' performance over that extended period.

Most notable amongst these were the ability to continuously reconfigure operations, structures, talent and methods of execution whilst still maintaining stability in overall vision. The outliers were also adept at learning and systematically and frequently disengaging from advantages rather than clinging on to outmoded ones. They had an exceptional ability to manage resources in more fluid ways, overcome cross-functional politics and rapidly organize resources around new opportunities. They had established governance and budgeting processes to embed continuous and systematic innovation and experimentation, and balance resource allocation better across core capabilities, growth opportunities and entirely new propositions. They had leadership that enabled talent to be oriented rapidly around emerging opportunity.

For too long we have largely seen strategy and innovation as separate competencies and areas of focus. Corporate strategy has become inflexible, often poorly articulated, and slow to respond to rapidly changing contexts. Innovation has become episodic, often poorly executed or scaled, and separated from the key functions of the business. If continuous innovation is to become a core capability of the business we need far better ways to system-atically and perpetually originate, commercialize and scale new concepts and propositions. We need far greater fluidity around how we allocate resourcing to be able to scale up and scale down rapidly as the need dictates. We need the cultures and the mindset that can support continual but produc-tive change, focused flexibility and adaptability and learning.

Changing the way that we work

Generating advantage from new technologies requires new ways of thinking and operating so that we might truly capitalize on the potential that they can deliver. Too often we look at the new through the lens of the old and misappropriate old thinking onto new technology paradigms. Too often we focus on applying new technologies to existing operating challenges, processes or methods without rethinking how we might need to fundamen-tally redesign the way in which we need to work.

One of the greatest lessons in how we can misappropriate new technolo-gies and fail to capitalize on their transformational potential comes from the introduction of electricity to factories and manufacturing in the 19th century. Thomas Edison, credited with inventing the phonograph, the light bulb, the motion picture camera amongst many other innovations, was also responsi-ble for patenting a system for electricity distribution. Yet despite Edison building the first electricity generating stations in 1882 and the first electric motors driving manufacturing machinery not long after that, 20 years later the vast majority of mechanical drive power in US factories still came from steam. This power came from a single, huge steam engine that typically turned a massive drive shaft that, in turn, powered a succession of subsidi-ary shafts, belts, hammers and presses. Factories were cacophonous, dangerous places to work, but the configuration, layout and organization of the factory was entirely driven by access to the shaft and the centralized steam-driven power source.

When electrification first came to factories, engineers simply replaced the big steam engines with big electric motors. But managers were disappointed with the level of productivity gain. In fact it took 20 to 30 years before significant benefits were seen.

Factory owners and managers failed to take advantage of the true poten-tial of this new power source because they made the mistake of viewing the new through the lens of the old. Electricity enabled power to be delivered efficiently to wherever it was needed, meaning that instead of one huge, centralized source powering everything, manufacturers could establish and maintain many smaller electric motors that could deliver localized power for localized needs.

This changed everything. As the economist Tim Harford notes:

> Steam-powered factories had to be arranged on the logic of the driveshaft.
> Electricity meant you could organize factories on the logic of a production line.[26]

The full potential of electrification could be realized only when entire working practices and processes were changed. The configuration of factories no longer needed to be organized around that centralized power source but could be far more decentralized and spread out. Economist Paul David has described how electrification made more lightly constructed, single-storey, linear factory layouts possible, within which machine placement could be configured in such a way to permit a far more rapid and reliable flow of materials through the plant.[27]

This meant that machines could be reoriented around the flow of materials rather than the flow of power, and only switched on when they were needed, so the pace of production could be set by the workers rather than the power source.

New ideas about manufacturing processes (like the automated production line) emerged as a result and became more widespread. But it wasn't just the architecture and production process that changed. This greater autonomy for workers changed the way that they were paid, recruited and trained, and the focus shifted towards quality of skills. There was resistance to change, of course, but as mains electricity became cheaper and more widespread change became inevitable. The previously unrealized productivity gains were achieved and exceeded but whilst the technology had now been around for 50 years, it was only when manufacturers implemented more fundamental changes in thinking, ways of organizing and working that the real potential became clear.

There is a stark parallel here with modern day digital transformation. In my first book, *Building the Agile Business Through Digital Transformation*,[28] we defined digital transformation as 'the transformation and reinvention of the resources, priorities and processes of a company in order to be fit for purpose in a digital-empowered world'. This definition is inspired by Clay Christensen who framed an organization's capabilities (what it can and cannot do) through those three broad areas: Resources (tangible ones like buildings and headcount, intangible ones like brands and IP); Priorities (the consensus on what's right to do, the values and the strategy); Processes (the formal or informal way in which the work gets done). As Christensen says, these aspects are mutually exclusive in that a part of a business cannot fit into more than one of the categories, but are also collectively exhaustive (put together the three categories account for everything inside of the business).

Digital technologies have been with us for years, but it is only through a fundamental reorientation of these elemental capabilities that the true potential can be realized.

References

1 Perkin, N and Abraham, P (2017) Building the Agile Business Through Digital Transformation, Kogan Page, London, https://www.koganpage.com/product/building-the-agile-business-9780749480394 (archived at https://perma.cc/6VH8-LG5D)

2 Trudeau, Justin [accessed 15 January 2019] The Pace of Change Has Never Been This Fast [Online] https://www.youtube.com/watch?v=fTl1YNTNb0g (archived at https://perma.cc/H7MV-RAKN)

3 The New York Times [accessed 5 February 2019] Consumption Spreads Faster Today [Online] https://archive.nytimes.com/www.nytimes.com/imagepages/2008/02/10/opinion/10op.graphic.ready.html (archived at https://perma.cc/XZN3-5D2E)

4 Innosight [accessed 15 January 2019] 2018 Corporate Longevity Forecast: Creative Destruction is Accelerating [Online] https://www.innosight.com/insight/creative-destruction/ (archived at https://perma.cc/9BSQ-MEZN)

5 Evans, Benedict [accessed 3 March 2019] Mobile Smartphones and Hindsight, February 2016 [Online] https://www.ben-evans.com/benedictevans/2016/2/19/mobile-smartphones-and-hindsight (archived at https://perma.cc/6ADB-HBXV)

6 Mace, Michael [accessed 3 March 2019] What's Really Wrong With BlackBerry, October 2010 [Online] http://mobileopportunity.blogspot.com/2010/10/whats-really-wrong-with-blackberry-and.html (archived at https://perma.cc/LLX6-7RKN)

7 Evans, Benedict [accessed 3 March 2019] Mobile Smartphones and Hindsight, February 2016 [Online] https://www.ben-evans.com/benedictevans/2016/2/19/mobile-smartphones-and-hindsight (archived at https://perma.cc/6ADB-HBXV)

8 Hemingway, Ernest (1994) The Sun Also Rises, New edn, Arrow [Online] https://www.goodreads.com/book/show/3876.The_Sun_Also_Rises (archived at https://perma.cc/V44W-ZN4A)

9 BlackBerry Sales ($ millions): [accessed 24 May 2011] Research In Motion Year-Over-Year Growth, Press Release, GuruFocus [Online] https://www.gurufocus.com/news/134176/research-in-motion-on-its-deathbed- (archived at

https://perma.cc/7FP9-FGJ4); [accessed 19 April 2015] 10 Year Financial Data of BlackBerry Ltd (NAS:BBRY), GuruFocus.com, *GuruFocus* [Online] https://www.gurufocus.com/symbollookup1.php?company=NAS:BBRY#bs (archived at https://perma.cc/9N4Y-66UL); Arthur, Charles [accessed 19 April 2015] Ten Things to Know About BlackBerry – and how much trouble it is (or isn't) in, *The Guardian* [Online] https://www.theguardian.com/technology/2014/sep/29/ten-things-to-know-blackberry-john-chen (archived at https://perma.cc/52RF-MCLF); BlackBerry Annual Information Form for Fiscal 2017 (PDF) [Online] https://www.blackberry.com/content/dam/blackberry-com/Documents/pdf/financial-reports/2017/q4fy2017/Q417_Financial_Statements.pdf (archived at https://perma.cc/TT5E-D3A5); BlackBerry Annual Information Form for Fiscal 2018 (PDF) [Online] https://www.blackberry.com/content/dam/blackberry-com/Documents/pdf/financial-reports/2018/q4fy2018/Q4FY2018_Financial_Information.pdf (archived at https://perma.cc/26GA-VTT6)

10 Mace, Michael [accessed 3 March 2019] What's Really Wrong With BlackBerry, October 2010 [Online] http://mobileopportunity.blogspot.com/2010/10/whats-really-wrong-with-blackberry-and.html (archived at https://perma.cc/LLX6-7RKN)

11 Shih, Will [accessed 12 March 2019] The Real Lessons from Kodak's Decline, Summer 2016, *MIT Sloan* [Online] https://sloanreview.mit.edu/article/the-real-lessons-from-kodaks-decline/ (archived at https://perma.cc/NY47-KEX3)

12 Manjoo, Farhad [accessed 12 March 2019] People Will Misunderstand You, August 2011, *Slate* [Online] http://www.slate.com/articles/technology/top_right/2011/08/people_will_misunderstand_you.html (archived at https://perma.cc/MU2E-NCFR)

13 Shih, Will [accessed 12 March 2019] The Real Lessons from Kodak's Decline, Summer 2016, *MIT Sloan* [Online] https://sloanreview.mit.edu/article/the-real-lessons-from-kodaks-decline/ (archived at https://perma.cc/NY47-KEX3)

14 Financial Times [accessed 12 March 2019] Fujifilm's Kenji Sukeno on Reinventing a Brand, January 2019 [Online] https://www.ft.com/content/c3bae264-fbb8-11e8-aebf-99e208d3e521 (archived at https://perma.cc/G93W-9677)

15 Inc. [accessed 10 February 2019] 20 Years Ago, Jeff Bezos Said This 1 Thing Separates People Who Achieve Lasting Success From Those Who Don't [Online]https://www.inc.com/jeff-haden/20-years-ago-jeff-bezos-said-this-1-thing-separates-people-who-achieve-lasting-success-from-those-who-dont.html (archived at https://perma.cc/5AN4-QQVB)

16 Netflix [accessed 5 February 2019] Where is Netflix Available? [Online] https://help.netflix.com/en/node/14164 (archived at https://perma.cc/M9X6-5LZZ)

17 Statista [accessed 6 April 2019] Global Wheat Production from 2011/2012 to 2018/2019 (in million metric tons) [Online] https://www.statista.com/ statistics/267268/production-of-wheat-worldwide-since-1990/ (archived at https://perma.cc/5JGL-3EJB)

18 Amazon [accessed 5 February 2019] Letter to Shareholders [Online] https:// www.sec.gov/Archives/edgar/data/1018724/000119312518121161/ d456916dex991.htm (archived at https://perma.cc/DRL5-8HS5)

19 Mukherjee, Arijit and Vasconcelos, Luis [accessed 24 August 2022] What Makes Agility Fragile? A dynamic theory of organizational rigidity, September 2022 [Online] https://pubsonline.informs.org/doi/10.1287/mnsc.2022.4512 (archived at https://perma.cc/F5KM-QXN7)

20 Mukherjee, Arijit and Vasconcelos, Luis [accessed 24 August 2022] What Makes Agility Fragile? A dynamic theory of organizational rigidity, September 2022 [Online] https://pubsonline.informs.org/doi/10.1287/mnsc.2022.4512 [last accessed 24.08.22] (archived at https://perma.cc/E4JT-DHPW)

21 Taleb, Nassim Nicholas (2012) *Antifragile: Things that gain from disorder,* *Penguin*

22 Evans, Benedict [accessed 2 February 2019] The End of the Beginning [Online] https://www.ben-evans.com/benedictevans/2018/11/16/the-end-of-the-beginning (archived at https://perma.cc/6DTE-67ZH)

23 Evans, Benedict [accessed 2 February 2019] The End of the Beginning [Online] https://www.ben-evans.com/benedictevans/2018/11/16/the-end-of-the-beginning (archived at https://perma.cc/6DTE-67ZH)

24 BCG [accessed 5 January 2019] BCG Classics Revisited: The growth share matrix [Online] https://www.bcg.com/en-gb/publications/2014/growth-share-matrix-bcg-classics-revisited.aspx (archived at https://perma.cc/TG3L-FVRS)

25 MacGrath, RG (2013) *The End of Competitive Advantage: How to keep your strategy moving as fast as your business*, Harvard Business Review Press

26 Harford, Tim [accessed 1 February 2019] Why Didn't Electricity Immediately Change Manufacturing? [Online] https://www.bbc.co.uk/news/ business-40673694 (archived at https://perma.cc/K2J6-AW4H)

27 David, Paul A and Wright, Gavin [accessed 18 June 2019] General Purpose Technologies and Surges in Productivity: Historical reflections on the future of the ICT revolution, Discussion Papers in Economic and Social History, Number 31, September 1999, *University of Oxford* [Online] https://www. nuffield.ox.ac.uk/economics/history/paper31/a4.pdf (archived at https://perma. cc/W5QJ-AVPJ)

28 Perkin, N and Abraham, P (2017) *Building the Agile Business Through Digital Transformation*, Kogan Page, London [Online] https://www.koganpage.com/ product/building-the-agile-business-9780749480394 (archived at https:// perma.cc/6VH8-LG5D)

02

The agile business

Defining the agile business

My first book *Building the Agile Business Through Digital Transformation*[1] defined a useful maturity model for understanding what a true digital-native, agile business should look like. This was focused around three key stages of development:

1 **Legacy:** this is the state before the agile transformation journey begins, where traditional approaches, thinking and processes still dominate.

   a. Customers – Multichannel, not omnichannel, company orients around efficiency rather than customer need.

   b. Planning and process – Rigid waterfall processes, fixed approaches to planning, waterfall project management, infrequent release cycle, control centralized.

   c. Resources – Siloed data sources, basic analysis tools, descriptive analytics, technology restricts, legacy platforms, isolated knowledge, vertical skillsets, poor training, organizational structures oriented around functional silos, rigid structures that don't adapt to opportunity.

   d. Strategy – Digital capability development not central to organizational strategy/KPIs, clinging to legacy advantage, episodic innovation, short-term view.

   e. Vision – Assumes retention of existing advantage, lack of clarity around organizational direction or purpose on the ground.

   f. Culture – Precise, slow, controlling, restrictive, focused on efficiency, incremental improvement, highly discursive.

2 **Enabled:** the business is in the midst of the journey, and has likely adopted many of the foundational shifts in mindset, strategy, process, resources and culture, but there is still work to do to fully embed, extend and realize the full potential value of these new elements.

   a. Customers – Organization orients around customer need, joined-up processes and data create coherent, consistent, high-quality customer experience.

   b. Planning and process – Agile development, SCRUM, test and learn, deployment of rapid prototyping and build, operations empowered by digital, strong governance, measurement frameworks.

   c. Resources – Software-as-a-service, integrated technology stack, flexible partnerships, joining up data, basic modelling, predictive analytics, centres of excellence, specialists and generalists, tech skills, more fluid structures, collaborative environment, integrated digital and online/offline.

   d. Strategy – Systematically designed innovation process, more fluidity to strategy and planning, innovation accounting.

   e. Vision – Compelling vision and strategy, strong link between vision and organizational priorities/KPIs, rigid execution of vision.

   f. Culture – Collaborative, customer-centric, data-driven, focus on talent, challenging norms, ownership mindset, greater autonomy, learning from failures as well as successes.

3 **Native:** the business is native to the fluid, rapidly changing environment in which it operates, and this is reflected right across the organization in the fabric of its culture and how it operates.

   a. Customers – Seamless, rapid customer feedback loops inform strategies, tactics, innovation and continuous improvement.

   b. Planning and process – Interdisciplinary agility, cross-functional, small, nimble teams, embracing of uncertainty, permission to fail, rapid test and learn embedded throughout, Lean methodologies, embedded digital operations, data-driven and adaptive processes.

   c. Resources – Structures and resourcing oriented around the customer, continuous reconfiguration of resourcing, flexible, adaptive structures, organizing around opportunity, joined-up data/tech, prescriptive analytics, empowered frontline staff, customized dashboards, scalability of the cloud, actionable modelling, real-time decisions, T-shaped, deep knowledge, human layer over tech, fluid flow of knowledge.

d. Strategy – Fully agile and adaptive strategy, systematic and embedded experimentation, healthy disengagement from legacy advantage, long-term view.

e. Vision – Clear organizational purpose and vision lived through leadership and operations, evident in explicit tactics and implicit behaviours, adaptive execution of vision.

f. Culture – Highly fluid/collaborative, agile culture, 'fast and roughly right', entrepreneurial, empowered teams, distributed authority, bias to action, 10X thinking, networked, embedded learning culture.

This model provides a useful vision for what good looks like in agile transformation, but as well as understanding the fundamentals of agile working and thinking, it is vitally important to acknowledge the critical mindset shifts that are involved in transitioning at scale from more traditional ways of working.

Following a comprehensive agile transformation one Asian insurer was found by McKinsey to have improved their speed to market by a factor of between 5 and 7, their productivity by 20–30 per cent, customer satisfaction by 20–30 percentage points and staff engagement by a similar margin. The benefits of applying agile ways of working are as broad as they are deep, with the opportunity of dramatically improving multiple facets of organizational and customer value.[2]

Scaling agile principles

The word 'agile' has become well worn as many businesses seek to become nimbler and more adaptive, and yet agile principles and ways of working are often poorly articulated, poorly understood and poorly applied. We might call this the 'agile gap' – the chasm that can often open up between a high-level, basic understanding of some agile terms and a scaled implementation of agile thinking and working that supports change, enables a sensible approach to the application of different methodologies to solve different problems, develops a broad appreciation of agile culture, and as I'll discuss later in the book enables a good balance between actually 'doing Agile' and 'being agile'.

There are many specific methodologies that have grown up around agile (including SCRUM, SAFe, XP, Kanban) and each of these have their passionate champions, but just as there is no single roadmap for transformation, there is no one methodology that is always best. Instead, it is far more important for an organization to find its own way and develop ways of working (often through prototyping the working methodology itself) that are suited to its unique context. This process may well draw on foundational principles from Agile, Lean and design thinking in order to create a scalable approach. Alongside this it is critical to understand the fundamental mindset shifts that are involved and how we can apply these principles effectively through the organization to support transformation.

In my first book[3] I took a detailed look at the working methodologies, so in this book I'm going to focus on the critical principles that are the foundation, and that are often the most challenging for organizations to apply well at scale.

Design thinking

It was David Kelley and Tim Brown, the founders of design business IDEO, who first adapted design thinking for wider business application. Tim Brown has defined design thinking as 'a human-centred approach to innovation that draws from the designer's toolkit to integrate the needs of people, the possibilities of technology, and the requirements for business success.'[4]

A design thinking process typically starts with empathy, seeking to understand customer or end-user needs in non-judgemental ways through observation and interviews. This is often followed by a definition phase that seeks to define the right problem to solve. Once a problem and its context has been explored, it may well be appropriate to reinterpret or redefine the problem to create a framing that will help lead to the solution. Design thinking then follows a solutions-focused approach characterized by divergent and convergent thinking, which involves originating multiple ideas and possibilities before converging around an optimal way forwards through prototyping, testing and learning.

Design thinking is important since it is adept at working through complex problems that cannot be solved by the application of rules or technical knowledge. The critical principles that are scalable and important to take out from design thinking are:

- the value of empathy, exploration and defining the right problem to solve;
- the importance of abductive thinking, using observation and creativity to imagine possibilities and create hypotheses;

- the benefit of divergent and convergent thinking in generating many possibilities before using prototypical approaches to narrow down and learn;
- the need to iterate, and continuously learn.

These principles are useful at scale since they support better problem definition, solutions-focused thinking, and a bringing together of human, technology and economic dynamics for business benefit.

Agile

Agile methodologies arose in software development in response to the challenges inherent in more traditional and rigid waterfall processes. A group of developers, meeting at the Snowbird resort in Utah in 2001 to discuss more lightweight development philosophies, published the Agile Manifesto[5] as a way of expressing a new way of working that captured some key shifts in value. Whilst there is value in the items on the right, they believed there to be more value in the items on the left:

- individuals and interactions over processes and tools;
- working software over comprehensive documentation;
- customer collaboration over contract negotiation;
- responding to change over following a plan.

Agile has revolutionized the way in which technology teams worked and software is built, but smarter businesses have also come to the realization that agile principles have significant value beyond technology teams in supporting more responsive and adaptive operations right across the organization. As I go on to discuss, there are key culture and leadership contexts that are necessary to enable a scaled application of agile thinking, but there are some essential principles that underpin Agile methodologies that are more broadly applicable:

- **Small, multidisciplinary teams:** agile teams are kept small in order to adapt and move fast, and comprise the competencies needed to achieve the outputs required of the team and no more. The teams are often self-organizing, co-located and characterized by a high level of autonomy.
- **Sprint working:** the team works iteratively in blocks of time or sprints (usually one to four weeks) against an agreed set of priorities. The sprints follow the same fundamental pattern, beginning with a prioritization of

the backlog and a sprint planning process to identify the highest priority items that will be taken into the sprint. The majority of the sprint is focused on doing the work to achieve the required outputs and using techniques like daily standups to help remove blockers to moving quickly. At the end of the sprint, a review captures what was achieved and a retrospective enables learning about ways of working that can empower continuous improvement.

- **Backlogs, epics and user stories:** rather than specify rigid, up-front requirements following a lengthy period of capturing requirements, teams break down large challenges/problems/projects into smaller components, which are then prioritized in a backlog. An epic can be thought of as a large body of work, often with one focused objective, that can be broken down into a number of smaller stories. Each user story is a high-level definition of a requirement, and might be expressed in these terms: 'As a (role) I want (goal) so that (benefit)'.[6] User stories can be used to express requirements working back from the customer or end-user, and usually contain just enough information to enable an estimate of the effort needed to fulfil it.

- **Adaptation and iteration:** since the backlog is reprioritized at the start of every sprint, allowing requirements to change over time, and keeping the team focused on realizing maximum value (wherever possible customer value) as early as possible, sprint working naturally embeds adaptation into the fabric of the way in which teams are working. Teams require the flexibility and autonomy (usually working with a product owner who oversees the product backlog) to flex and adapt as they go.

- **Velocity:** agile teams predict and track their velocity through effort estimates relating to user stories. This means that they can more accurately predict how long a project will take to complete and avoid planning fallacy, the concept first described by Daniel Kahneman and Amos Tversky, which shows that we are inherently overoptimistic when predicting how much time is needed to complete a future task, which results in underestimation of time and effort.[7] Teams track their velocity and progress in transparent ways, often using physical displays near the team.

- **Retrospective:** a good retrospective is an opportunity to focus on improving ways of operating. Questions addressed in a typical retrospective might focus on what to stop doing, what to start doing, what to continue, what to do more or less of. The 'after action review' from the US military is an example, simple framework for retrospective that aligns the team around agreed facts (What was supposed to happen? What actually happened?) and shared opinions (Why was there a difference? What can we learn from this?). Retrospectives are useful since they embed continuous learning and improvement into the fabric of how teams work.

- **Definition of done and the sprint demo:** the 'definition of done' in an agile team is a consistent, agreed set of criteria that outputs have to fulfil in order to be counted as 'done'. This is useful in supporting high quality of outputs, consistency and continuous governance of outputs. In a sprint demo, working outputs are demonstrated to stakeholders in order to solicit feedback that can be incorporated into future work and sprints. The demo can therefore be very useful in keeping stakeholders updated on progress and running an inclusive development process.

- **Product owners and scrum masters:** the product owner plays a key role in owning the vision for the end product and also representing the voice of the customer and also key stakeholders in the business. Scrum masters facilitate interaction on the team to ensure good communication and alignment, help remove barriers to moving quickly, ensure the team is sticking to agile values, and protecting the team from outside interference or distraction. Both are key roles but neither is there to directly tell the team what to do – the team decides the best way to solve the challenges set (Figure 2.1).

FIGURE 2.1 The Agile process

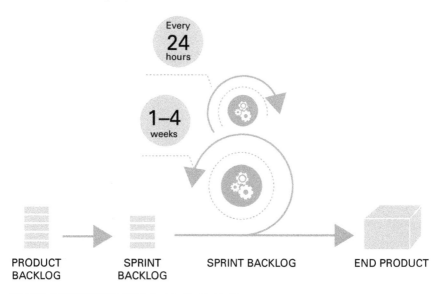

Every **24** hours

1–4 weeks

PRODUCT BACKLOG   SPRINT BACKLOG   SPRINT BACKLOG   END PRODUCT

SOURCE © TPX Manifesto. Reproduced with permission

These are principles and practices that have grown up around Agile but have much broader application and benefit:

- the ability to embed continuous learning, adaptation and responsiveness into everyday operations;
- the approaches to prioritization around a more balanced understanding of customer and business needs;
- the understanding of the ability of small teams to create disproportionate value;
- the inclusive approach to development to help support ongoing buy-in and mitigate surprises and distraction;
- the recognition of the benefits of accurately predicting time and effort and tracking velocity and progress;
- the appreciation of team autonomy and the role of leadership in removing barriers to moving fast.

All of these practices are now fundamental to how organizations need to operate in complex adaptive environments.

Agile is no silver bullet, and it is essential to take an intelligent approach to how we apply different thinking and value creation techniques across a business. But, as I discuss later, agile working and thinking have the potential to transform large, slow organizations to become far more responsive, yet they involve some fundamental mindset shifts that challenge entrenched belief systems and habits that have grown up over decades in companies. This is no small shift, and organizations that underestimate the significance of this change or under-commit to both doing Agile and being agile, will fail to truly adapt for the modern world.

Lean Startup

Building on the practices that have long been a key part of Lean manufacturing and philosophies like the Toyota Production System (TPS), Lean Startup set out a product development methodology which, in keeping with Agile, is about starting small and scaling fast. Fundamental to Lean manufacturing and TPS was the idea that anything in a process that sits outside of the creation of value for the end-customer is potentially wastage that can be systematically removed. The process sought to bring in inputs only at the point they were needed (hence 'just in time' production), minimize correction time by eliminating imperfections in output as early as possible, and focus on 'Kaizen' or continuous improvement.

Similarly, the principles of Lean Startup, expounded in Eric Ries' book of the same name,[8] are about eliminating unnecessary waste, continuous improvement through learning, iterative product development and fast customer feedback loops. Like scientific method it seeks to test hypotheses about customer needs through prototyping, removing assumptions and turning them into validated learning. Like Agile, Lean Startup is as much about the mindset as it is about the process and it involves some fundamental principles that have much broader application than product development:

- **The build–measure–learn loop:** like Agile, Lean Startup uses an iterative cycle that seeks to identify a hypothesis (all customer needs or solutions or product features are hypotheses until tested), design a test or prototype (wherever possible to be directed at real end-users, developing validated learnings that can then inform the next hypothesis and learning loop. This process is useful in identifying what Eric Ries calls 'leap of faith' assumptions – all the things that need to be true in order for an outcome to happen – and testing them one by one to create validated learnings. The process therefore mitigates risk through learning, adaptation and eliminating uncertainty.

- **The minimum viable product (MVP):** the MVP has become another piece of jargon that is often misunderstood or misapplied. Eric Ries described this as the *'version of a new product which allows a team to collect the maximum amount of validated learning about customers with the least effort'.*[9] The principle is to start small with simple tests and prototypes in order for you to learn fast and scale by moving through successive learning loops quickly. As I'll discuss later, there can be some significant mindset and cultural challenges around starting small in organizations that are used to big up-front investments.

- **Innovation accounting:** traditional accounting and budgeting methods work well with established propositions and in stable environments but can be problematic when an organization needs to innovate at scale and move quickly with fluidity. A focus on short-term payback and metrics governed by ratios and cash flow analysis for example can act to stifle innovation. Overly rigid budgeting and forecasting processes can hamper adaptiveness. Lean Startup's focus on actionable rather than vanity metrics (that is, measures that better represent customer interaction, performance and business drivers) enables a more sophisticated approach to understanding project trajectory and budget prioritization. Dave McClure's 'Pirate Metrics' framework, for example, sets out a hierarchy of measures around Acquisition, Activation, Retention, Referral and Revenue (AARRR – hence Pirate Metrics) that flows from customer usage to growth to financial measures in a way that enables a better appreciation of the potential of early-stage ideas to deliver value. Innovation accounting therefore involves finance teams acting more like venture capitalists in releasing successive rounds of funding for projects based on measures and trajectory.[10] Small teams should be enabled to spend small amounts of money to demonstrate how they can progress value and reduce risk of scalability.

- **The pivot:** another overused but poorly understood term, the pivot is described by Ries as a '*structured course correction designed to test a new fundamental hypothesis about the product, strategy, and engine of growth*'.[11] Pivots keep one foot in maintaining the guiding vision for the product or project whilst still enabling a refocus of proposition or key features. Pivots can be challenging to execute in environments that don't support adaptation and change, and there are not insignificant mindset challenges around avoiding well-known biases that may lead to poor decision-making. The ability to make smart choices about whether to continue, stop or pivot in an initiative is an increasingly valuable yet underrated leadership skill.

Lean Startup is structured around continuous involvement of customers and so, like Agile, works back from the end-user, defines value in customer-centric ways, and enables businesses to stay closer to changing contexts. Yet it also speaks to more fundamental practices that support breadth as well as depth of innovation, the mitigation of risk, and learning fast at scale. Like Agile, a poor or half-hearted implementation of Lean Startup can easily lead to poor decision-making, under-realized value, and a drift back to more traditional linear ways of working and thinking.

Design thinking, Agile and Lean Startup (and the many variant processes that they have spawned) all offer related practices that enable far greater flexibility and adaptiveness for a complex, changing, non-linear world. But the value inherent in the mindset, culture and approaches that they all speak to applies way beyond product development, design and technology teams.

Given how fundamental this way of thinking can be to supporting transformation, let's consider some of the key mindset challenges involved with a broad shift towards agile culture and working.

The key shifts from linear thinking

The transformation from traditional linear thinking, exemplified by waterfall project management, to more iterative, agile ways of operating involves some critical mental and operational leaps that can mean the difference between success and failure in agile transformation. If we are to become more agile as an organization, then a wider appreciation and application of these core ways of thinking is critical to success. This is about recognizing that agile principles are more than just a process and working methodology to be used in technology teams. Applied correctly and judiciously it is a way of operating and thinking that equips organizations to become more responsive and manoeuvrable in complex adaptive environments.

The processes themselves can teach us about these wider mindset shifts and can also act as a catalyst for embedding new approaches and positive habits. Take, for example, a service design process. Here's an example, drawn from the public sector, of the sequential flow that characterizes Waterfall methodologies:

1 Gather requirements and inputs.

2 Agree a plan.

3 Pick a supplier and set goals.

4 Plan the project.

5 Start implementation.

6 Finish implementation.

7 Handover and evaluation.[12]

Waterfall methodologies grew up in the manufacturing and construction industries in highly structured environments where design changes in the development process would quickly become prohibitively expensive. So the design needed to be defined at the start in great detail and then remain relatively unchanged through the manufacturing or construction process. It is therefore a process methodology that is specifically designed to mitigate change and adaptation. We take all our inputs at the start and finish that process before moving to the next stage and designing the solution to those requirements, which we would also do in great detail. We would complete the design or the plan before moving towards implementation or build. The design or the plan remains relatively unchanged and we build to those exact specifications. Once this stage is complete, we move to test or verify, and then launch to the end-users or customers.

Waterfall thinking and processes work well in stable, slow-moving environments where plans need to be fixed, development approaches more rigidly structured, and the environment and conditions are largely unchanging and widely understood. Their linear nature means that they are relatively simple to follow and to understand. So perhaps inevitably, these kinds of approaches have become embedded not just in technology development, but much more broadly in business process, thinking and strategy. Business decision-making and business cases, for example, often follow this one-size-fits-all approach of gathering comprehensive inputs, creating a detailed plan and forecasts, big investment and a lengthy programme of implementation that deviates little from the plan. In the fast-moving, complex environments in which we now conduct much of our business this opens up a number of significant vulnerabilities to those operating in this way. Key to these are the compounding, interrelated challenges of time, complexity and adaptability:

- **Adaptability:** contexts, customer needs, requirements, competitive challenges are all changing much faster, and linear process thinking is poor at capturing and responding to change. This often means that solutions are shipped at the end of a process that are no longer fit for purpose, or that require immediate changes to be made. Requirements gathering processes can not only be lengthy, but can also fail to capture real user need since people often don't know what they really want. Problem definition needs to be a continual process, and the response to evolving problems requires flexibility and adaptation.

- **Complexity:** since an increasing degree of business focus is about operating in relatively unknown environments or uncharted territory (either because of the growing complexity of markets and technological change, or rapidly shifting competitive situations, or the need to innovate and grow into new and less familiar territory) there is a heightened need for experimentation, testing and rapid learning. Waterfall thinking does not lend itself well to any of these. Complex scenarios also require concurrent, multidisciplinary problem solving and collaboration, and cognitive diversity, which traditional linear processes do not support well.

- **Time:** detail-driven, sequential processes may work well for the construction industry, but may well be lengthy developments and are not suited to situations in which speed-to-market is key, or advantage resides in solving customer problems better, easier, faster. Unforeseen problems that crop up in development and that inevitably were not captured in requirements gathering can further delay timing.

Complex, rapidly changing environments with high levels of uncertainty require a different response and different thinking. They require us to begin with the users, to work out what they need, to test solutions and then be ready to flex and change as contexts and requirements change. We still have a vision and a direction for where we are going and what we want to achieve, but we iterate in an informed way and stay closer to changing needs and contexts as we go:

1 Meet the users.

2 Understand the users' needs.

3 Build a prototype.

4 Get feedback from real users.

5 Iterate, with constant feedback.

6 Make it live.

7 Continue to improve.[13]

Flexibility, adaptability and continuous learning are built into these processes. They are inherent to the fabric of this whole way of thinking.

The big opportunity here, as this book sets out, is to take agile, iterative principles and culture and to scale this way of operating and thinking to help entire businesses transform to become more agile and responsive to a very different world: to develop a far more informed and nuanced view of where in the business it is right to stick with traditional, linear approaches to value creation, and where it is right to implement more iterative ways of operating. But also to BE more agile as a business and adopt the kind of thinking and culture that can enable more flexible, adaptive processes and working to scale and to thrive.

In order to do that well we need to fully appreciate the key mindset shifts involved in the adoption of more agile approaches, most notably in relation to value creation, risk and visibility. These conventions are applicable to working methodologies and projects but beyond this capture the wider strategic differences, mindset changes, and fundamental assumptions that are at play when an organization wants to become more agile. These shifts represent not only opportunities to manage these dynamics differently, but also potential cultural and attitudinal barriers that can prevent agile transformation from being successful.

Value creation

As we mentioned before, embedded ways of creating value, making decisions and business cases in businesses are strongly Waterfall focused. It's all about gathering comprehensive inputs, setting out detailed plans, and quality of execution against those fixed plans. Somehow, we feel more comfortable with a PowerPoint presentation or a spreadsheet that sets out a linear progression for the initiative with set stage gates and forecast outcomes at every stage, even when those forecasts are based on contexts that are highly likely to change, or projections extrapolated from past data that are already out of date. It's false certainty, and simply creates more work in justifying why you've moved away from those forecasts as the project progresses.

Far better surely to acknowledge when contexts are likely to shift, to set a directional course and a vision for the project outcome, but then be more fluid and adaptive in how you achieve that vision. Tracking progress towards a goal is important, but we need to be more adaptive than a linear set of rigid targets set out at the start allows for and instead be smarter about how we fund projects and track leading indicators.

One of the key mindset shifts involved here is around value creation. In any initiative or project, we often imagine value creation to be roughly proportionate to the effort that we put in, and to progress in a reasonably linear fashion with value being created steadily as we go. In reality, of course, if we frame this as both customer and business value, waterfall approaches have a rapid delivery of value at the end of the process. We do a whole bunch of work speaking to stakeholders, designing and building, where the business or customer sees very little value before launching the proposition at the end. If we do agile correctly we do the complete opposite; we concentrate on delivering as much value as early on in the process as possible, and then iterating from there to continually deliver more value. The business and the customer are able to benefit far earlier. We might represent these differences as in Figure 2.2.

If we were to substitute time on the x-axis with effort, the same will often be true. We're focused always on how we can deliver maximum value as early as possible, particularly to customers (because if customers are happy the business is usually happy, right?) but also to the business.

This conceptual change requires a mental leap that if not achieved, can become a cultural and behavioural barrier to change. There is comfort in detailed plans, so we need to reappraise our understanding of the level of inputs that we need up front and be more comfortable with learning along

FIGURE 2.2   Agile vs Waterfall value creation

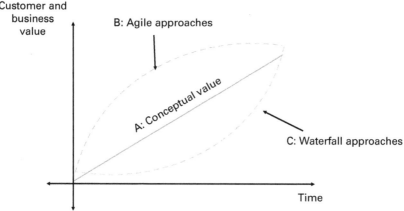

the way. There is comfort in rigid, linear time-planning and stage-gate review processes so we need to be more comfortable with not knowing in advance exactly where we will be at any given stage in the project (but then we never really knew anyway). And there is comfort in spending huge amounts of time and resource building a highly sophisticated solution that we're all excited about before launching it to market, so we need to get better at 'fast and roughly right' combined with proper agile governance.

Adaptability

Another key mindset shift is around the flexibility that we need to adapt easily, judiciously and rapidly. In a business world characterized by linear thinking, change and flex become hard to do. We might conceptually believe that we are maintaining a consistent level in the potential to change through a project, but the reality is often different. In a Waterfall-dominated environment the more we progress through a project the more time and resource we spend on it and the more invested we become in a particular course of action that we believe will determine success. The recognition and support of our superiors depends on it. We become path dependent, and increasingly less likely to make significant changes the further we go on. With more iterative approaches, however, the ability to flex, learn and adapt is built in to the process and so whilst we may lose some degree of flex as we go on, it is far less than in a linear model. We might represent these differences in Figure 2.3.

FIGURE 2.3 Agile vs Waterfall adaptability

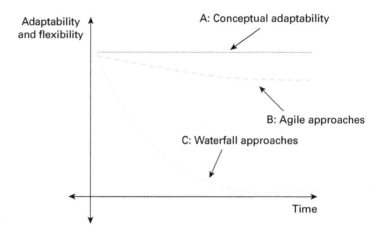

At a broader level within business, this problem can mean that it is very easy for businesses to become path dependent on particular strategies and versions of what success looks like. It can dramatically reduce manoeuvrability and result in the business becoming stuck.

Approaches to risk

In his book on rethinking risk management (*Rethinking Risk Management: Critically examining old ideas and new concepts*[14]) Rick Nason, Associate Professor at Rowe School of Business, makes the case for why we need to redefine how we manage risk in organizations. Traditional approaches, he argues, see risk management teams as the 'department of no', overly reliant on third-party frameworks, and lacking in independent thinking: 'Very quickly, frameworks tend to become risk management, rather than a guide for risk management. In other words, people manage to the framework, rather than manage risk – two very different things.'[15]

A more balanced approach takes into account upside or good risk whilst also mitigating the impact and probability from bad risk. It is, Nason says, a balance between art and science, process and judgement. This positions risk management much more as a strategic contributor to value creation. Problem definition, and understanding whether an issue is simple, complicated or complex, is the first step in developing that strategic understanding. I'll talk later in the book about how this approach to problem definition can support more sophisticated thinking around the methodologies that we use to solve challenges, and where we do Agile and where we don't. But in managing risk it is helpful to have an appreciation that simple and complicated challenges can largely be solved by rules and processes whereas solving complex issues requires judgement but also a 'manage, not solve' approach that involves trying, learning and adaptation, where it is less important to define the exact solution at the start than it is to take a broad, creative approach to how you might find the right solution. Structured approaches to managing risk in simple and complicated domains make sense, but in complex areas we need structure to get out of the way so that a flexible, emergent approach to risk management is possible.

The risk culture that an organization carries with it can be a significant barrier or enabler to change. If the culture is set up in a way that people are fearful that there will always be blame and consequence for risk outcomes, they are more likely to hide events from risk management that can amplify rather than mitigate risk. Risk homeostasis, or risk compensation, was developed as a theory by Gerald JS Wilde, a professor of psychology at Queen's University, Ontario, Canada, and it posits that everyone has an acceptable level of risk that they like to operate to. People may well adjust their behaviour in response to a perceived level of risk in a situation in order to come more in line with that acceptable risk level. So they may become more careful where they believe a greater amount of risk exists but conversely they may also take more (perhaps unnecessary) risks in situations that are heavily locked down by risk management.

When in 1967 Sweden changed from driving on the left to driving on the right, the next 18 months saw a marked reduction in traffic fatalities that Wilde hypothesized this was due to drivers responding to increased danger by taking more care. In a well-known 1994 traffic study in Munich, a group of taxi drivers were given cabs that were equipped with anti-lock brakes (ABS) and a control group were given cabs that were identical in every way except that they didn't have ABS. When the results were analysed by Wilde, they showed that a very similar number of accidents happened in each group, leading him to conclude that those drivers who had been given the extra safety features then drove more aggressively, so maintaining a similar accident rate.[16]

Risk-averse culture can easily generate more unintended risk. When in 2013 the Obama administration launched Healthcare.gov, the online insurance market for US citizens to access affordable health insurance, the system immediately crashed when it went live and it took weeks to get it working properly. Citizens couldn't even log in to what was meant to be a one-stop hub for insurance that had cost more than US $400 million to build.[17]

A whole series of managerial, technical and financial errors contributed to the site collapsing at launch, but author Clay Shirky wrote an analysis at the time that highlighted how the culture in the team that worked on the system made it very hard to pass bad news back up the line and the environment was one in which failure was not an option. Shirky noted how sticking to rigid waterfall-type processes had mitigated the ability to learn from tests, to adapt as necessary and so had built up huge risk over time:

> An effective test is an exercise in humility; it's only useful in a culture where desirability is not confused with likelihood. For a test to change things, everyone has to understand that their opinion, and their boss's opinion, matters less than what actually works and what doesn't.[18]

The result was a bloated site that reportedly had 500 million lines of code, a giant house of cards, and a disastrous launch. Rather than avoiding failure, the lack of early and aggressive testing simply stored it up. Rather than taking smaller, acceptable risks in public early on, they accumulated risk. It was not simply a procurement problem; it was a management and a cultural problem.

Many large organizations are hampered by risk-averse cultures that prevent them from experimenting widely and frequently. An organization needs to be very focused in where it chooses to place its bets, but then it needs to test solutions, learn and scale rapidly in order to identify where the real opportunity is. That means a systematic allocation of resource towards testing hypotheses and iterating value, and the fluidity and flexibility to recognize when a given path is no longer valid and to shift focus and resources. The reality, of course, is that the more experimentation you do, the more you learn, the more you innovate, the less risk there is of your future being decided for you. A focus on learning rather than avoiding risk at all costs creates a more resilient organization.

Similarly, a culture of openness and transparency can encourage managers to take prudent risks within understood parameters of risk tolerance, which results in more progress, creativity and motivation. Establishing clear 'safe to fail' parameters means that you're not betting the company through risky experimentation but instead setting people free to test and learn within an environment that rewards them to do this whilst mitigating unnecessary risk.

When moving to more agile ways of working this can involve a challenging mindset shift in the relation between risk and reward. In a Waterfall world we're used to taking all of our inputs at the beginning of the process, making a decision and betting big by investing heavily in a limited number of ways to realize the value we believe there is to be had. In a complex adaptive world, however, it is more appropriate to have a clear view on what the future looks like, to be decisive about your direction, but then to start small and learn and scale fast. This requires multiple small bets, rapid learning, quick scaling and/or disengagement and an appreciation that rather than betting big on two initiatives in the hope that one will succeed, we're placing ten smaller bets but out of those ten perhaps nine will fail and one will pay back really big.

In a Waterfall world, since investment comes up front and value creation and customer feedback come towards the end of the process, the risk largely stays with us until the end. In Agile, we seek to mitigate risk as early as possible by learning as we go, ensuring that we're not investing resource, time and money unnecessarily on things that the customer doesn't actually want. We might represent the differences as in Figure 2.4.

One of the key principles of iterative processes such as Lean and Agile is that we are listing our leap-of-faith assumptions as a backlog and then looking to test them one by one to turn them into validated learnings. In rigid, linear processes it's easy to bake-in untested assumptions right at the beginning of the process and then only find out that it is an incorrect assumption at an advanced stage of development, perhaps even when we put the finished

FIGURE 2.4 Agile vs Waterfall approaches to risk

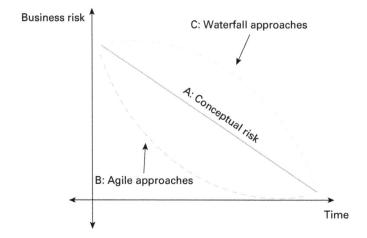

product live to end-users. This creates heightened risk and vulnerability, particularly when things around you are changing fast. With linear processes the cost of change goes up as you progress. With iterative processes you are deliberately reducing risk as you go.

CASE STUDY
Airbus A380

Later in the book we'll discuss the importance of aligned autonomy as a way to empower moving fast whilst still retaining strong directional alignment and governance. One story of what happened in the development process of the new Airbus A380, the world's largest commercial airliner, is a stark reminder of what can happen in the absence of proper alignment, but also how significant assumptions that are baked-in to a development process can be.[19]

The essence of the story focuses on how different design groups working in different countries on the project had used different versions of the same Computer Aided Design (CAD) software. As the engineering drawings were being developed across multiple teams, German and Spanish designers were using version 4 of the CATIA software, whilst British and French teams had upgraded to version 5. The trouble with this was that version 5 of the software was a significant upgrade from the previous version, meaning that there were notable inconsistencies that emerged only as the first aircraft prototype was being built in Toulouse.

Despite being manufactured to specification, as the 530 kilometres of wiring and cables began to be woven into the airframe, engineers quickly noticed that many of the wires were a few centimetres too short. The complexity of the wiring system (more than 100,000 wires) coupled with the discrepancies between the software meant that the redesign, rebuild and consequent multiple project delays (at one point more than 1,100 German engineers were camped out at the Toulouse production facility trying to rectify the problems[20]) resulted in months of delays and a huge overspend.

The situation was exacerbated by a complex organizational structure that originated from the history of the Airbus business as a consortium of separate companies. Not creating a single project team across different centres, ongoing pressure to keep the project moving forwards to fulfil an overly aggressive schedule, and misdirected emphasis on keeping different parts of the company happy rather than focusing on what was best for the aircraft also hindered the development. Delays in the A380 development project cost the business a reported US $6.1 billion.[21] It's a clear example of the potential cost of not testing assumptions and adding unnecessary complexity to an important project.

Approaches to visibility

It can be easy to believe with waterfall approaches that since we're building in regular stage gates we have good visibility of progress throughout the initiative, yet the reality can be very different. As the project progresses through stages that involve intensive and detailed work by individual teams or functions it can easily happen that we lose visibility on exactly what is happening with progress and, as I've already mentioned, even to have a significant assumption baked-in to the development without realizing it. With iterative approaches it might be difficult to predict with certainty at the start of a project where we will be at a given stage (if you do, you're not being agile), but with proper agile governance we can actually maintain a good level of clarity throughout. We might represent the key differences as in Figure 2.5.

The key point here is that these are all key mindset shifts that if not addressed can become significant barriers to the adoption of new ways of thinking and cause us to drift back to more comfortable, linear practices. As we seek to not only use iterative methodologies more widely through the business but to adopt agile mindsets throughout, these differences become critical representations of success and failure.

FIGURE 2.5 Agile vs Waterfall visibility

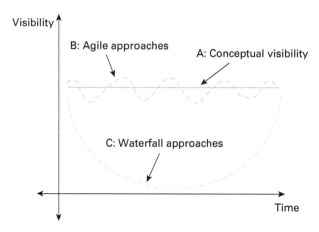

Principles of agile business

In my first book, *Building the Agile Business Through Digital Transformation*, we developed 12 principles of agile business, inspired by the original Agile

Manifesto, which was a blueprint for a better way of developing software. Taking these original principles we defined some fundamental principles for doing better business in the complex adaptive world we know today (Table 2.1).

These agile business principles set out a blueprint for a truly adaptive, responsive organization.

TABLE 2.1 Agile business principles

	Agile Manifesto Principle	Agile Business Principle
1	Our highest priority is to satisfy the customer through early and continuous delivery of valuable software	The primary orientation is towards customer need delivered through constant improvement of customer experience
2	Welcome changing requirements, even late in development. Agile processes harness change for the customer's competitive advantage	Strategies and tactics are highly adaptive and responsive, and change is welcomed
3	Deliver working software frequently, from a couple of weeks to a couple of months, with a preference to the shorter timescale	Iterative, sprint working delivers customer value through continuous progress and momentum
4	Business people and developers must work together daily throughout the project	Effective cross-functional collaboration, supported through clear intent, is critical for success
5	Build projects around motivated individuals. Give them the environment and support they need, and trust them to get the job done	Build companies with motivated individuals. Empower teams to deliver through a flexible working environment characterized by trust and comfort with dissent
6	The most efficient and effective method of conveying information to and within a development team is face-to-face conversation	Bureaucracy and politics are minimized, co-location and face-to-face communication maximized wherever possible
7	Working software is the primary measure of progress	Working outputs are the optimum measure of progress and success
8	Agile processes promote sustainable development. The sponsors, developers and users should be able to maintain a constant pace indefinitely	Agile business supports relentless and sustainable innovation and progress. Change and iteration is constant, and the pace of progress never slows

(continued)

TABLE 2.1 (Continued)

	Agile Manifesto Principle	Agile Business Principle
9	Continuous attention to technical excellence and good design enhances agility	Technical excellence and good design are central to maintaining pace and agility
10	Simplicity – the art of maximizing the amount of work not done – is essential	Minimize wasted effort, duplication and resources
11	The best architectures, requirements and designs emerge from self-organizing teams	The best results emerge from small teams with a high degree of autonomy
12	At regular intervals, the team reflects on how to become more effective, then tunes and adjusts its behaviour accordingly	Continuous improvement is achieved through embedded reflection time, and behaviours and culture that support learning

The impact of rising customer expectation

Customer experience has become THE area of focus over the past few years for organizations from the broadest spread of sectors. As more products become services, and even physical goods are augmented with layers of software-driven service interaction, the operational focus of many organizations is shifting from a focus on value chain efficiency to ecosystems of value where customer experience becomes a critical component.

There can be little doubt about just how important customer experience is to business value creation. A survey by Defaqto Research found that 55 per cent of consumers would pay more for a better customer experience.[22] A report by Walker Group predicted that by 2020 customer experience will overtake price and product as the key brand differentiator.[23] Respondents to Econsultancy's annual Digital Trends Report[24] (published in association with Adobe and based on a global survey of more than 14,000 digital professionals) named 'optimizing customer experience' as the most exciting business opportunity for the coming year. The same answer has been top of the list for the last four iterations of this research, demonstrating that this is a long-term, but game-changing priority.

So it is for future potential advantage. When asked what are anticipated to be the primary ways in which their organization (or their client's organization in the case of agency respondents) will differentiate themselves over the next five years from competitors, participants in the same Econsultancy survey named customer experience as the primary focus.

There are evidently many challenges wrapped up in this focus on delivering exceptional customer experience, not least those inherent in joining up disparate data sources and effectively extracting insight and value through application, the challenge of legacy systems, and the reinvention of the business itself (structures, processes, priorities) to be more responsive to rapidly shifting consumer and competitive contexts.

This is an ongoing challenge, not least because for every slick new service that comes to market, customer expectation rises with it. Author Adam Morgan once described this phenomenon as 'Uber's children' – the idea that this ongoing rise in customer expectation creates a continually shifting context that businesses need to deliver to and the need for continuous (not episodic) improvement.[25]

In 2015, the Uber Data Team did an analysis on whether increased efficiency (shorter time to get a cab) resulted in increased expectations over time from Uber users. They found that the cities that Uber had been in longest had experienced the sharpest decay in the willingness to wait for a car.[26] The greater the efficiencies Uber gained from improvements in supply and optimizing despatch algorithms, the more impatient people became in their expectation – a pattern that was replicated regardless of geography. As the Uber team said: 'The bottom line is that we realize we have to continually raise the bar, to get you home from the bar.'[27]

The bottom line for just about every business is that as customer experience increasingly becomes the differentiator, the agility to respond to shifting user expectation becomes one of the key competitive advantages or disadvantages. This is no small change. It means a reorientation of the entire business towards far more customer-centric structures, processes, practices and behaviours.

Yet somehow despite the obvious importance of customer experience in driving business value, and the fact that just about every business professes to be customer-centric, so much of the reality of consumer experience is anything but customer-centric. Still now, years after the importance of customer experience as a differentiator and profit driver became evident, we have a myriad of examples of businesses doing things for distinctly company-centric rather than customer-centric reasons. So we have contact numbers buried in websites behind FAQs because it's more convenient for companies not to have to pay someone to answer customer questions. We have poorly implemented automation that fails to give customers what they want when they need it, that pushes customers through automated menus rather than just being able to ask a person a question, or worse bombards them with unnecessary and wasteful messages when they don't want or need it. We have complicated log-in and security procedures that have failed to keep up with new technology, and unnecessarily complex customer journeys that are not joined up, awkward to navigate and anything but customer-centric.

In spite of all the promise we have ended up in an age of multiple inboxes, payment and identity systems that are far from seamless, competing ecosystems that don't talk to each other, and creaking back-end infrastructure that leaks data or crashes services.

Tom Goodwin (author of *Digital Darwinism: Survival of the fittest in the age of business disruption*[28]) has described this as the 'mid-digital age' – an age of peak complexity when we have all the possibilities of new technologies but are still burdened with the thinking of the past, resulting in too much complexity, poor interoperability and clunky customer experience:

> This energy – the disruptive forces, the vast feeling of change, the acceleration of
> complexity, the stress of companies fighting for the profit margins of the past –
> is where we now lie. The complexity is found in every aspect of our lives and we
> tend not to notice it because we're enamoured by the wonder of the new.

As customer expectation continually rises, businesses of all types need to always be adapting, evolving and transforming in response. This is not about periodic investments and innovation; it is about rapid customer feedback loops that enable continuous iteration and new thinking.

CASE STUDY
How the music industry became its own worst enemy

Sometimes entire industries can implement strategies that make no sense for the customer and can create strategic vulnerability. In the 1990s, the record industry made specific efforts to try to kill retail sales of the single in favour of the more lucrative album format. The result was a salutary lesson for businesses of all types.[29]

The album had, of course, been the prominent format from the 1960s, with singles frequently seen as a way of boosting sales of the accompanying long-player, particularly in the 1980s when albums like *Thriller*, *Hysteria* and *Born in the USA* all put out a high proportion of tracks as singles (*Thriller*, for example, had seven out of nine tracks released).

In the 1990s, however, record companies (starting with Capitol Records and MC Hammer believe it or not) went to war on the retail single by promoting hits to radio that you could buy only on a full-length album (think Alanis Morissette) giving rise to the phenomenon in the late 1990s of consumers being forced to shell out for an entire album that likely had one good song on it (think Chumbawamba). The reason for this was, of course, that the labels could make more money that way, but inevitably they generated resentment amongst their customers, which would eventually come back and bite them in a big way. The story of how Napster disrupted the music business in the run-up to the turn of the century is well documented, but it also provides a lens through which to see how the industry's own practices had set it up for a spectacular fall.

It's a great example of how easy it is for entire industries to misalign incentives and goals and pursue strategies that might make sense on the balance sheet in the short term but make no sense in the long term and build up the kind of fragility that makes them highly vulnerable to genuinely far-reaching disruption.

The 'platformization' of capability

The word 'platform' is perhaps a little overused these days, but it speaks to perhaps one of the most significant transitions inherent to business economics in the digital age. The internet has always been great at facilitating relationships between nodes in a network, but the shift from traditional 'pipeline' businesses to so-called 'platform' organizations capitalizes on this in a way that neatly characterizes truly digital-native thinking and models.

A good exploration of this concept comes from Van Alstyne, Parker and Choudary in their article that talks about the new rules for strategy in which they make the point that platforms are not entirely new – like many things, the digital age simply serves to give certain concepts a heightened importance, or a brand-new context or application.[30] Yet the internet era has changed some key dynamics: the need to own infrastructure and assets; scalability becoming faster and cheaper; interaction and participation more frictionless; the flow and exchange of data and value more fluid. These new dynamics have enabled a new type of business to take shape: 'Platform businesses bring together producers and consumers in high-value exchanges. Their chief assets are information and interactions, which together are also the source of the value they create and their competitive advantage.'[31]

The classic value chain model that we discussed earlier (originated by Michael Porter, of course) fits the linear idea of 'pipeline' businesses, where inputs go in at one end, go through a series of processes and activities in the organization to result in outputs, and the margin is the difference between the resultant value that is created and the cost of creating that value. In contrast, platform businesses sit within an ecosystem that typically comprises four key components:

- owners of the platform;
- providers who serve as the platform's interface;
- producers who create their offerings;
- consumers who use those offerings.

As an example, Google owns the Android platform, but partners with mobile device manufacturers (the providers), third-party app developers (the producers), and consumers (who utilize the platform but also return value in the form of usage data and revenue). It's perfectly possible for companies to be both a pipeline and a platform business (as indeed Google and Apple are with their device manufacturing business, and app store marketplace and services business) but the difference between the two involves a few key strategic and mindset shifts, which Van Alstyne, Parker and Choudary capture as:

1 **From resource control to resource orchestration:** instead of a model strongly focused on ownership and control of (perhaps scarce or unique) resources (which may be tangible or intangible, like IP), the main value asset (and what is difficult to copy) comes from the community, assets and contributions of the producers and consumers.

2 **From internal optimization to external interaction:** rather than a (internal) primary focus on efficiency in value chain activities, the value in platform businesses comes from facilitating the (external) interaction between producers and consumers. As the authors note, this means a focus on ecosystem governance rather than costs of production.

3 **From a focus on customer value to a focus on ecosystem value:** the difference here is that between optimizing lifetime customer value and the value that comes from optimizing an expanding ecosystem powered by iterative, fast-feedback loops (the example they give is perhaps subsidizing one type of consumer in order to attract another type).

Key to platform business thinking then, are concepts like network effects – the principle that the more participants there are in the system the better and more attractive the system becomes (better supply–demand matching, more data to apply), driving scalability, demand-side economies of scale, and advantages in average value per transaction. Network effects create the kind of virtuous feedback loop that has enabled companies like Alibaba to scale in the way that they have.

This is very different from linear 'pipeline' businesses that are focused on avoiding traditional threats (like those expressed in Porter's 'Five Forces' framework: the threat of new entrants; the threat of substitutes; the bargaining power of customers; the bargaining power of suppliers; competitive rivalry), or on 'building a moat' to counteract competition, and on controlling as much of the process as possible in order to gain from efficiencies. Traditional 'pipeline' thinking, say the authors, generally regards external forces as 'depletive' (ie extracting value from the company), yet in demand-side economies they can actually be 'accretive' (ie adding value). Powerful suppliers and customers can be beneficial rather than threatening, but the trick is in understanding that dynamic in order to shape an ecosystem.

This kind of platform thinking is a critical element in empowering organizational agility. If we understand how ecosystems work, how we can capitalize on network effects, and how we might facilitate relationships to create value, we can not only survive but also thrive in the digital age.

And it's worth noting that is as true of public sector organizations as it is of businesses. When Mike Bracken of the UK Government Digital Service talked about 'government as platform' (a phrase originated by Tim O'Reilly some time before[32]) back in 2015, he talked about how siloed approaches to digital transformation create duplication and waste. Instead, the vision he was setting out was about establishing 'a common core infrastructure of shared digital systems, technology and processes on which it's easy to build brilliant, user-centric government services'.[33]

The principles that underpin this way of thinking are about frictionless access, efficiency in matching supply with demand, understanding how value flows through a system, and reinforcing feedback loops that enable continuous improvement. And surely they are all things that every organization wants to understand.

ASOS Marketplace

Digital fashion retailer ASOS launched its Marketplace proposition in 2010 as a platform to support emerging and established boutique fashion businesses. These boutiques are smaller businesses, each selling their own unique styles of clothing, and in many ways are essentially competitive to ASOS. The launch of Marketplace is is perhaps counterintuitive to more traditional thinking, which would be concerned with direct competition and cannibalization of sales. Why would ASOS choose to host potentially competing sellers on its own site?

ASOS Marketplace launched with 20 sellers but since then it has become a leading platform for independent fashion brands and vintage stores with more than 1,000 boutiques from 50 different countries. Marketplace is a destination, giving customers a reason to come back to the retailer's site again and again (according to analytics business SimilarWeb, Marketplace has 1.8 million visits a month[34]), but it is also a distributed community across social platforms. ASOS takes 20 per cent commission from every sale on the platform. It speaks of a confident brand that is taking a leadership position in its market. But perhaps one of the most valuable yet relatively hidden benefits of the Marketplace platform for ASOS is the learning that it gets from a high volume, broader base of sales. More sales equals more data equals more learning, and for ASOS this means the ability to identify and respond to changing consumer demand faster, to capitalize on trends in product areas that are at the fringes of its product domain. What might the ASOS Marketplace for your business look like?

Systems thinking for business

Since most businesses are operating in increasingly complex adaptive environments it has become more important to develop an appreciation of high-level systems thinking as a way to navigate, solve problems and support change. Emergent strategies are more needed to navigate effectively through complex scenarios and shifting contexts. Businesses increasingly operate as role players within ecosystems that comprise suppliers, partners, customers and other third parties in value-driven networks. And understanding organizational change in terms of systems change (businesses are systems) is progressively more useful. These are all systems related, so the basic principles of systems thinking have never been more relevant.

Australian designer and innovator Leyla Acaroglu has usefully defined six fundamental concepts of systems thinking: interconnectedness; synthesis; emergence; feedback loops; causality and systems mapping.[35]

One of the core concepts of systems thinking is interconnectedness. Using a definition drawn from systems theory, which was first introduced by biologist L von Bertalanffy in the 1930s, we might first define a system as: 'a set of related components that work together in a particular environment to perform whatever functions are required to achieve the system's objective'.[36]

At the most basic level, there are really three main types of system:[37]

1 **Social:** human-created systems that are created to facilitate and progress human society (including things like education, finance, government and legal systems).

2 **Industrial:** any systems to do with products, services, goods and infrastructure that might facilitate and support social systems (examples include transport systems and the parts that comprise them).

3 **Ecosystems:** natural systems that provide the raw materials that support industrial systems, and ultimately sustain life on Earth (examples include the carbon cycle, minerals and fuels – whilst everything in nature is circular, humans have a tendency to make industrial systems linear which, as we've discussed, can make them unsustainable).

All elements in a system are reliant on something else (and often a complex array of things) for survival. As Leyla Acaroglu puts it:

> when we say 'everything is interconnected' from a systems thinking perspective, we are defining a fundamental principle of life. From this, we can shift the way we see the world, from a linear, structured 'mechanical worldview' to a dynamic, chaotic, interconnected array of relationships and feedback loops.[38]

The shift in mindset is therefore from linear to circular, and systems thinking seeks to untangle the relationships between these interconnected things.

If analysis is about breaking complexity down into manageable components and is therefore more reductionist and appropriate for the mechanical, linear view of the world, the goal in systems thinking is synthesis, or how the elements combine to create something new. So this requires an appreciation of not only the individual components, but also the relationships and dynamics between those individual components, and how they combine to create the whole: 'synthesis is the ability to see interconnectedness'.

Emergence is the result of things interacting and coming together to produce something different. What emerges as a result of the interaction might be completely different from what we set out with or had in mind. As R Buckminster Fuller once said: 'There is nothing in a caterpillar that tells you it will be a butterfly'.[39]

Emergent strategy therefore involves organizations undertaking a series of actions, each perhaps informed by the results of the last action that over time may turn into a consistent pattern of behaviour. In this way it differs from deliberate strategy where a linear set of actions result in something that matches the intended course of action. Deliberate strategy might be akin to rigid, linear business planning that may work well in slow-moving, stable environments but is far less suited to climates that see rapid change and need a more adaptive response. Emergent strategy is that which is constantly evolving, perhaps in diverse ways, in response to changing contexts. Managing it involves not dismissing anything that deviates from the original plan but continually identifying better options and then managing resources flexibly to nourish them.

When elements interact in a system they create constant feedback loops between the components. These feedback loops can either be reinforcing or balancing. A reinforcing feedback loop can happen when elements in a system encourage more of the same thing, which may have a positive impact but which can cause problems if one element continually refines itself to the point where it takes over. An example of this might be how methodologies can become doctrines in business as they reinforce certain behaviours that can then reduce flexibility and adaptability.

Strategist John Willshire has called this the 'pattern problem':[40]

- An example becomes a lesson.
- A lesson becomes a method.
- A method becomes a practice.
- A practice becomes a doctrine.
- A doctrine becomes death.

Conversely, balancing feedback loops are self-correcting and produce stability rather than bolstering more of the same (like a predator/prey situation in natural ecosystems). But dramatic changes in the ecosystem can turn balancing feedback loops into reinforcing ones.

In a dynamic constantly evolving system, understanding feedback loops and causality, or how elements influence each other, becomes important.

It's useful to map systems, particularly when we're looking to change them. When we map systems, we need to take account of not only the component elements, but also the connections, relationships and feedback loops between them. We can then develop insights around interventions or strategies that can shape the system in the most effective way. Simple approaches to systems mapping include:

- actor or stakeholder maps: these show individuals and/or organizations that are important players in the system and how they are related and connected;
- mind maps: these can be used to show influences, changes or trends in the external environment that might influence the issue;
- issue maps: these can be used to set out a given set of issues (social, political, economic) around an entity or problem;
- causal-loop diagrams: these are designed to show the feedback loops (both positive and negative) between players that might impact behaviour or outcomes.

There are various methodologies for mapping systems including cluster maps, where the problem, question or topic goes in the centre, and all the related elements of the system are mapped around that with the connections between them drawn on. Or we might use interconnected circles to investigate the relationships inherent in a system, where the elements of that system are placed around a large circle and the relationships between them connected up. Or we might map out the feedback loops involved in a system as a way to consider how it works.

The point is that every organization is a system, and more than ever in the digital world every company sits within a system and a network of connections. Mapping that system and the relationships within it is a good starting point for informing our understanding of where we are now, and how we might change it. In business, modern value generation is less about rigid, linear processes and more about networked relationships. If businesses increasingly operate as part of more complex ecosystems, we need to be able to map the component parts, to appreciate the relationship, feedback loops and causality between them, and how we can establish and orchestrate successful networks that work for everyone involved.

Genuine (and pretend) customer-centricity

Enough has been written about customer-centric approaches for there to be a high level of understanding about exactly what they mean. Enough businesses have put the phrase in their mission statements and strategy documents for there to be little doubt of its importance. And yet so many customer experiences remain poor; so many customer journeys are broken; so many customers are left frustrated and annoyed rather than surprised and delighted.

Some of this may well be a result of the fact that, in spite of the promise of new technology and the fact that many smart technologies have been around for a relatively long time, we still find it so hard to reimagine experiences, simplify complexity, and empathize well. We're often stuck in looking at the new through the lens of the old and not rethinking from the ground up. This is the 'mid-stage' of digital that Tom Goodwin, author of *Digital Darwinism: Survival of the fittest in the age of business disruption*, describes: 'We're in a hybrid period between two ages. We live in an analogue world augmented by the new possibilities of digital, but not rethought or rebuilt for this era.'[41]

The intentions of many executives are often good, but the real challenge with being genuinely customer-centric is that businesses have ingrained habits to do things for business-centric reasons. They create experiences that make sense for an organization's operating procedures, or structures, or efficiency requirements, but which make no sense for the customer. When it actually comes down to it, most leaders in businesses are actually incentivized and rewarded for doing things that are business-centric, not customer-centric. We undervalue qualities such as empathy or skills like good design because there is no immediate payback. The more senior you get in a company the further away you tend to get from real customers, so it becomes harder to understand real needs, real problems, and connect execution with the reality of experience.

The only way around this is to completely orient your business towards the customer. To not let a few teams or departments be the only ones that get in front of real customers. To embed customer needs in organizational mission, strategy, priorities, tactics and execution and measures. It has to be inherent to the working methodologies. And it has to be part of the very culture of the organization.

CASE STUDY
Amazon working backwards

Amazon's 'working backwards' approach is widely used in the business as a way to pitch new propositions and provide a north star for customer-centric product development and continuous iteration of customer value. Working backwards from the customer is the opposite of the more traditional approach of starting with an idea for a new product or service and then trying to find customers who actually want it.

When pitching a new idea, for example, a product manager begins by writing an internal press release targeting the new/updated product's customers and announcing the finished product. Time is spent finessing this press release as it contains key information about the customer's problem, why or how the current solutions are failing, and why and how the new proposition is going to address this. This provides not only a guiding vision for what the proposition is that can be used at all stages of development, but also acts as a gut-check for whether or not the product or service is exciting enough to actually build. If it's not exciting enough, the product manager needs to iterate or abandon the release. This prevents unnecessary spend as iterating on the release is a lot more cost effective than iterating on the product itself. An example outline for the press release is:[42]

- Heading – Name the product in a way the reader and target customers will understand.
- Subheading – In one sentence below the heading, describe who is the market for the product and what benefit end-users get.
- Summary – An important paragraph to summarize the product and the benefit. This needs to assume that the customer/reader will not read anything else to make sure it captures exactly what the product is.
- Problem – Answering the question of what problem the product is solving.
- Solution – Exactly how the product is solving the problem better and more elegantly.
- Quote from you – An imaginary quote from a company spokesperson about why the product is exciting.
- How to get started – How can you make it easy to get started?
- Customer quote – A quote from a hypothetical customer describing the experience and the benefit that he or she gets.
- Closing and call to action – Pointers for more information, where the reader should go next, and wrap up.

It's worth keeping the press release short and simple, perhaps a maximum of two pages, with no wording that doesn't add to the quality of the description, no jargon, and a good flow to the narrative. If there is a need for more information, that can be included in an accompanying FAQ as a way of ensuring that the press release stays focused on the customer benefit. As Ian McAllister, Director at Airbnb and ex-Amazon staffer notes about working backwards, once the project moves into development the release can act like a guiding light for the team to ensure that they are building what was in the release and no more: 'This keeps product development focused on achieving the customer benefits and not building extraneous stuff that takes longer to build, takes resources to maintain, and doesn't provide real customer benefit.'[43]

References

1 Perkin, N and Abraham, P (2017) *Building the Agile Business Through Digital Transformation*, Kogan Page, London

2 Lorenz, Johannes-Tobias, Mahadevan, Deepak, Oncul, Batu, and Yenigun, Mehmet [accessed 20 August 2022] Scaling Agility: A new operating model for insurers, McKinsey, September 2020 [Online] https://www.mckinsey.com/industries/financial-services/our-insights/scaling-agility-a-new-operating-model-for-insurers (archived at https://perma.cc/PQ7S-3HEG)

3 Perkin, N and Abraham, P (2017) *Building the Agile Business Through Digital Transformation*, Kogan Page, London

4 ideou.com [accessed 6 April 2019] Design Thinking, *IDEO U* [Online]http://www.ideou.com/pages/design-thinking (archived at https://perma.cc/A2TL-DP27)

5 AgileManifesto.com [accessed 24 October 2016] Manifesto for Agile Software Development [Online] http://agilemanifesto.org/ (archived at https://perma.cc/GX8F-Y5CC)

6 Agile Modelling [accessed 6 April 2019] User Stories – An Agile Introduction [Online] http://www.agilemodeling.com/artifacts/userStory.htm (archived at https://perma.cc/ND5J-9PKX)

7 Pezzo, Mark V, Litman, Jordan A and Pezzo, Stephanie P [accessed 6 April 2019] On the Distinction Between Yuppies and Hippies: Individual differences in prediction biases for planning future tasks, *Personality and Individual Differences*, **41** (7), pp 1359–71 [Online] https://www.sciencedirect.com/science/article/pii/S0191886906002194?via%3Dihub (archived at https://perma.cc/Q6SJ-RFT8)

8 Ries, Eric [accessed 24 October 2016] The Lean Start-up, *The Lean Start-up* [Online] http://theleanstartup.com/ (archived at https://perma.cc/U69X-SYZV)

9 Ries, E (2011) *The Lean Startup: How constant innovation creates radically successful businesses*, Portfolio Penguin

10 McClure, Dave [accessed 6 April 2019] Master of 500 Hats: Startup Metrics for Pirates: AARRR! [Online] http://500hats.typepad.com/500blogs/2007/09/startup-metrics.html (archived at https://perma.cc/5H9X-9S2W)

11 Ries, Eric [accessed 6 April 2019] Lean Startup Principles [Online] http://theleanstartup.com/principles (archived at https://perma.cc/U69X-SYZV)

12 Reynolds, Roo [accessed 13 March 2019] Agile in the Public Sector, May 2016 [Online] http://rooreynolds.com/2016/05/25/agile-in-the-public-sector/ (archived at https://perma.cc/H6WF-BLFN)

13 Reynolds, Roo [accessed 13 March 2019] Agile in the Public Sector, May 2016 [Online] http://rooreynolds.com/2016/05/25/agile-in-the-public-sector/ (archived at https://perma.cc/H6WF-BLFN)

14 Nason, R (2017) *Rethinking Risk Management: Critically examining old ideas and new concepts*, Business Expert Press

15 Nason, R (2017) *Rethinking Risk Management: Critically examining old ideas and new concepts*, Business Expert Press

16 Wilde, Gerald [accessed 30 March 2019] Challenges to Accident Prevention: The issue of risk compensation behavior [Online] https://www.researchgate.net/publication/292792694_Challenges_to_accident_prevention_The_issue_of_risk_compensation_behavior (archived at https://perma.cc/QYX5-CWVB)

17 The New York Times [accessed 30 March 2019] From the Start, Signs of Trouble at Health Portal [Online] https://www.nytimes.com/2013/10/13/us/politics/from-the-start-signs-of-trouble-at-health-portal.html (archived at https://perma.cc/B9SU-4NKU)

18 Shirky, Clay [accessed 30 March 2019] Healthcare.gov and the Gulf Between Planning and Reality, November 2013 [Online] http://www.shirky.com/weblog/2013/11/healthcare-gov-and-the-gulf-between-planning-and-reality/ (archived at https://perma.cc/U94P-URNX)

19 International Project Leadership Academy [accessed 9 March 2019] Why Do Projects Fail? [Online] http://calleam.com/WTPF/?p=4700 (archived at https://perma.cc/465R-S3PS)

20 International Project Leadership Academy [accessed 9 March 2019] Why Do Projects Fail? [Online] http://calleam.com/WTPF/?p=4700 (archived at https://perma.cc/465R-S3PS)

21 BBC News [accessed 9 March 2019] Q & A, A380 Delays, October 2006 [Online]: http://news.bbc.co.uk/1/hi/business/5405524.stm (archived at https://perma.cc/U757-LVU2)

22 SalesForce Customer Experience Statistics [accessed 14 February 2019] [Online] https://www.salesforce.com/blog/2013/10/customer-service-stats-55-of-consumers-would-pay-more-for-a-better-service-experience.html (archived at https://perma.cc/9PJG-3YVQ)

23 Walker [accessed 14 February 2019] Customer 2020 [Online] https://www.walkerinfo.com/knowledge-center/featured-research-reports/Customers-2020-A-Progress-Report-OLD (archived at https://perma.cc/ZH72-5T8H)

24 Econsultancy [accessed 14 February 2019] Digital Intelligence Briefing [Online] https://econsultancy.com/reports/digital-intelligence-briefing-2017-digital-trends/ (archived at https://perma.cc/2A5M-KQDZ)

25 MadebyMany [accessed 14 February 2019] Uber's Children vs Conscious Consumers [Online] https://www.madebymany.com/stories/uber-s-children-vs-conscious-consumers (archived at https://perma.cc/V33U-F7KU)

26 Uber [accessed 14 February 2019] Expectations as We Grow [Online] https://www.uber.com/newsroom/uber-expectations-as-we-grow (archived at https://perma.cc/322V-YGN2)

27 Uber [accessed 14 February 2019] Expectations as We Grow [Online] https://www.uber.com/newsroom/uber-expectations-as-we-grow (archived at https://perma.cc/322V-YGN2)

28 Goodwin, T (2018) *Digital Darwinism: Survival of the fittest in the age of business disruption*, Kogan Page, London

29 Slate [accessed 30 January 2019] Hit Parade: The Great War Against the Single Edition [Online] http://www.slate.com/articles/podcasts/hit_parade/2017/09/the_story_of_how_the_recording_industry_made_you_pay_a_premium_for_90s_hit.html (archived at https://perma.cc/5H8D-YWR4)

30 Harvard Business Review [accessed 14 February 2019] Pipelines, Platforms, and the New Rules of Strategy [Online] https://hbr.org/2016/04/pipelines-platforms-and-the-new-rules-of-strategy (archived at https://perma.cc/UT8D-8FH6)

31 Harvard Business Review [accessed 14 February 2019] Pipelines, Platforms, and the New Rules of Strategy [Online] https://hbr.org/2016/04/pipelines-platforms-and-the-new-rules-of-strategy (archived at https://perma.cc/UT8D-8FH6)

32 O'Reilly, Tim [accessed 15 February 2019] Government as a Platform [Online] https://www.mitpressjournals.org/doi/pdf/10.1162/INOV_a_00056 (archived at https://perma.cc/Y62R-C2U8)

33 Bracken, Mike [accessed 15 February 2019] Government Digital Service, Government as a Platform [Online] https://gds.blog.gov.uk/2015/03/29/government-as-a-platform-the-next-phase-of-digital-transformation/ (archived at https://perma.cc/ZJF3-MAKU)

34 SimilarWeb [accessed 15 February 2019] ASOS Traffic [Online] https://www.similarweb.com/website/marketplace.asos.com#overview (archived at https://perma.cc/P9BD-48XS)

35 Tools for Systems Thinkers [accessed 17 February 2019] The 6 Fundamental Concepts of Systems Thinking [Online] https://medium.com/disruptive-design/tools-for-systems-thinkers-the-6-fundamental-concepts-of-systems-thinking-379cdac3dc6a (archived at https://perma.cc/S4ZJ-5UD6)

36 Systems Theory Overview [accessed 17 February 2019] [Online] http://www.cs.unb.ca/~fritz/cs3503/system35.htm (archived at https://perma.cc/J3T2-M4LM)

37 Disrupt Design [accessed 14 February 2019] The Three Main Systems at Play in the World [Online] https://www.disruptdesign.co/blog/the-3-main-systems-at-play-in-the-world-are (archived at https://perma.cc/3QKK-FASA)

38 Tools for Systems Thinkers [accessed 17 February 2019] The 6 Fundamental Concepts of Systems Thinking [Online] https://medium.com/disruptive-design/tools-for-systems-thinkers-the-6-fundamental-concepts-of-systems-thinking-379cdac3dc6a (archived at https://perma.cc/S4ZJ-5UD6)

39 Montana Institute [accessed 14 February 2019] R Buckminster Fuller [Online] http://www.montanainstitute.com/blog/2014/4/20/there-is-nothing-in-a-caterpillar-that-tells-you-its-going-to-be-a-butterfly-richard-buckminster-fuller (archived at https://perma.cc/SSZ5-UDL8)

40 Google Firestarters [accessed 14 February 2019] Patterns of Behaviour [Online] https://www.onlydeadfish.co.uk/only_dead_fish/2017/09/google-firestarters-25-patterns-of-behaviour.html (archived at https://perma.cc/55K7-QHEN)

41 Goodwin, T (2018) *Digital Darwinism: Survival of the fittest in the age of business disruption*, Kogan Page Inspire

42 McAllister, Ian [accessed 9 March 2019] Director at Airbnb, ex-Amazon, Quora answer to 'What is Amazon's Approach to Product Development and Product Management?' [Online] https://www.quora.com/What-is-Amazons-approach-to-product-development-and-product-management (archived at https://perma.cc/6YCB-JLMR)

43 McAllister, Ian [accessed 9 March 2019] Director at Airbnb, ex-Amazon, Quora answer to 'What is Amazon's Approach to Product Development and Product Management?' [Online] https://www.quora.com/What-is-Amazons-approach-to-product-development-and-product-management (archived at https://perma.cc/6YCB-JLMR)

03

A new agile operating system for business

The key technology dynamics in companies

As technology develops at pace and empowers new capabilities throughout the business, not least through emerging areas such as machine learning, leaders will increasingly need to make smart choices about how they balance critical dynamics in order to maximize opportunity.

Marketing Technologist Scott Brinker has described these dynamics as the need to achieve the right balance between technology and people (between automation and humanization), and centralization and decentralization (between scale and speed).[1] When considering the latter dynamic, we need to recognize the advantages that can come from centralizing key processes, data and tools to achieve the benefit of scale across the organization. This enables us to share common practices and standards, deliver more consistent customer experience through shared data, cut out duplicated effort and tools, and establish repeatable processes that enable efficiency. But the counterpoint to this is the need to also optimize workflow for local context, empower teams to experiment and respond at speed, and enable the serving of more personalized customer experiences based on local context (Figure 3.1).

When it comes to the other axis, we have the opportunity to harness automation at scale through a coherent technology stack evaluated, integrated and maintained at a global level, and orchestrate the flow between decentralized and centralized data and technology. Yet we also need to invest in the people end of this spectrum to capitalize on human judgement and oversight, to encourage continuous learning, experimentation and knowledge sharing, to tie strategies and activity back to values and culture, to empower individuals to override automation when it's necessary to protect

FIGURE 3.1 Organizational technology dynamics

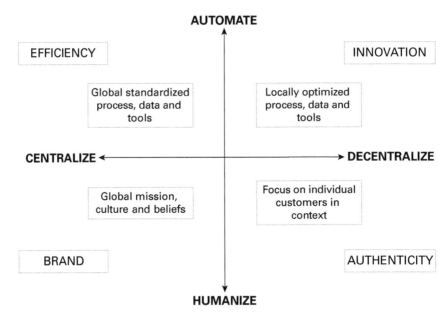

SOURCE Reproduced with kind permission of Scott Brinker, The 4 Forces of Marketing Operations and Technology, August 2018 [Online] https://chiefmartec.com/2018/08/4-forces-marketing-operations-technology/

customer and brand experience, and to enable and inspire empathy and creativity. We need to avoid what Scott calls 'Jurassic Park' (using a quote from the film): 'Your scientists were so preoccupied with whether or not they could that they didn't stop to think if they should.'[2]

Scott originated this matrix in the context of marketing technology, but this model captures the critical dynamics across the wider technology organization. It's easy for businesses to gravitate to extremes when considering the impact of technology but, of course, the truth always lies somewhere in the middle.

Small teams can drive big change

Greater organizational agility comes from empowered teams that perform well in solving the challenges that really matter to the business. But those teams don't need to be big. Small, multidisciplinary teams empowered by digital technologies can generate a disproportionate amount of change and value in transformation programmes and beyond.

There is a temptation in large businesses to throw resource at problems in the assumption that more brains and bodies mean better solutions. Internal politics results in people being included in the process who don't really need to be there and don't contribute much value. Representatives of functions that may be needed only at key points get included in the project team from the beginning and have to attend every update meeting. The result is 20+ people sat in a room trying to move a project forward. Everything slows down.

The reality is that more is not better for team effectiveness. Harvard professor (and specialist in team dynamics) Richard Hackman has shown that one of the key challenges with large teams is in the growing burden of communication.[3] Put simply, as group size increases the number of unique links between people also increases, but exponentially (Figure 3.2).

Communication in teams is subject to a combinatorial explosion. In other words, as people are added to the team the lines of communication are

FIGURE 3.2 Impact of team size

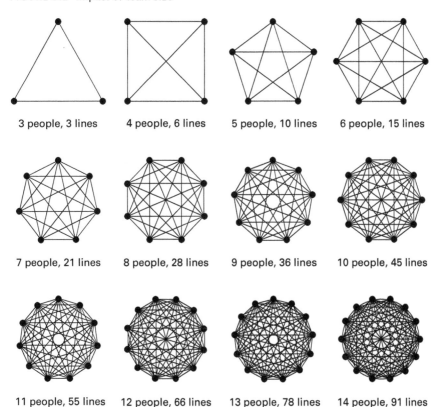

3 people, 3 lines   4 people, 6 lines   5 people, 10 lines   6 people, 15 lines

7 people, 21 lines   8 people, 28 lines   9 people, 36 lines   10 people, 45 lines

11 people, 55 lines   12 people, 66 lines   13 people, 78 lines   14 people, 91 lines

subject to a rapidly accelerating increase. Communication overhead increases dramatically, which very quickly comes at the expense of productivity.

Small teams have other benefits beyond the ability to align, iterate and move fast. They are also more likely to generate new ideas. An analysis of more than 65 million papers, patents and software projects from science and technology found that whilst larger teams more often develop and consolidate existing knowledge small teams are far more likely to introduce new and breakout ideas.[4] James Evans, one of the authors of the study and Professor of Sociology and Director of the Knowledge Lab at the University of Chicago, described how larger teams have a tendency towards building on recent successes: 'Big teams are almost always more conservative. The work they produce is like blockbuster sequels; very reactive and low-risk.'[5] Small teams, on the other hand, are more likely to come up with disruptive and innovative ideas and research and appreciate the potential of the work that they are doing.

Hackman defined four key features that are critical to create an effective team in an organization:

- common team tasks that work towards fulfilling a compelling vision;
- clear boundaries in terms of who is in the team, information flow, and alignment with other resources, priorities, policies and teams;
- autonomy to work within these boundaries;
- stability.

It is therefore critical that we understand the difference between a real team and a looser 'co-acting' group, and how a (surprisingly common) lack of clarity, direction and autonomy impairs the ability to move fast.

Jeff Bezos, focused on retaining agility as Amazon scales, has famously described how teams in the company should get no larger than the number of people it takes to feed with two large pizzas (six to eight people). An effective small, multidisciplinary team is comprised of the people and skills areas needed to achieve key outcomes and no more (in the book we outline an effective way of managing dependencies across multiple small teams to ensure that the core team is kept small). This is important since it avoids not only communication problems, but also team-scaling fallacy (the tendency for people to overestimate team capability and underestimate task completion time as team size grows), and relational loss (the feeling that it is difficult to get support in large teams).

The multidisciplinary composition of the team is important not only in achieving outputs, but in encouraging diversity. As Richard Hackman points out, homogeneity of team membership can often be a real problem in project teams since we tend to pick like-minded people to work with. Yet performance and creativity improve with greater diversity (including cognitive diversity and having a substantive range in views about how the work should be structured and executed): 'It is task-related conflict, not interpersonal harmony, that spurs team excellence.'[6]

Digital technologies have transformed the dynamics of team contribution. Small, empowered teams can originate transformational ideas and successfully apply their capability to build and execute those ideas well. It's time we reimagined how we resource value creation in business.

Moving away from strict hierarchies

There has been a reasonable amount of focus over the last few years questioning the value of strict hierarchical structures in business and asking whether, particularly in the context of today's digital-empowered and networked operating models, this traditional approach to organization needs to change.

It's a good question to ask. Despite the fact that the context in which business operates has changed substantially due to the impact of digital technology, most businesses are still structured in ways that made more sense in an industrial age where control, efficiency, scale and minimization of deviance were all important. But does that really make sense in a world that is increasingly characterized by horizontality, networks, data and value flows, systems thinking and platform business models?

The challenges inherent in hierarchy as an organizing principle have already been addressed by some. A broad meta-study of 54 prior studies (covering analysis of over 13,000 teams) conducted by Lindred Greer, Bart de Jong, Maartje Schouten and Jennifer Dannals at Stanford Graduate School of Business ('Why and When Hierarchy Impacts Team Effectiveness: A meta-analytic integration'[7]) found that the net effect of hierarchy on performance was broadly negative. Whilst some expert-based hierarchies helped improve team performance, many others were dysfunctional.

Yet hierarchy is not inherently bad. It can bring order, clarity, governance and leadership. But an over-reliance on hierarchy, and an overly fixed view of top-down organizational design can hamper agility and the kind of continuous innovation, team and individual autonomy, customer-centric approaches and strategic and tactical adaptability and responsiveness that are quickly becoming table-stakes for organizational resilience and survival. Functional silos act against the ability to create joined-up, exceptional customer experiences. They hamper the ability to collaborate quickly. They get in the way of cross-functional design and innovation. They limit flexibility of job activity. It's no accident that (often self-organizing) small, multidisciplinary teams have become the engine of change in many forward-thinking companies. With near-universal access to information, the old ideas of leadership as having all the answers and solutions, which then flow downwards, have become grossly outdated.

Yet there are challenges at the other end of the organization design spectrum too. Some brave businesses have taken a radical approach to the adoption of flatter structures using methodologies like Holacracy,[8] which distributes power more horizontally at scale across the company. Shoe retailer Zappos is perhaps the most renowned example of a business that has adopted Holacracy, yet in spite of Holacracy being around for over a decade there are still very few examples of it being applied successfully at scale and Zappos have admitted that they've had to significantly evolve the way it works in their organization since its deployment in 2014.[9]

So as always, the answer is somewhere in the middle. Organizations need to balance the benefits that can accrue from hierarchy (efficiency, clarity of authority, concentration of specialist expertise, clear lines of communication and simplified career path) with those of a more fluid, evolving structure (agility, adaptiveness, cross-functional collaboration and innovation, speed of delivery). Since many businesses are structured in relatively rigid functional disciplines and hierarchies, the direction of change is clearly towards greater fluidity and challenging the long-standing orthodoxies about the optimal way to organize teams. We need to reinvent organization design around a more nuanced understanding of where hierarchy is beneficial, and where it is not in order to balance the extremes, adeptly manage the interplay between them, and bring a new level of flexibility to structures that can enable far greater organizational agility.

CASE STUDY
Haier's Microenterprises

The transformation of Chinese company Haier from an ailing fridge factory in
Qingdao to one of the world's largest consumer electronics businesses is an
exceptional exemplar of bold thinking in bringing agility to life through culture,
management practice and organizational design.

In the 1980s, the Haier factory was deep in debt, and suffering from poor
management, dilapidated infrastructure and producing around 80 refrigerators a
month. New CEO Zhang Ruimin began to turn the fortunes of the business around
through a spotlight on improving product quality, which had been a major problem
for the firm. Yet as the company became more successful and grew ever larger,
Ruimin was passionate about embedding a culture of entrepreneurship, innovation
and agility.

As the company scaled, Ruimin cut back on middle management and separated
his 75,000 workforce into more than 4,000 microenterprises (MEs), many of which
have only 10 to 15 employees. These MEs act as a network of small companies
within the larger company, each with their own profit and loss account, and focused
on specific business and customer needs and groups, and have a high level of
flexibility to adapt as required without lengthy, bureaucratic sign-off.

There are three main varieties of ME within Haier. 'Transforming' MEs are
market-facing units that are focused on reinventing legacy propositions for the
web-enabled world. A smaller number of 'incubating' MEs help to originate entirely
new businesses to capitalize on emerging markets or technologies and ensure a
continuous stream of breakthrough innovation. A much larger number of 'node'
MEs sell component products and services (from HR support to design to
manufacturing) to Haier's other market-facing MEs. In this internal contracting
approach, MEs are free to go externally for access to services if they so desire,
meaning that services that would traditionally be internal monopolies (anything
from R&D, to finance, IT, HR and so on, where departments have no choice but to
use them) are exposed to market competition and therefore forced to be efficient
and best in class.

Haier has turned its own company into a flat organization that is an open
marketplace of ideas, talent and resources, with the MEs often in competition for the
best. Instead of rigid functional silos, employees are empowered to propose new
ideas, which are then put to a vote, and those that are successful become project
leaders who can recruit other employees for their venture. Employees have freedom
to work on the projects that they find most compelling, and once a project is over
the people working on it go back in to the marketplace. Effectively Haier has become

like a fast-moving, networked startup characterized by high levels of agility, self-organization, talent development and entrepreneurship.[10]

Ruimin instigated a 'zero distance to customers' principle designed to create greater customer intimacy alongside responsiveness, with everything being focused on the end-value that is being created for the end-user whether that be a customer in the market, another ME within Haier, or a partner of the business. Compensation is aligned to business performance but also customer value in a concept they call *rendanheyi*, a mashup of Chinese characters that represents a close link between the value created for customers and that which is received by employees. Base salaries are low but a combination of bonuses, dividends and profit-sharing mean that earning potential is high. This ensures exceptional levels of service and customer experience, greater flexibility in enabling MEs to configure their network of service providers as needed, faster lines of communication between the company and its customers and external partners, but also a collaborative approach to resolve problems to help MEs hit their targets.

Rather than using last year's performance as a starting point, each ME is set challenging targets for growth 'outside in', by a dedicated research unit that looks at what is possible. Those MEs that are market facing are often expected to grow revenues and profit at multiples of the industry average, but the targets do adapt in response to shifting circumstances. A series of metrics that consider user involvement in development, extent of profits derived from ecosystem value and unique customer value are used to track performance alongside more traditional targets and measures.

Haier believes in the principles of open innovation, opening the business up to external cooperation and input in order to generate new propositions, but it also believes that in many instances of corporate open innovation the speed of innovation is very fast outside of the organization, but then slows down dramatically as soon as it comes into the business when it is subjected to embedded processes and rules. In order to mitigate this, employees are empowered to become entrepreneurs and create their own ME to serve specific business needs.

One example of this is when the company needed to move into the three-door refrigerator market (two fridge doors and one freezer door at the bottom). The company put a request for proposals on its intranet as an invitation to bid. One of the employees won the bid and was given seed money to begin building a team and a business. He sensibly brought in some of the other employees that had bid but not won yet had good ideas, and they then hired manufacturing, research, development and marketing capability and talent. They started a business that two years later was generating around US \$1.5 billion in revenues.[11]

To become more native to the digital world, market-facing MEs are encouraged to innovate to support the move from providing products and services to developing platforms and ecosystems. One example of this is Community Laundry, which grew from a mobile app that enabled Chinese university students to schedule and pay for dormitory laundry facilities, to an ecosystem that hosts many other businesses, retaining a share of the revenue that it takes from the 9 million users of the service.[12]

The MEs are brought together into groups (called platforms), which are focused mainly on product categories or sometimes key competencies, as a way to coordinate major investment initiatives. Platform owners identify opportunities for cross-platform collaboration, set relevant standards that the rest of the organization can use, and are incentivized to drive platform growth.

Haier's fast-flowing network of MEs has empowered not only a unique level of agility, but exceptional success, from a failing factory in Qingdao to a multinational consumer electronics giant with revenues of US $35 billion. Over the last decade the gross profits of its core appliance business have grown by 23 per cent annually, performance that has enabled them to acquire other manufacturers including GE Appliances. And the company has generated over US $2 billion in market value from new ventures.[13]

A central vision focused on quality and service provides a north star for strategy. The lack of hierarchy enables the company to move quickly and means that frontline sales staff can bring customer ideas straight back to top management in order to inform innovation and strategy. The fluidity of their modular structure means that employees are used to continuous change, more comfortable with uncertainty, and can more easily embrace opportunities for entrepreneurialism. It is an organization built for continuous innovation, that is adaptive yet resilient and coherent.

Changing innovation horizons

McKinsey's Three Horizons model for innovation[14] has long been a definitive way of categorizing the different types of innovation that a company needs to focus on to create lasting advantage. The impact of highly scalable and accessible digital infrastructure and technologies, however, is challenging the model in some critical ways.

The model famously seeks to define the different types of innovation that businesses need to focus on if they are to survive and thrive:

- Horizon 1 is about incremental improvements or continuous innovation around a company's existing products, models, or core capabilities. This type of innovation typically focuses on existing markets or utilizes existing technologies that the company is familiar with, and is likely the easiest and most common form of innovation.

- Horizon 2 innovations are more about adjacencies, next-generation products and likely focused on extending the company's existing business model or core capabilities to new markets or customers, perhaps using new technologies. Since this extends into areas that the company is less familiar with, it likely requires thinking and techniques different from Horizon 1.

- Horizon 3 innovations are entirely new, breakthrough products or categories that are pushing the boundaries, responding to or taking advantage of disruption, and pushing the company to explore new markets or technologies.

Originally articulated in the book *The Alchemy of Growth* in 2000 by Baghai, Coley and White,[15] the model has become a well-referenced way of describing the need for organizations to shape focus and funding on the different types of innovation and how the ability to create ongoing competitive advantage depends on all three types. Whilst it's easier for businesses to focus on incremental innovation that is closer to existing, well-understood models (Horizon 1), there is a requirement for a more comprehensive approach that recognizes the need for continuous exploration in lesser known areas (Horizons 2 and 3).

Three Horizons presents a way that organizations can concurrently manage optimizing for current growth opportunities whilst discovering and building potential future opportunities for growth. But it is important for businesses to recognize the differences in the way in which you manage each one, for example: approaches to risk and payback; sources of value creation; measures; and the allocation of senior management time.

The source of value creation in Horizon 1 comes from superior execution, in Horizon 2 from 'positional advantage' (where you are trying to gain a better position relative to your competitors), and in Horizon 3 from insight and foresight around changing customer and market contexts and opportunities.

McKinsey found that Horizons 2 and 3 required more time from senior leaders, but also a commitment to avoid starving these innovations of resources due to short-term financial pressures. They also found that in

Horizon 3, whilst the general hit rate may be lower, successful innovators clustered their experiments into between two to five themes depending on the size of the organization.

Measures through the Horizons also differed. Horizon 1 is more about profit, cash flow and return on invested capital, overseen by experienced business managers. Horizon 2 is more entrepreneurial, so is supervised by 'business builders' whose metrics for success might be revenue milestones and net present value. Horizon 3 is far more emergent and so requires visionaries and 'champions' who are focused on emerging technological and commercial value milestones.

Yet as Silicon Valley entrepreneur Steve Blank has noted, some of the dynamics that characterize the model, most notably the delivery time for each horizon, have fundamentally changed.[16]

The McKinsey model accounts for the fact that different industries may have different timescales for innovations to return value (short-cycle industries, for example, may see value created quicker), but in general the impact on profit and cash flow, and current market value is far longer with more emergent innovations than it is for extending core capabilities. Horizon 1 may therefore deliver impact in the short term since it is focused on models and capabilities that are already contributing the majority of value and profit today. Horizon 2 may take three to five years to see a return since it involves extending existing businesses and capabilities. And Horizon 3 may take as long as five to twelve years as it involves more disruptive creation of value.

In the modern environment, however, Blank notes that the time it can take for disruptive ideas to be researched, engineered and scaled to market has been radically transformed by digital technologies and networks. Horizons 2 and 3 may now happen at speed. The potential for new, emergent, even disruptive, ideas to be rapidly prototyped and then to generate scale and take on a life of their own has added an entirely new dynamic: 'These rapid Horizon 3 deliverables emphasize disruption, asymmetry and most importantly speed, over any other characteristic. Serviceability, maintainability, completeness, scale etc are all secondary to speed of deployment and asymmetry.'[17]

The Three Horizons, whilst still a valid and important way of understanding the different types of innovation that businesses need to continuously focus on, is no longer bound by time. Disruptive businesses, unencumbered by legacy technologies and systems, and entrenched, slower moving processes, can move faster towards generating return from newer, disruptive technologies and models.

Blank defines four key ways in which incumbents can counter this kind of rapid disruption:

- Incentivizing third-party resources to focus on your goal or mission – open innovation initiatives, allowing external parties to innovate from your data through APIs, creating new marketplaces through platform thinking (Apple and the App store), partnering with entrepreneurs to venture build around aligned goals (Diageo and Distill Ventures[18] would be an example of this), setting incentivized, inclusive challenges (DARPA Prize Challenges is an example of this,[19] as is Elon Musk's Hyperloop Pod Competition which since 2015 has challenged teams of University students around the world to support the development of functional Hyperloop prototypes[20]).

- Acquiring external innovators that can operate at the speed of the disruptors. The challenge here though is the not-insignificant potential for corporate culture, processes, and approaches to stifle any speed advantage that the newer business has.

- Rapidly copying new, disruptive models (like Google copying Overture's pay-per-click model) – this carries with it the risk of not properly understanding customer needs and contexts and so failing to do it well.

- Innovating better than the disruptors (like Amazon and AWS, Apple and the iPhone). This is, of course, extremely difficult for a large, incumbent organization to pull off when it is focused on execution, optimization and protecting legacy value creation.

Three Horizons remains an extremely useful taxonomy, but the trap is that we underappreciate the impact of repurposing existing Horizon 1 technologies into new models at speed, and the rapidity with which new, emergent propositions can be iterated and scaled.

The real challenge with transformation

Futurologist and Google's Director of Engineering Ray Kurzweil famously described the life cycle of a technology (or inventions based on technology) as an 'S-curve'. They begin with a slow adoption, which is then followed by a period of high growth and rapid development, before the growth plateaus into maturity (Figure 3.3).

FIGURE 3.3 Technology S-curve

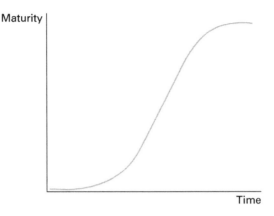

It's important to understand the impact of this trajectory on innovation. Artificial Intelligence, for example, was birthed in the 1950s and has progressed in some critical ways since then but only in the last few years has reached the point of real democratization and more universal business application. Kurzweil noted that it was important that inventions should take account of a future world and not just current contexts,[21] but timing is also critical. Thus, the cycle begins as the enabling factors for the technology innovation come into place, it is then invented, refined and developed, it then matures and becomes a part of everyday life and seems immune from disruption (a belief that is perhaps reinforced by the failure of early disruptors), before being usurped by newcomers and sliding into obsolescence.

The S-curve is a useful way of representing the development of technological innovations but it was Charles Handy who (in his book on making sense of the future, *The Empty Raincoat*[22]) originally used the S-curve as a way of describing the trajectory of many successful systems. His pattern of overlapping S-curves demonstrates the need for regular reinvention, but also the challenge inherent in disruption and transformation. It's an excellent metaphor to express the real challenge inherent in transformation.

Let's say an organization is represented by Curve 1 in Figure 3.4. It's doing well in exploiting its existing advantage and so may be approaching the top of its S-curve. When the new wave of technology or next wave of disruption comes in at Point A that is the moment when it needs to innovate and yet there is little reason to do so since everything looks pretty good.

FIGURE 3.4 S-curves and the ambiguity zone

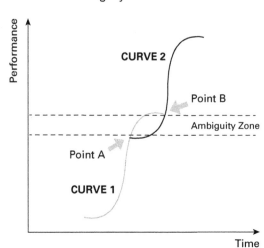

The business is making more money than ever before and is well optimized. There is no reason to look forwards and anticipate a different future and yet that is precisely what they should do.

As the new technology or disruptive force starts to scale, the incumbent organization may well find itself at Point B, caught out by the speed of change. In this instance, it could well already be too late since the incumbent is set up around an existing advantage and has not yet done the work to understand how to create value in the new paradigm. New entrants to the market or nimble, disruptive incumbents *have* done the work and so can scale fast – too fast for the slow-moving incumbent to catch up. Many organizations, of course, wait until they reach crisis point before actioning significant change but by then leadership credibility and competitive position may already have been damaged irrevocably. As Ray Kurzweil said, we need to invent for what will be rather than what is now. We have to look forwards to Point B and work back to understand when and how we need to make the transition.

There is a second challenge inherent with the shift from one curve to the next, represented by the 'ambiguity zone' in the chart. During this transitionary period the business needs to be managing business as usual and delivering to its quarterly targets, shareholder value, and all of the priorities characterized by the existing S-curve, whilst concurrently inventing the business of the future and making the shift to the new S-curve. This is the 'messy middle' of transformation. The period when a business is effectively trying to change the wheels on the car as it is driving along; the period when it will need to balance resources carefully between the old and the new; the period when it may need to be willing to be misunderstood, to experiment and learn fast, to make intelligent bets on the future.

The real challenge with all of this, however, is that businesses are not only facing one S-curve that they will have to deal with but successive, overlapping S-curves. Continual and restless reinvention is therefore the new normal.

The problem with corporate innovation

One of the greatest challenges with corporate innovation is the ability to step outside of existing (often hidden or toxic) assumptions to reimagine existing propositions, relationships or processes from the ground up. It's hard to argue for a disruptive idea when everything the business currently knows detracts from how viable that idea looks. It's even harder to execute.

JFC Fuller was an officer in the British Army, a military strategist and historian, and one of the founders of modern armoured warfare. He became chief of staff of the British tank corps from late 1916. His 'Plan 1919' from the First World War was a pioneering and ambitious strategy to use new British tanks to roll over the German trenches and strike a decisive sledge-hammer blow to the German army that would end the war.[23] The plan involved amassing 5,000 heavy and medium British tanks, 3,000 of which would be used to penetrate German defences along a 90-mile front supported from the air. Then 800 faster-moving medium tanks would proceed to attack the German army's string of headquarters miles behind the trenches to disrupt the command structures. A further 1,200 medium tanks, supported by artillery, airpower, cavalry and truck-mounted infantry would then move rapidly to penetrate far behind enemy lines.

Fuller's lightning thrust plan was revolutionary. Tanks had until then only been used to open up gaps in the enemy trenches through which foot infantry could advance a few miles. But Fuller was proposing a new form of mechanized warfare that could end the attritional stalemate of trench warfare and focus on disorganizing the enemy. He wrote: 'Tactical success in war is generally gained by pitting an organized force against a disorganized one.'[24]

Yet the plan was never used. Fuller's biographer Brian Holden Reid called Plan 1919 'the most famous unused plan in military history'.[25] Yet as Tim Harford, writing in the *Financial Times* notes, Fuller had actually created an entirely new military strategy that would be studied by the Germans and implemented to devastating effect in 1940. Fuller had in fact invented Blitzkreig.[26]

After Fuller's plan failed to see the light of day in the First World War, many nations still resisted his ideas and believed that tanks should be used in small pockets to support infantry. The army even went as far as stopping the publication of Fuller's book for several years yet Heinz Guderian, the mastermind behind Hitler's blitzkrieg, managed to read Fuller's work after the war and, of course, used it to great impact.

The story is an excellent analogy for why organizations so often look at the new through the lens of the old and ignore the kind of ideas and concepts that can be truly transformational, even if those concepts are originated inside their own organizations: Xerox Parc's personal computer with mouse and graphical user interface; Steven Sasson's first digital camera for Kodak; Sony's Memory Stick Walkman; the IBM Simon; the first touchscreen phone.

In 2010, author and technologist Kevin Kelly wrote about Clay Shirky's quote that: 'Institutions will try to preserve the problem to which they are the solution.'[27] He called it the 'Shirky Principle', in reference to the Peter Principle, which says that people in organizations get promoted to their 'level of incompetence'. Their promotion is based on their previous successes but since skills for one job don't necessarily translate to another job they eventually reach a level at which they are no longer competent. Their previous achievements prevent them from being fired but they can't progress further so they stagnate in their incompetence. The Shirky Principle speaks to the idea that complex entities like a company or an industry can become so dedicated to the problem that they are the solution to that often they inadvertently perpetuate or prolong the problem. Companies get stuck in the strategies and thinking that have made them successful before. Path dependence means that decisions and choices are made based on past or present knowledge, limited by the current competency, rather than thinking about what might be possible.

Tim Harford references a 1990 paper by Rebecca Henderson and Kim Clark (Architectural Innovation: The reconfiguration of existing product technologies and the failure of established firms[28]) in which the authors distinguish between different types of innovation based on the components of a product and the way that they are integrated into the system, setting out four key types of product innovation:

1   **Incremental innovation:** this may strengthen the core components of the product but it also maintains the existing linkages between them (an example would be improving the performance of a car component like a driveshaft without impacting the way in which the car is put together).

2   **Modular innovation:** which may change the fundamental technology of the component but still doesn't change the way in which the system links together (like an automatic transmission).

3   **Architectural innovation:** this may change the design but whilst the components may not change significantly the way in which they link together does (like front-wheel drive transmissions).

4   **Radical innovation:** which is the most extreme, and involves changing both the technology of the components and also the way in which they link together (electric vehicles, for example).

Henderson and Clark make the case that architectural and radical innovation can more fundamentally challenge the existing organizational structure and processes, which makes it more difficult for incumbents to respond: 'architectural innovations destroy the usefulness of the architectural knowledge of established firms, and... since architectural knowledge tends to become embedded in the structure and information-processing procedures of established organizations, this destruction is difficult for firms to recognize and hard to correct.'[29]

Incremental and modular innovation are less challenging to established structures since the system doesn't fundamentally change. Radical innovation establishes a new dominant design and a new set of design concepts embodied in components that are linked together in a new architecture. Architectural innovation involves the reconfiguration of an established system, linking together existing components in new ways. So it can be harder to perceive and make sense of since it involves similar component parts to the problem that are put together in new ways and so have very different relationships with each other. When an organizational structure and information flow has grown up around the old system, it becomes very difficult for the company to respond in suitable ways. The structure gets in the way.

Henderson uses the example of IBM to demonstrate how a company can respond well even to radical innovation if it fits the structure that already exists. IBM successfully dealt with significant developments such as the semiconductor, the integrated circuit, the hard drive, and the shift to mainframe computing since it was not dissimilar in structure to producing mechanical tabulating machines. Yet when it came to the PC revolution IBM's initial success came only from going against existing strengths and the advantages of its extant structure, and eventually internal politics rose up and the PC division struggled to cope and was sold off. Similarly, in the First World War, the invention of the tank did not fit existing systems and structures for fighting the war and so the real potential to use it in a very decisive way was missed.

In 1968 programmer Melvin Conway wrote that: 'organizations which design systems… are constrained to produce designs which are copies of the communication structures of these organizations.'[30]

'Conway's Law' as it became known, was based on the observation that building software requires multiple engineers to communicate with each other frequently in order for the software to work properly, so the interface structure of software naturally shows congruence with the social structure of the organization that created it. This similarity between organizations and designs he called homomorphism, noting that: 'the very act of organizing a design team means that certain design decisions have already been made, explicitly or otherwise.'[31]

US computer scientist Fred Brooks noted the wider application of this concept in management theory, observing in his early book on software engineering (*The Mythical Man-Month*[32]): 'Because the design that occurs first is almost never the best possible, the prevailing system concept may need to change. Therefore, flexibility of organization is important to effective design.'

The point is that when we've started to design any system the choices that we've already made can fundamentally affect the final output. Organization structure and the design/architecture of propositions are intrinsically linked meaning that architectural or radical innovation become very difficult since they require a fundamental rewiring of the way in which the component parts are linked together. Put simply, the existing way in which the business is organized constrains any innovation that is not incremental or modular. Greater organizational flexibility and fluidity is therefore required to organize quickly to fix mistakes and adapt around new models.

In writing about Conway's Law, strategist Noah Brier references the work of Harvard Business School professor Carliss Baldwin.[33] Baldwin's work around the so-called 'mirroring hypothesis' shows that mirroring between technical dependencies and organizational ties becomes evident as a way of preserving scarce cognitive resources in solving complex problems:

People charged with implementing complex projects or processes are inevitably faced with interdependencies that create technical problems and conflicts in real time. They must arrive at solutions that take account of the technical constraints; hence, they must communicate with one another and cooperate to solve their problems. Communication channels, collocation, and employment relations are organizational ties that support communication and cooperation between individuals, and thus, we should expect to see a very close relationship – technically a homomorphism – between a network graph of technical dependencies within a complex system and network graphs of organizational ties showing communication channels, collocation, and employment relations.[34]

In other words mirroring makes outputs and new products easier to understand when they align nicely to current ways of organizing. This effect, as Noah points out, can be circular: 'Companies organize themselves and in turn design systems that mirror those organizations which in turn further solidify the organizational structure that was first put in place.'[35]

It may be that in some instances (particularly in the context of incremental or modular innovation) mirroring will result in effective innovations and outputs. But with more radical, architectural innovation that challenges the architectural knowledge, information flows and structure of an organization, mirroring can be counterproductive.

Rapidly changing contexts or emergent capabilities characterized more by higher levels of uncertainty do not suit rigid systems and ways of working that mirror existing ways of doing things. Instead, we need to enable greater fluidity in structures to work back from the system design that we need into a structure that can reflect it. Rigid and deeply hierarchical structures may be good at delivering incremental and modular innovation and supporting optimization and efficiency, but do not lend themselves to the flexibility required for adaptive, emergent problem solving. These types of challenges require small, cross-functional teams that can move quickly, unconstrained by ingrained systems, architecture and thinking.

We need to fundamentally redesign our organizations to reflect both of these needs.

Beyond innovation: the need to constantly renew

Transformation is about more than just innovation. In fact, there's much to be said for the argument that becoming an agile business is really about large companies remembering what it's like to be small again: to do the basics well; to simplify complexity well; to be nimble and not averse to change; to avoid getting stuck.

Yet there is also a distinct mindset shift involved with moving on from being continuously focused on protecting your existing advantage (the obsessive focus on incremental market share changes, or being willing to learn only from the narrow confines of your own sector or industry and not thinking about a broader view of your own capabilities) and the kind of business that can imagine a different future, create the proposition to self-disrupt and then ruthlessly execute against it.

Agile businesses do not wait until the next inflection or crisis point. They are actively exploring the future and their place in it, and remaking the business on a continual basis. Perpetual reinvention.

CASE STUDY
Netflix, and disrupting your own business

Netflix launched as a DVD rentals business in 1997 but in its short history has reinvented itself as a business not once but twice on its journey to where it is today. The ability to optimize business as usual whilst also building the business that will potentially cannibalize and disrupt your existing one is a critical area of tension for many organizations. Saying it is easy. Actually doing it is terribly hard, not least because of the economic, resource and emotive challenges that this brings. Netflix is one of the relatively few companies that have shown themselves to be willing to continually reinvent themselves as new waves of technology, market dynamics and consumer contexts hit.

CEO Reed Hastings has talked about how important it was to him on that journey for the company to retain agility as it scaled, as the company grew for it to have fewer rules, not more,[36] but also the importance of focus and context in enabling the big changes to happen. They spend, for example, very little time thinking about what the competition are doing and instead focus their time and their thinking on how they can improve the service for customers. Where you choose to focus your attention is, of course, a key determinant of organizational orientation. Many incumbents, he says, look at you as you are now rather than envisaging what you could become as technology inevitably improves.

Reed takes issue with Andy Grove's maxim that only the paranoid survive. A key part of selecting where they put their attention, he says, is about having a point of view on the future. Netflix has long made public a point of view on its long-term future, which does just this.[37] His point is that if you see everything as a threat then it becomes a distraction from following your own path, like a game of chess where you need to anticipate several moves in advance.

But the importance of focus and commitment has been critical in their successive transitions. If you need to develop an entirely new muscle as a business, he says, it has to be positioned as essential to survival. You can't dabble in it. Consequently, when the streaming business began to take shape he deliberately created space between the two competing businesses and teams and even went as far as separating the key management meetings to ensure that the streaming business should and could be built to stand on its own merits.

The ambidextrous organization

The concept of the 'ambidextrous organization' was first described by Charles O'Reilly and Michael Tushman in their 2004 HBR article[38] as a way to capture the challenge inherent in businesses being able to make steady improvements to existing models whilst still developing breakthrough innovations. This, they said, was akin to the challenge of constantly looking backwards in attending to the products and processes of the past whilst also gazing forwards and preparing for the innovations that will define a new future.

They studied 35 different attempts to launch breakthrough innovations that were undertaken across nine different industries, looking for those instances where the business was able to simultaneously pursue incremental innovations for existing customers whilst also developing breakthrough innovations for new customers.

The research showed that the companies that had successfully balanced simultaneous exploitation of existing models and more radical exploration of future models shared some common characteristics – most notably in maintaining a degree of separation between the traditional areas and the exploratory ones, so allowing for different processes, structures and cultures to emerge, whilst also keeping links between the units tightly integrated at the senior executive level. More than 90 per cent of these ambidextrous organizations ended up achieving their goals, far higher than the other ways of structuring for breakthrough innovation.

The commonalities and differences between the exploratory and exploitative areas of the business and how they link and interact are key. O'Reilly and Tushman showed that successful ambidextrous organizations had been able to set up structures that were independent enough to enable break-through innovation and different ways of working to emerge whilst connected enough at the senior level to keep them aligned to vision, strategic goals or needs. This requires the senior teams and management to be ambidextrous in understanding the divergent needs of the different kinds of business areas, combining the ability to make difficult trade-offs or decisions with the visionary thinking required of entrepreneurs. The senior team must also be committed to operating ambidextrously. A compelling vision relentlessly communicated by that senior team can articulate a goal and direction that can enable the exploitation and exploring parts of the business to coexist and thrive, and bring to life the benefits of both types of operating model for employees.

The need for breakthrough innovation has certainly not declined since the research was done in 2004, and the business environment has if anything become even more characterized by rapid change and unpredictability. So the concept of an organization that can ambidextrously optimize for the present whilst simultaneously creating the future is a powerful one. Particularly when we consider what happens when there is too much focus on just one of these facets. When 3M, long revered as one of the world's most innovative companies, appointed James McNerney as CEO in 2000 he brought in many practices that he was familiar with from his time at GE. McNerney focused on driving efficiencies and introduced Six Sigma, the disciplined and data-driven process methodology that seeks to eliminate waste and defects and favours incremental improvements, predictability and repeatability. For the first few years this had the benefit of increasing operating margins from 17 per cent in 2001 to 23 per cent in 2005.[39] But as Six Sigma was applied to the research and development processes it killed creativity and disruptive innovation and there was a dramatic fall-off in the number of new, innovative products produced. The company that had been famous for innovations including the Post-it note and Scotch Tape had stifled the very thing that made it successful and unique. It took a new CEO who from 2005 exempted key areas of the business from Six Sigma to take a more balanced approach to exploitation and exploration and rekindle the innovation potential in the business.

In the modern environment where value is increasingly shifting from long-term, sustainable competitive advantage to generating and exploiting a series of transient advantages, businesses need a continuous flow of new propositions and breakthroughs. This can only happen if there is enough separation in the early stages to ensure that new thinking, cultures and ways of working are given sufficient space to thrive and are not suffocated by legacy and hierarchy. But then the bigger opportunity is for these new ideas and operating models to catalyse a much wider transformation across the entire organization. For that to happen, as concepts are commercialized and scaled there should be growing commitment and integration not just at the most senior level, but at all levels through the organization, and a more seamless flow between exploit and explore.

Shaping demand and fulfilling demand

One example way of thinking about organizational ambidexterity is BCG's classic experience curve.[40] Developed in the mid-1960s as a way of showing the relationship between production experience and cost, the curve expresses how a company's unit production costs would fall by a predictable amount as its 'experience', or accumulated production volume, increased (Figure 3.5). The founder of BCG Bruce Henderson noted that the curve could result in significant advantage for market share leaders as they could more rapidly accumulate experience leading to a self-perpetuating cost advantage.

FIGURE 3.5 The experience curve

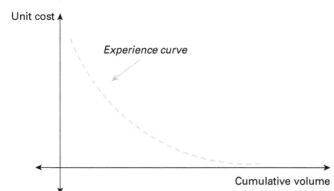

SOURCE Adapted from the BCG experience curve [Online] https://www.bcg.com/en-gb/publications/2013/growth-business-unit-strategy-experience-curve-bcg-classics-revisited.aspx

The experience curve is all about exploitation and fulfilling demand but as we discussed earlier, the shifting nature of advantage has added some very different nuance to this. The experience curve works well in stable climates but is challenged in the context of more volatile and rapidly changing environments, which require more frequent innovations and launches. This means that in addition to fulfilling and exploiting demand, businesses need a far more significant focus on creating demand for a succession of new products, services, or propositions – what BCG call shaping demand. This can be represented as a succession of experience curves which are concerned with exploiting existing demand, with a series of repeated 'jumps' from one experience curve to the next, as companies generate new waves of product or proposition innovation and value. Similarly, we might represent this as a succession of experience curves through which the agile organization becomes adept at exploiting existing advantage, with a series of related jumps from one advantage to the next (Figure 3.6).

BCG notes that the two types of experience are characterized by different approaches and strategic needs, as mentioned earlier. Since the experience curve is shaped by exploiting and fulfilling demand it is defined by logical, more linear and deductive processes structured around repetition, generating greater efficiency and incremental improvement. We might capture data relating to transactional costs, look for opportunities to improve, and put in

FIGURE 3.6 Exploiting demand and shaping demand

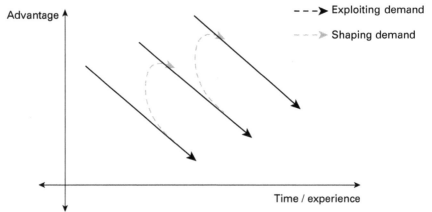

SOURCE Adapted from the BCG experience curve [Online] https://www.bcg.com/en-gb/publications/2013/growth-business-unit-strategy-experience-curve-bcg-classics-revisited.aspx

place changes: in other words, inductive thinking (based on directly observable facts) and deductive thinking (logic and analysis, typically based on past evidence). The experience of shaping demand on the other hand, is characterized by *abductive* thinking where we might think creatively, imagine what is possible, form hypotheses about customer needs, new sources of advantage, the potential of new technologies, and then test and prototype, learn based on empirical results and either shut, pivot or rapidly expand. Businesses tend to become highly proficient at inductive and deductive reasoning but are generally poor at abductive thinking. All three are essential.

Ultimately, long-term competitive advantage has perhaps always been about being adept at both types of experience but in today's fast-moving, complex environments it is the degree of focus placed on each that is important (most companies get very good at fulfilling demand over time at the expense of shaping demand), and the fact that the required speed with which you cycle between the two has increased dramatically.

Netflix is a great example of a business that has been adept at getting this balanced ambidexterity right, undertaking a succession of pivots from mailing DVDs to streaming films to investing now in original content. They successfully anticipated the shift to content streaming, and were able to manage the existing business whilst still growing a disruptive new proposition. Now, in a relatively short space of time, they have grown their investment in original content to a reported US $13 billion for 2018, more than HBO and even CBS.[41] In shaping demand in this way they are raising customer expectation significantly and generating significant advantage.

From scalable efficiency to scalable learning

Small teams can be engines for change in a large organization. The team, as strategist Russell Davies once described it, is the unit of delivery.[42] But the team can also catalyse learning and transformation since we learn better when we learn together. Large organizations are typically dominated by a focus on efficiency and execution – managing repeatable tasks, minimizing variance and rewarding conformity. Qualities that work well in stable environments with well-understood contexts that change slowly but ones that work less well in rapidly changing circumstances characterized by greater uncertainty. Qualities that can bring operational cost savings and improved productivity and process efficiency, but which can also act as a brake on cross-discipline collaboration, and knowledge and insight development. We need to break down these barriers to effective learning and reorient the organization to learn at scale.

Harvard Business professor Amy Edmondson (in her book *Teaming: How organizations learn, innovate, and compete in the knowledge economy*[43]) talks about how organizing to learn should be reflected in the broadest possible set of approaches, functions and processes right across the organization:

> To keep up with developments in their field, people must become lifelong learners, and success will belong to those who can master new skills and envision novel possibilities. Employees must absorb, and sometimes create, new knowledge while executing. Because this process typically happens among individuals working together, collective learning – that is, learning in and by smaller groups – is regarded as the primary vehicle for organizational learning.[44]

We should look to recruit experimenters and problem solvers rather than conformers and rule followers, we should train to learn by doing rather than always learning before doing, we should champion the integration of knowledge over separate and siloed know-how, we should empower staff to explore and experiment, use variance as an opportunity to improve rather than try to drive it out, ask 'what did we learn?' more than 'was it done in the right way?'.

The point is that lifelong learning is something that we should pursue not only as individuals but is also something that is critical at a team and an organizational level. We hear a lot these days about 'failing fast', 'fail happy', 'embracing failure'. This is not that helpful. Failure in isolation is a redundant standard. Far better to talk about learning, and how we can support continuous improvement from understanding, reflecting on and responding to both successes and failures. As Amy says:

> When facing an uncertain path forward, trying something that fails, then figuring out what works instead, is the very essence of good performance. Great performance, however, is trying something that fails, figuring out what works instead, and telling your colleagues all about it – about both the success and the failure.[45]

This shift in value towards organizational learning over leveraging dominance in scale and efficiency represents one of the most impactful disruptions in corporate advantage. John Hagel and John Seely Brown at Deloitte have described this as the shift from 'scalable efficiency' to 'scalable learning'.[46]

Corporate history has long been characterized by the advantages that can be derived from size and volume and the ability to drive down costs, improve margins and gain scaled efficiencies over time. As new transportation, communication and manufacturing technologies emerged in the 1800s so did a new breed of company, structured to leverage the scaled benefits of new production, distribution and marketing capabilities. These organizations were architected around efficiency, concentrating transactions into a single enterprise in order to reduce transaction costs in much the same way as Ronald Coase describes in his famous essay on the nature of the firm.[47] Firms, said Coase, exist to economize on the cost of coordinating economic activity.

This focus on leveraging scaled efficiency has long shaped organizations around the need for control, consistency, stability, certainty and predictability, resulting in top-down command-and-control hierarchies, longer-term planning and forecasting, vertical functional silos and standardized, rigid processes. Through the 20th century this has served companies well, but in the process, there has been a significant corporate trade-off between scaled efficiency and the ability to learn quickly, to be flexible, adaptive and experimental.

Put simply, it's very difficult to find the space to explore new possibilities, to try out new things and even to adapt quickly when the organizational structure, processes and culture have grown up specifically around mitigating divergence from the norm, risk, exploration, deviance and non-conformity. Experimentation, curiosity and improvisation are the fuel for rapid learning. Limit those, and organizational learning is also limited.

In times of stability and slower moving contexts the pre-eminence of scalable efficiency makes sense. But when the environment changes to be characterized by much higher levels of disruption, unpredictability and rapid change, the trade off with the ability to learn at scale and at speed becomes a distinct disadvantage. Digital technologies and models can (and have) dramatically reduce transaction costs; for example, the ability to leverage third-party capability, knowledge and investment, thereby reducing the advantage that comes from vertical integration and scale.

Hagel and Seely Brown write about the need to develop new relationship architectures within, across and outside institutions to break these performance trade-offs, expand what's possible, and value scalable learning over scalable efficiency. As competitive, market and customer contexts change ever more rapidly the value of existing, relatively static stocks of knowledge within the organization can depreciate fast, emphasizing the need to create mechanisms, relationships and spaces that are designed to increase the flow of information, learning and adaptation. An inability to learn quickly in these contexts creates vulnerability and fragility:

> We have reached an important turning point where success is not defined by scale, but by the ability to learn (and unlearn) more rapidly. The traditional model of 'punctuated equilibrium' in which companies move from one stable state to another is dead, and companies need to adopt a state of 'continually becoming' to keep up with rapid changes in the environment.[48]

Digital technologies have enabled radically different ways to connect with more diverse and useful sources of knowledge and information both inside and outside the organization, whether through the power of open-source, crowd-sourcing, talent-pools, a myriad third-party insight sources, or through the flow of data through APIs. It has ensured that potential complexities and transaction costs around connecting with multiple external sources of value have been mitigated and reduced. It's never been easier to get rapid answers to questions, to access exceptional expertise, and to create and maintain communities focused around collaboration, expertise and knowledge. These kinds of knowledge-based networks can benefit from the easy flow of information, the exponential value curve that comes from network effects (every additional participant in the network increases the value of the network as a whole), and thereby increase the speed and scope of learning of everyone involved. New potential can be realized.

This is no small shift. As Hagel and Seely Brown noted in their Deloitte report: 'Fundamentally different types of institutions may be necessary that break those constraints and harness new tools and practices to simultaneously drive both accelerated learning and high levels of efficiency in rapidly evolving environments. To do so, we need to rethink the rationale for firms.' In order to remodel from scaled efficiency to scaled learning we need a fundamentally different type of organization.

Advantage was for many years defined by scale. Then, more recently, it became about adaptive scale. Now advantage is firmly rooted in the ability to learn fast at scale (Figure 3.7).

FIGURE 3.7 Learn fast at scale

CASE STUDY
Amazon Marketplace and Fulfilment by Amazon

Launched in 2006, Fulfilment by Amazon (FBA)[49] is an end-to-end service that Amazon created to enable millions of third-party sellers to utilize the Amazon platform to sell and fulfil orders. Used by sellers in more than 100 countries, the service enables sellers to take advantage of the full suite of Amazon service propositions from storing product in Amazon's estate of local fulfilment centres, to using their thousands of employees to sort, pack and ship products to customers, taking advantage of Amazon's Prime benefits and delivery services, to export products easily to customers in 185 countries around the world, and even to handle returns and make use of Amazon's customer service team.

Through FBA, Amazon provides a suite of tools to enable better sales management including pricing optimization, business analytics and recommendations that effectively allow third-party sellers to manage their business from any device wherever they are.

FBA is an excellent example of digital-native thinking. Instead of being concerned that third-party sellers would cannibalize Amazon sales, the company has established a platform ecosystem that facilitates a productive relationship between Amazon, third-party sellers and customers, which is beneficial for all. As sellers sell more on the Amazon Marketplace platform, the value increases for everyone in the ecosystem.

As of the fourth quarter of 2018, 52 per cent of paid units sold on Amazon were sold by third-party sellers and in the whole of 2018, they generated over US $42 billion of sales in seller-service revenues (an increase of over a third from the previous year), a revenue segment that is second only to Amazon's retail product sales in value.[50]

Marketplace and FBA give Amazon greater scale and leverage, but critically they also give the company scaled learning at speed. As more sellers come onto the platform and more transactions go through Amazon systems, they accumulate ever-increasing amounts of data that enables them to learn better and faster than anyone else.

Explore, execute, extend and exploit

So, as we've established, the agile organization is one that is characterized by continual change, reinvention, responsiveness and manoeuvrability: able to capitalize on the potential of small teams to support transformation, agility and adaptiveness at scale; able to maintain a high level of fluidity around resourcing to avoid the mirroring challenges inherent in architectural and radical innovation; able to manage high levels of ambidexterity in managing business as usual whilst concurrently inventing the business of the future; able to be adept at both fulfilling and shaping demand.

The Austrian-born economist Joseph Schumpeter, who taught at Harvard for many years, defined the process of technological change as being divided into three key stages: Invention (ideas); Innovation (the development of new ideas into marketable products and processes, or commercialization); Diffusion (scaling or adoption).[51] Given the need for not just episodic innovation but continuous innovation that is both broad and deep, we need to structure a new type of organization that is defined by a perpetual cycle of exploration, execution, extension and exploitation (Figure 3.8):

Exploration: the search for underserved customer needs, new customer problems to solve, new propositions, new efficiencies, new relationship structures, value from new technologies, better ways of working. Exploration needs to be embedded and continuous.

Execution: the ability to commercialize, generate early value, to build scalable models around new propositions, to shape resourcing, technology and processes in ways that can enable rapid growth. Without this stage there is often a 'missing link' between early-stage ideas and scaled solutions that have real business impact.

Extension and exploitation: a focus on operationalizing, extending and growing the proposition to maximize the potential, exploiting the advantage created through experience and greater efficiency over time. This stage is necessary for fully optimizing the opportunity from existing advantage.

FIGURE 3.8 Explore, execute, extend and exploit

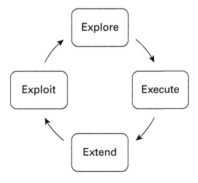

Innovation cycles needs to be expedited so that they operate in months, not years, generating a continuous flow of new experiments and initiatives. But beyond this, the whole organization needs to be set up to support this flow of new value.

If you were to design organizations from the ground up for today's complex adaptive environments you would not design a business that is shaped overwhelmingly by exploitation of existing advantage, functional silos that inhibit horizontal collaboration, and slow-moving bureaucratic practices. There is a need for an entirely new type of organization that is set up around continuous innovation and change.

A structure for continuous innovation

Having defined the key jobs that an agile organization is required to do in terms of exploration, execution and extension and exploitation, we need to align resourcing, process and people around these tasks. Researcher Simon Wardley has articulated a useful way of framing the unique skills and different resourcing characteristics needed to bring products and services to life but also that typically characterize these stages – pioneers, settlers and town planners.[52] Each of these archetypes are brilliant in their own way, but draw on different capabilities that enable us to map them to the organizational job-to-be-done:

- **Pioneers:** seek out new territory for the business, originate entirely new concepts, use foresight to create new future possibilities. Their failure rate is likely to be the highest out of the archetypes, but they will generate the concepts that can shape a new future value for the organization. Pioneers map to the exploration stage.

- **Settlers:** take the possible future and make it a reality, partial ideas and make them complete, early-stage ideas and ensure they are commercially viable. They build business models around great ideas, make new products and services scalable, understandable, build trust and cohesion. Settlers map to the execute stage.

- **Town planners:** industrialize, operationalize, optimize. They make models, products and services work at scale, benefit from economies of scale, and then extend them into new areas of opportunity, make them faster, better, more efficient over time. Town planners map to the extend-and-exploit stage of the cycle.

FIGURE 3.9 Proposition Evolution

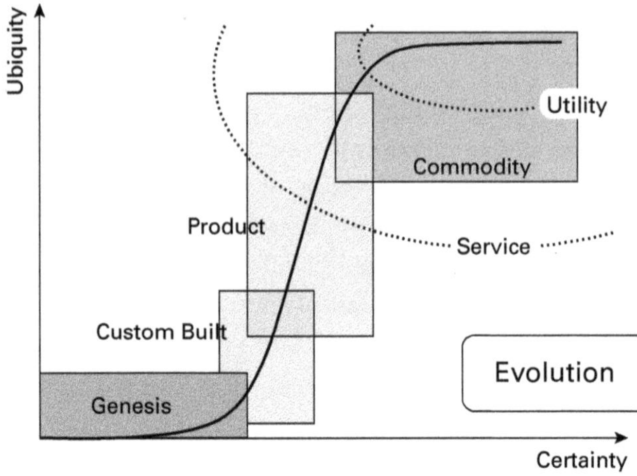

SOURCE Adapted from content created by Simon Wardley, available under Creative Commons Attribution-ShareAlike 4.0 International (CC BY-SA 4.0) https://medium.com/wardleymaps/anticipation-89692e9b0ced

Simon represents the traditional product or proposition evolution cycle as an S-curve with early-stage solutions beginning by being largely custom built, before being scaled, and ultimately reaching the point where it is increasingly commoditized and becomes more of a utility. As the product life cycle progresses over time, certainty will increase as the organization develops experience, but so does the ubiquity of the proposition (Figure 3.9).

We can also map our people archetypes on to this graph. Pioneers will work in the earliest genesis stages of the proposition. Settlers will create custom-built versions and create scalability. Town planners will operate at the volume end, drawing value from more commoditized and ubiquitous services and propositions. As a result of this, the way in which each of these archetypes works is different:

- **Pioneers:** will be experimenting iteratively, prototyping in-house, and likely using Agile or Lean Startup working and techniques. They will be operating in environments of high uncertainty, looking for the novel or potential to differentiate, perhaps high-potential future value but propositions or markets that are currently poorly understood or defined. They understand early prototyping, MVPs, future potential.

- **Settlers:** are focused on developing understanding, differentiating specific features that will be useful, growing a market, generating profitability.

They work with constant feedback and improvement and so will likely still use iterative working methodologies. They understand growth, trends, working with customer feedback loops.

- **Town planners:** operate in mature markets, high-volume and more stable environments, understand well-defined segments, optimization, operational efficiency, analytics, building what the business needs. Are familiar with process efficiency focused processes, such as Six Sigma.

Later in the book I'll be looking at how an organization might map the different jobs-to-be done and apply appropriate resourcing and processes to these different domains. Being an agile organization doesn't mean that agile is the default process, but it does mean more sophisticated thinking around the application of different working methodologies, and where we do Agile, and where we need to simply BE agile.

The dual operating system

Given the need for organizations to be ambidextrous and to continue to deliver against existing competitive advantage whilst still inventing the business of the future, we need to rethink our approach to organization design.

Harvard Business School professor John Kotter (in his book *Accelerate: Building strategic agility for a faster-moving world*[53]) has argued that in order to create true agility and responsiveness businesses need to create a 'dual operating system' designed to enable the rapid development of new ideas and models whilst still maximizing the operational efficiencies needed to manage business as usual. When companies start out as startups, they are naturally small and highly networked organizations but as they scale, they require management and greater efficiencies and so the hierarchical side of the business grows over time. But as innovation slows and competitive pressure grows, the need for ever-greater efficiency results in an entirely hierarchical business, which has lost that networked capability. Kotter's thought was about the need, in a rapidly changing business environment, to reintroduce some of the networked model to the organization.

As organizations become larger, they often become more internally focused, and innovation becomes additive to those in the hierarchy who are busy enough dealing with the day job. This lack of space for continual experimentation is a real challenge. Leaders and managers taking responsibility for new projects are often expected to run the new initiative whilst still doing everything that they were before. No one ever thinks about what we can stop doing in order to free up time and resource to start something new. Another critical challenge in strictly hierarchical organizations is just how difficult cross-disciplinary collaboration becomes. Departments operate to their own agendas. Leadership status is determined by size of team or budget. Making quick decisions that involves different inputs or disciplines becomes problematic. Over time the primary orientation becomes what's right for the department rather than what's right for the customer.

As we discussed earlier, strict hierarchies get very good at exploiting existing advantage but are pretty terrible at being responsive to rapid change and embedding exploration and experimentation into the fabric of how they work. Given the modern business environment, businesses need to more proactively create structures that can deliver greater agility. The big opportunity is that alongside the ability to deliver business-as-usual and optimize existing advantage via traditional hierarchies, we can use small, multidisciplinary teams to create a more networked element to the business (Figure 3.10).

Later we'll discuss some of the opportunities and challenges that arise when shifting to this way of operating, but it is important to understand that there is no one blueprint for how this should happen. Small cross-functional teams may be aligned to significantly different objectives from optimizing customer journeys, to specific innovation projects, to solving key business challenges. Every business will have its own contexts and objectives that will dictate a different approach. And there will be significant challenges along the way as the organization learns how to balance different

FIGURE 3.10 Hierarchy and networks

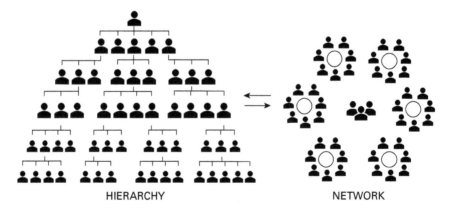

HIERARCHY   NETWORK

ways of working, manage different priorities, and be adaptive with the change so that it might be successful in the long term.

But the point is that through doing this the business is proactively embedding more nimble ways of working whilst still hitting its targets. You're not breaking the business, nor are you playing at the edges of transformation. You're bringing greater agility to the company, enabling more fluidity to resourcing, more adaptability in addressing key customer and business challenges, and capitalizing on the ability of small teams to drive big change.

Building a service-oriented architecture

Traditional organizational structures organize functional expertise into silos that can benefit from shared learning, and greater efficiency. This works well in a vertical sense, to align a functional team more easily around common practices, approaches and standards, and to provide functional governance and a career path. But it is terrible for horizontal collaboration. In an age that requires a step-change in cross-functional working we need to find new ways to empower concurrent multidisciplinary running. Alongside the ability to scale small, multidisciplinary teams as an engine for continuous change, we need to catalyse more seamless cross-functional working through the development of a service-oriented architecture and the use of APIs (Application Programming Interface – a set of definitions and protocols that can connect systems and services and enable data and utility exchange between them). There are three key types of API:[54]

- open or public APIs that have no restrictions on access;
- partner APIs that are made available only to strategic partners;
- private or internal APIs that expose systems or capabilities internally, and which are most often not open to external use.

Internal APIs can enable an organizational operating model to be built around a service-oriented architecture (SOA) where individual teams and functions can make data and resources available as a service to other teams that might need them. Whilst this approach is not without its challenges (including the discovery of relevant resources, managing demand, and also support), it has the potential to support far greater agility by making more data and capability available on demand as and when they are needed. Consider how frequently in a large organization one team requires information, resources or numbers from another team and just how slow that process can be through manual processes and e-mail. This is compounded by the fact that most organizations have grown up with multiple systems that don't share data or talk to each other meaning that breadth of access to relevant data becomes difficult.

Amazon was, of course, the first scaled organization to realize the potential of APIs to enable a truly innovative operating model that has given them (and continues to give them) considerable advantage. As far back as 2002, Jeff Bezos issued an infamous mandate concerning how software was to be built at Amazon (paraphrased here):

1 All teams will henceforth expose their data and functionality through service interfaces.

2 Teams must communicate with each other through these interfaces.

3 There will be no other form of interprocess communication allowed: no direct linking, no direct reads of another team's data store, no shared-memory model, no back-doors whatsoever. The only communication allowed is via service interface calls over the network.

4 It doesn't matter what technology they use.

5 All service interfaces, without exception, must be designed from the ground up to be externalizable. That is to say, the team must plan and design to be able to expose the interface to developers in the outside world. No exceptions.

6 Anyone who doesn't do this will be fired.[55]

The mandate was undoubtedly provoked by the increasing cost and sluggishness in not having a consistent way of exchanging capabilities and data between different teams and functions. But it resulted in the business transforming internally into a SOA where every team interacts through APIs, defines what resources they have and makes them available through web services so that other teams can independently access and reuse them to support business outcomes. Amazon had created its own internal API economy and a business that thinks of everything in a services-first way, but it had also created the platform on which it could build an almost unassailable advantage.

This SOA approach was taken to a whole new level by the successive externalization of capability, effectively establishing separate parts of the company as individual platforms, opening them up to external competition and ensuring that they avoid the inefficiencies that can come from internal monopolies or vertically integrated businesses (in other words avoiding the danger of becoming fat and complacent from having a captive, internal customer without external competition).

This approach means that Amazon gains greater leverage and learning through scale, services have to compete on the open market ensuring greater efficiency, and in effect that Amazon becomes Amazon's largest customer. Amazon Web Services (AWS) is perhaps the most obvious example of where they have turned their own technology infrastructure into a hugely valuable externalized product. In 2018 AWS brought in US $25.7 billion, which represented a 47 per cent year-on-year increase and is more than McDonald's brought in in that entire year.[56] AWS taught Amazon the true value of creating externally facing, service-driven platforms from internal services, so future-proofing operational capability against inefficiency, complacency and stasis. A succession of services including fulfilment infrastructure, contact centres, and even pricing have been turned in revenue generating platforms that exist by their own merits in the open marketplace. Their open approach to the development of the Alexa platform, for example, has enabled developers to create an ecosystem of 'skills', immeasurably increasing its value to customers (as of December 2018 there are over 70,000 skills on the platform[57]). Opening up the capability to integrate Alexa into third-party devices means that it is now being incorporated into everything from TVs to lighting to clocks to cars. It is now fast becoming an Amazon Operating System and in the process on its way to positioning itself as the default voice Operating System for the smart home and smart car.

Yet it is the internal API economy, and SOA that has truly enabled them to retain agility as they have scaled. In this scenario teams become partners of each other, loosely coupled but able to draw on copious resources at will. Able to collaborate horizontally at speed, capitalizing on free-flowing access to data and resources. Open to innovation from anywhere, not limited by core systems that are locked up.

The post-digital organization

The concept of going 'beyond digital' was first mooted as far back as 1998 by Nicholas Negroponte in a *Wired* essay that talked about how 'digital' will ultimately become quite banal. He wrote: 'Its literal form, the technology, is already beginning to be taken for granted, and its connotation will become tomorrow's commercial and cultural compost for new ideas. Like air and drinking water, being digital will be noticed only by its absence, not its presence.'

Fast-forward 20 years and there remain organizational challenges around adapting mindsets, cultures and approaches to become more native to what is now a truly digital world.[58] Yet the aspiration for organizations has to be that we can move beyond instances where 'digital' is any way a separate thing. Where projects and propositions begin with questions that ask whether the thing we're working on is a digital thing or an analogue thing. We should simply be doing the right thing, whether that is digital or not.

The practice of digital may still require defined, specialist expertise but every organization should be aiming for a place where thinking and evaluation is neutral to platform or channel. Where digital is truly integrated. And where culture and practice reflect this. Digital should be lived, breathed, known, understood to the extent that is habitual behaviour to do things in ways that are native to the digital empowered environment. To quote strategist and blogger Russell Davies:

> The only way to be a Post Digital business is to be a thoroughly, deeply, massively digital one. To be digital in culture not just in capabilities. To know how to iterate in public, to do experiments not research, to recognize that it's quicker and better to code something than it is to describe it in meetings. You need to be part of the wider digital culture, to have good sharing habits, to give credit where it's due.'[59]

It's a good aspiration to have.

References

1   Brinker, Scott [accessed 30 April 2019] The 4 Forces of Marketing Operations and Technology, August 2018 [Online] https://chiefmartec.com/2018/08/4-forces-marketing-operations-technology/ (archived at https://perma.cc/5K63-2GYZ)

2   Brinker, Scott [accessed 30 April 2019] The 4 Forces of Marketing Operations and Technology, August 2018 [Online] https://chiefmartec.com/2018/08/4-forces-marketing-operations-technology/ (archived at https://perma.cc/5K63-2GYZ)

3   Hackman, Richard [accessed 3 January 2019] Leading Teams: Setting the stage for great performances – the five keys to successful teams, July 2002, *HBS* [Online] https://hbswk.hbs.edu/archive/leading-teams-setting-the-stage-for-great-performances-the-five-keys-to-successful-teams (archived at https://perma.cc/6Q2P-NT6F)

4 Wu, Lingfei, Wang, Dashun and Evans, James A [accessed 7 April 2019] Large Teams Develop and Small Teams Disrupt Science and Technology, February 2019, *Nature*, [Online] https://www.nature.com/articles/s41586-019-0941-9 (archived at https://perma.cc/7JZA-UMLP)

5 University of Chicago [accessed 7 April 2019] Bigger Teams Aren't Always Better in Science and Tech, February 2019, *Science Daily* [Online] https://www.sciencedaily.com/releases/2019/02/190213132304.htm (archived at https://perma.cc/S4W9-W2R4)

6 Hackman, Richard [accessed 3 January 2019] Leading Teams: Setting the stage for great performances – the five keys to successful teams, July 2002, *HBS* [Online] https://hbswk.hbs.edu/archive/leading-teams-setting-the-stage-for-great-performances-the-five-keys-to-successful-teams (archived at https://perma.cc/6Q2P-NT6F)

7 Greer, Lindred Leura, De Jong, Bart, Schouten, Maartje and Dannals, Jennifer [accessed 30 March 2019] Why and When Hierarchy Impacts Team Effectiveness: A meta-analytic examination, *Journal of Applied Psychology*, 2018, **103**, pp 591–613 [Online] https://www.gsb.stanford.edu/faculty-research/publications/why-when-hierarchy-impacts-team-effectiveness-meta-analytic (archived at https://perma.cc/H7EU-MW7Z)

8 Holacracy [accessed 4 April 2019] [Online] https://www.holacracy.org/ (archived at https://perma.cc/KZL9-57ZR)

9 Zappos Insights [accessed 4 April 2019] Holacracy and Self-Organization [Online] https://www.zapposinsights.com/about/holacracy (archived at https://perma.cc/3GCC-RENN)

10 Mahajan, Neelima [accessed 30 March 2019] Haier is Disrupting Itself – Before Someone Else Does, October 2015, *CKGSB Knowledge* [Online] http://knowledge.ckgsb.edu.cn/2015/10/05/china-business-strategy/haier-is-disrupting-itself-before-someone-else-does/ (archived at https://perma.cc/XV8P-8M3J)

11 Fischer, Bill [accessed 30 March 2019] How CEO Zhang Ruimin Re-Invented Haier, September 2014, *CKGSB Knowledge* [Online] http://knowledge.ckgsb.edu.cn/2014/09/02/china-business-strategy/how-ceo-zhang-ruimin-reinvented-haier-three-times-over/ (archived at https://perma.cc/RZ6Z-PXMN)

12 Hamel, Gary and Zanini, Michele [accessed 29 March 2019] The End of Bureaucracy, November 2018, *Harvard Business Review* [Online] https://hbr.org/2018/11/the-end-of-bureaucracy (archived at https://perma.cc/6NC6-NQKR)

13 Hamel, Gary and Zanini, Michele [accessed 29 March 2019] The End of Bureaucracy, November 2018, *Harvard Business Review* [Online] https://hbr.org/2018/11/the-end-of-bureaucracy (archived at https://perma.cc/6NC6-NQKR)

14 Coley, Steve [accessed 5 February 2019] Enduring Ideas: Three horizons of growth, *McKinsey & Company* [Online] https://www.mckinsey.com/business-functions/strategy-and-corporate-finance/our-insights/enduring-ideas-the-three-horizons-of-growth (archived at https://perma.cc/QAB4-5PP7)

15 Baghai, M, Coley, S and White, D (2000) [accessed 5 February 2019] *The Alchemy of Growth*, New edn, Basic Books [Online] https://www.amazon.com/gp/product/0738203092/ (archived at https://perma.cc/Y9UE-2FBW)

16 Blank, Steve [accessed 5 February 2019] McKinsey's Three Horizons Model, *Harvard Business Review* [Online] https://hbr.org/2019/02/mckinseys-three-horizons-model-defined-innovation-for-years-heres-why-it-no-longer-applies (archived at https://perma.cc/EC27-C22E)

17 Blank, Steve [accessed 5 February 2019] McKinsey's Three Horizons Model, *Harvard Business Review* [Online] https://hbr.org/2019/02/mckinseys-three-horizons-model-defined-innovation-for-years-heres-why-it-no-longer-applies (archived at https://perma.cc/EC27-C22E)

18 Distill Ventures [accessed 5 February 2019] [Online] https://www.distillventures.com/ (archived at https://perma.cc/9T2G-FYF5)

19 DARPA [accessed 5 February 2019] Prize Challenges [Online] https://www.darpa.mil/work-with-us/public/prizes (archived at https://perma.cc/U5XS-8YVP)

20 SpaceX [accessed 12 March 2019] Hyperloop Pod Competition [Online] https://www.spacex.com/hyperloop (archived at https://perma.cc/338G-CTDY)

21 Kurzweil, Ray [accessed 28 January 2019] Kurzweil's Rules of Invention, *MIT Technology Review* [Online] https://www.technologyreview.com/s/402705/kurzweils-rules-of-invention/ (archived at https://perma.cc/WMD7-623K)

22 Handy, C (1995) *The Empty Raincoat: Making sense of the future*, Random House, London

23 Fuller's Plan 1919 – First Edition; May 24, 1918 [accessed 6 April 2019] Source: JFC Fuller's Autobiography; *Memoirs of an Unconventional Soldier* (1938) [Online] http://www.alternatewars.com/WW1/Fuller_1919.htm (archived at https://perma.cc/R2K7-NRGC)

24 Peck, Michael [accessed 6 April 2019] 5,000 Tanks: The Allies' World War I Plan 1919 Might Have Been the First Blitzkrieg in History, October 2016, *The National Interest* [Online] https://nationalinterest.org/blog/the-buzz/5000-tanks-the-allies-world-war-i-plan-1919-might-have-been-17893 (archived at https://perma.cc/K2ZC-9B7N)

25 Reid, BH (1987) *JFC Fuller: Military Thinker*, Studies in Military and Strategic History, Palgrave Macmillan

26 Harford, Tim [accessed 6 April 2019] Why Big Companies Squander Good Ideas, *FT Magazine*, September 2018 https://www.ft.com/content/3c1ab748-b09b-11e8-8d14-6f049d06439c (archived at https://perma.cc/USE6-G7UT)

27 Kelly, Kevin [accessed 6 April 2019] The Shirky Principle, *The Technium* [Online] https://kk.org/thetechnium/the-shirky-prin/ (archived at https://perma.cc/92QB-3UZV)

28 Henderson, Rebecca and Clark, Kim [accessed 6 April 2019] Architectural Innovation: The reconfiguration of existing product technologies and the failure of established firms, *Administrative Science Quarterly*, March 1990 [Online] http://dimetic.dime-eu.org/dimetic_files/HendersonClarkASQ1990.pdf (archived at https://perma.cc/H5JE-6K97)

29 Henderson, Rebecca and Clark, Kim [accessed 6 April 2019] Architectural Innovation: The reconfiguration of existing product technologies and the failure of established firms, *Administrative Science Quarterly*, March 1990 [Online] http://dimetic.dime-eu.org/dimetic_files/HendersonClarkASQ1990.pdf (archived at https://perma.cc/H5JE-6K97)

30 Conway, Melvin E [accessed 6 April 2019] How do Committees Invent? *Datamation*, **14** (5), pp 28–31 [Online] http://www.melconway.com/Home/Committees_Paper.html (archived at https://perma.cc/892C-85RK)

31 Conway, Melvin E [accessed 6 April 2019] How do Committees Invent? *Datamation*, **14** (5), pp 28–31 [Online] http://www.melconway.com/Home/Committees_Paper.html (archived at https://perma.cc/892C-85RK)

32 Brooks, F (1995) *The Mythical Man-Month: Essays on software engineering*, Anniversary edn, Addison Wesley

33 Brier, Noah [accessed 6 April 2019] Conway's Law, October 2018 [Online] https://www.noahbrier.com/archives/2018/10/conways-law/ (archived at https://perma.cc/KG5D-7PYA)

34 Baldwin, Carliss and Colfer, Lyra [accessed 6 April 2019] The Mirroring Hypothesis: Theory, evidence and exceptions, Harvard Business School Finance Working Paper No. 16-124, Apr 2016, [Online] https://papers.ssrn.com/sol3/papers.cfm?abstract_id=2770675 (archived at https://perma.cc/4UNH-U5GU)

35 Brier, Noah [accessed 6 April 2019] Conway's Law, October 2018 [Online] https://www.noahbrier.com/archives/2018/10/conways-law/ (archived at https://perma.cc/KG5D-7PYA)

36 Andreessen Horowitz [accessed 13 March 2019] a16z Podcast: Tech and Entertainment in the 'Era of Mass Customization', February 2015 [Online] https://a16z.com/2017/02/25/reedhastings-netflix-entertainment-internet-streaming-content/ (archived at https://perma.cc/RYF8-TMHS)

37 Netflix [accessed 5 January 2019] Long-Term View [Online] https://www.netflixinvestor.com/ir-overview/long-term-view/default.aspx (archived at https://perma.cc/ZXU4-ZJRW)

38 O'Reilly, Charles and Tushman, Michael [accessed 13 February 2019] The Ambidextrous Organization, *Harvard Business Review* [Online] https://hbr.org/2004/04/the-ambidextrous-organization (archived at https://perma.cc/M67J-AULQ)

39 Peppers, Don [accessed 14 April 2019] How 3M Lost (and Found) its Innovation Mojo, *Inc.* [Online] https://www.inc.com/linkedin/don-peppers/downside-six-sigma-don-peppers.html (archived at https://perma.cc/D2XN-5Z2A)

40 Reeves, Martin, Stalk, George and Scognamiglio, Filippo [accessed 10 January 2019] BCG Classics Revisited: The experience curve, *BCG* [Online] https://www.bcg.com/en-gb/publications/2013/growth-business-unit-strategy-experience-curve-bcg-classics-revisited.aspx (archived at https://perma.cc/PLX6-4GRR)

41 Feldman, Dana [accessed 13 February 2019] Netflix's Content Budget is Updated to $13B for 2018, *Forbes* [Online] https://www.forbes.com/sites/danafeldman/2018/07/09/netflixs-content-budget-is-updated-to-13b-in-2018/#7880ab972b8c (archived at https://perma.cc/E3SH-YSD3)

42 Davies, Russell [accessed 14 April 2019] A Unit of Delivery, April 2013 [Online] https://russelldavies.typepad.com/planning/2013/04/the-unit-of-delivery.html (archived at https://perma.cc/C8KS-NSL7)

43 Edmondson, A (2010) *Teaming: How organizations learn, innovate, and compete in the knowledge economy*, Jossey Bass

44 Edmondson, A (2010) *Teaming: How organizations learn, innovate, and compete in the knowledge economy*, Jossey Bass

45 Edmondson, A (2010) *Teaming: How organizations learn, innovate, and compete in the knowledge economy*, Jossey Bass

46 Hagel, John and Seely Brown, John [accessed 13 February 2019] Institutional Innovation, *Deloitte Insights* [Online] https://www2.deloitte.com/insights/us/en/topics/innovation/institutional-innovation.html (archived at https://perma.cc/U2HJ-WURZ)

47 Coase, Ronald [accessed 13 February 2019] The Nature of the Firm, *Wiley* [Online] https://onlinelibrary.wiley.com/doi/pdf/10.1111/j.1468-0335.1937.tb00002.x (archived at https://perma.cc/5LZ4-YJXX)

48 Hagel, John and Seely Brown, John [accessed 13 February 2019] Institutional Innovation, *Deloitte Insights* [Online] https://www2.deloitte.com/insights/us/en/topics/innovation/institutional-innovation.html (archived at https://perma.cc/U2HJ-WURZ)

49 Amazon Services Europe [accessed 14 February 2019] Fulfilment by Amazon [Online] https://services.amazon.co.uk/services/fulfilment-by-amazon/features-benefits.html (archived at https://perma.cc/P33X-YGEE)

50 Statista [accessed 14 February 2019] Percentage of Paid Units Sold by Third-party Sellers on Amazon Platform as of 4th Quarter 2018 [Online] https://www.statista.com/statistics/259782/third-party-seller-share-of-amazon-platform/ (archived at https://perma.cc/J388-YTLD)

51 Proven Models [accessed 7 April 2019] Invention Innovation Diffusion Trilogy [Online] http://www.provenmodels.com/14/invention-innovation-diffusion-trilogy/joseph-a.-schumpeter (archived at https://perma.cc/L74J-W5VX)

52 Wardley, Simon [accessed 9 April 2019] On Pioneers, Settlers, Town Planners and Theft, *Gardeviance.org* [Online] http://blog.gardeviance.org/2015/03/on-pioneers-settlers-town-planners-and.html (archived at https://perma.cc/T47J-TQJJ)

53 Kotter, J (2014) *Accelerate: Building strategic agility for a faster-moving world*, Harvard Business Review Press

54 API Friends [accessed 4 April 2019] What Are the Different Types of APIs? September 2017 [Online] https://apifriends.com/api-creation/different-types-of-apis/ (archived at https://perma.cc/4XZU-U5N6)

55 CIO [accessed 4 April 2019] Have You Had Your Bezos Moment? What You Can Learn from Amazon, August 2017 [Online] https://www.cio.com/article/3218667/have-you-had-your-bezos-moment-what-you-can-learn-from-amazon.html (archived at https://perma.cc/57FG-WBQ6)

56 Quartz [accessed 4 April 2019] Amazon Web Services Brought in More Money Than McDonald's in 2018 [Online] https://qz.com/1539546/amazon-web-services-brought-in-more-money-than-mcdonalds-in-2018/ (archived at https://perma.cc/5FAJ-WEWF)

57 Voicebot.ai [accessed 4 April 2019] There Are Now More Than 70,000 Skills on Alexa, December 2018 [Online] https://voicebot.ai/2018/12/14/there-are-now-more-than-70000-alexa-skills-worldwide-amazon-announces-25-top-skills-of-2018/ (archived at https://perma.cc/NRE8-WP7Q)

58 Wired [accessed 14 February 2019] Negroponte [Online] https://www.wired.com/1998/12/negroponte-55/ (archived at https://perma.cc/8JKY-Q7Q4)

59 Davies, Russell [accessed 14 February 2019] Post Digital – An Apology [Online] https://russelldavies.typepad.com/planning/2010/11/post-digital-an-apology.html (archived at https://perma.cc/845H-TBAK)

04

Changing change management

The messy middle of transformation

It's no accident that a caterpillar's metamorphosis into a butterfly is often used as a metaphor for business and digital transformation. It reflects well the degree of challenge and change that organizations can go through with transformation programmes. In one of nature's most remarkable feats we see the larva become a chrysalis and then out comes a completely different adult animal.

Yet this process is an excellent metaphor for another reason. The chrysalis represents a 'messy middle' stage between larva and adult in which the caterpillar radically transforms its body. To become a butterfly, the caterpillar effectively dissolves all of its tissues to create a kind of 'soup' of cells, but certain groups of cells survive this process – one for each of the adult body parts that it will need as a mature butterfly. These groups of cells then use the protein-rich soup around them to fuel rapid cell division that forms wings, antennae, legs and eyes. The chrysalis stage in a butterfly's life cycle is a metaphor for the 'messy middle' of transformation. Rather than follow an ordered, incremental change, the messy middle can involve significant uncertainty, complexity and change.

The shift away from big-bang, linear change management

Without wanting to stretch the metaphor too far, it's also worth noting that there are actually two distinct types of insect metamorphosis – complete and incomplete. Complete (or holometabolous) metamorphosis involves the insect passing through four distinct life stages (egg, larva, pupa, adult) that produce an adult that is very different from the larva. This is the caterpillar turning into a butterfly. With incomplete (or hemimetabolous) metamorphosis the insect does not go through a full transformation but instead transitions from a nymph to an adult by moulting its exoskeleton multiple times as it grows. So the adult still resembles its younger form.

Just as there are two types of metamorphosis, there are two types of organizational transformation. There is genuine transformation in which the organization may keep foundational attributes that still distinguish it as the organization it has always been but it commits to truly change the way in which it works, the way it is structured, the way it realizes its strategy, and the kind of cultures and behaviours it supports and rewards. Then there is partial or incomplete transformation where the organization does not commit fully to the degree and scale of change that is truly required, plays at the edges of change, gets distracted by shiny objects, drifts back to what it knows and what it feels comfortable with and ends up looking like a more mature version of the same company that it was before.

The point is that unless you really commit to making real change happen, it won't happen. A well-known piece of analysis by Boston Consulting Group discovered that only 25 per cent of transformation programmes outperformed in the long term and that 75 per cent of programmes effectively failed.[1] The research showed that such programmes typically follow a trajectory typified by 'chapter one' and 'chapter two' stages. The first stage may involve an initial streamlining process designed to produce efficiencies but the critical second stage is either characterized by long-term growth and reinvigoration of the business or by long-term decline. The minority of companies that made a success of 'chapter two' were those where there was a real commitment to drive lasting change, a compelling vision, a clear shift in strategy, a refocus on growth and innovation, an appetite to challenge norms and reinvent business models and commitment to a vision whilst allowing for flexibility and adaptation in how it was delivered. BCG published 'seven traps' that can most often cause transformation efforts to fail and these included being too focused on efficiency savings, not taking the scale of response seriously enough, giving up too soon, underestimating the inputs or time needed, not moving on from legacy assumptions and ways of working, not creating enough space between the legacy and the new business, and sticking too rigidly to a fixed transformation plan rather than adapting in response to new knowledge or changed contexts.

Inevitably, true transformation will involve a 'messy middle' stage and significant complexity. The only way to navigate that complexity is to learn your way through it. Every company will have very different operational contexts that implicate on the process, and those contexts will, of course, change significantly over time. For this reason, fixed and linear transformation programmes in complex adaptive environments will inevitably fail.

Traditional approaches to change management are very waterfall in nature. Change programmes are all about big upfront investments in technology, consultants and inputs, and then a relatively fixed, stage gate process to lay down a linear progression of change. When contexts change, as they inevitably will, the programme struggles to adapt and either becomes increasingly irrelevant, or results in drift back to old ways of thinking. In highly uncertain and adaptive environments, the reality is that it is far better to take an adaptive approach to change.

In other words, we need to BE agile about how we BECOME agile.

Agile change management

As I've discussed, modern digital and business transformation is far from being the linear process with a beginning, middle and an end that many take it to be. The trajectory instead should be towards creating a new type of organization that is, in itself, designed around continuous change and the ability to respond to rapidly changing contexts. In that sense the process of change management never ends. More than ever we are in the business of continuously managing change.

Given that change management processes need to be more adaptive and responsive to the changing contexts there are some critical shifts needed in how we approach change programmes:

- **The balance between vision and iteration:** achieving a new level of organizational agility requires continuous iteration and adaptation but we also need a compelling vision and an understood organizing direction. This means that one of the key questions we have to answer is what is fixed and what is flexible. We need to establish the parameters to understand what needs to change rapidly, and what might change far more slowly. And beyond this, to understand how feedback from faster iteration can inform the slower-changing strategy.

- **Barriers to organizational change:** removing blockers and barriers to change was previously seen as one part in a multistep process. Now, continuously shifting contexts mean that the barriers to moving fast are themselves always changing and emergent, so we need to work consistently and unceasingly at overcoming them.

- **Parallel, not linear:** one of the most famous models for change management is John Kotter's eight steps:
  - Establish a sense of urgency.
  - Form a powerful coalition.
  - Create a vision.
  - Communicate that vision.
  - Empower others to act on the vision.
  - Plan for, and create short-term wins.
  - Consolidate improvements and build on the change.
  - Institutionalize new approaches.[2]

This linear approach works well in stable, slow-moving environments such as those existing in the late 1990s when he first described it. Kotter's later thinking acknowledged the need to accelerate the change process itself, and to shift from a strictly linear approach to one in which we are enabling change to happen on multiple fronts and where we are in effect running the stages concurrently and continuously.

- **Fluid, not fixed:** just as planning needs to be constantly adaptive, so the very process of change management should be subject to continuous review and the application of learning as the process unfolds. Many companies may think that they are doing this but in reality few build in the opportunity for regular retrospectives and reflection, and enable enough fluidity for the process itself to be adaptive.

- **Open, not closed:** traditional efforts in change management tend to be inwardly facing, focused on the internal structures, cost savings, efficiency drivers. All of which may well be relevant. But cost savings and efficiencies in themselves do not create a new organization. Large companies become very inward facing over time and yet in the digital world the exact opposite is what is required. A focus on creating a truly networked organization (through technology, data and people) creates greater opportunity. We need to understand all sides of the ecosystem (customers, employees, partners, suppliers) in which the company exists and the most beneficial connections that we can create. We need to be transparent about the transformation process. The digital team from the retail and banking business Co-op, for example, have taken a very open approach to their change programme, posting updates, learning and best practice advice on their blog and social media accounts.[3] Or publishing code and design patterns on GitHub or similar entities to enable other teams to reuse the work and reduce duplication. The transparency is an inclusive way to bring key audiences (employees, customers, suppliers) on the journey with you but also helps support the recruitment of digital talent.

- **Experience, over efficiency:** customer and employee experience are two of the most powerful pillars that can support transformation. Truly reorienting the organization around the customer means fundamental change for many businesses. Yet alongside the customer experience we need to focus on reorienting employee experience: the human side of digital transformation. Employees who are intrinsically motivated towards achieving a new vision are powerful enablers for change.

- **More leadership, less management:** as I discuss later in the book management is a brilliant invention but in the context of a fluid change process we need to accept that not everything can be tightly managed, and that there is real value in leadership at all levels of the organization. People who are willing to lead the change, model the behaviours, set the course, create the exemplars, show the way.

Above all, modern transformation programmes need to be adaptive, responsive and build from continuous learning. We need to think big. We need to start small. We need to scale fast.

CASE STUDY
LEGO's digital transformation, putting agile at the heart

In 2003/04 LEGO was facing something of an existential threat. Jørgen Vig Knudstorp was appointed the new CEO of the struggling company and recognized that many of the issues that the company faced were as a result of supply chain and enterprise-level inefficiencies that had arisen over time. Perhaps ironically, the company's commitment to innovation had led to it becoming inefficient in key areas including production, planning, purchasing and distribution as successive innovations were implemented.

The introduction of a company-wide Enterprise Platform gave them the foundation upon which to transform their processes, costs and subsequently revenues and helped to bring a culture of continuous improvement and greater efficiency to the management of the business. Integrated product lifecycle management and supply chain systems meant that product could be supplied to stores on a far more on-demand basis. Digitization of products and propositions had been a key part of this programme and by 2016 the company had a series of innovations which capitalized on the potential of digital technologies. These included sales of video games and programmable robots alongside the traditional LEGO blocks, a plethora of fan-created LEGO YouTube videos, and investment in online communities such as the 'LEGO ideas' forum through which fans could submit new ideas which could then be pre-tested easily, shortening the go to market time.[4]

Yet the senior leadership team still felt that the company was at risk of not being responsive enough to rapidly changing opportunities and challenges in the digital world. Alongside the efficiencies brought by the Enterprise System, it was clear that there was a need for an engagement platform that could meet customer expectation around its increasingly digitized set of products. This meant a faster turnaround time for new functionality, the ability to cope with rapid increases in demand without system down-time, and the ability to scale changes to platforms rapidly across the company.[5]

To implement the change, operations needed to implement agile ways of working at scale and shift from a structure based on functions to one which was organized around products and services.[6] The transformation to agile at scale began from the top down with workshops for global LEGO leaders to understand the shift in mindset and methodology from traditional linear processes to more adaptive ways of working focused on continuous delivery of value. Product and programme managers break down large, organizational goals into product backlogs for teams to deliver iteratively. Product-focused, multidisciplinary teams are tasked with delivering complete solutions to the market by working in rapid two-week sprints, supported by a funding model which evolved from being constrained by annual budget processes to a more project-based approach. Each agile team has particular areas of expertise but the teams are comprised of the skills and capabilities needed to deliver working outputs.

The company also focused on how it could align multiple agile teams across different areas and domains. Larger releases or changes in functionality were coordinated at a 'programme level' which sits above the team level and ensures that the work of individual teams is aligned in a way that supports business outcomes.[7] Two-weekly Product Implementation Planning meetings regularly agree priorities based on the latest known information and inputs, and areas of work are allocated to specific teams through discussion and conversation. The planning events themselves are highly collaborative and social but also work to identify potential risks and dependencies as well as priorities. This ensures that teams can be set up for success in their delivery of outputs.[8] Managers regularly review the risks which have been identified to assess how significant blockers can be tackled (the objective being ROAM – that the risk is Resolved, Owned, Accepted or Mitigated).[9]

The application of agile ways of working across LEGO was no short-term programme. During the COVID-19 pandemic the company was able to respond to significant changes in customer shopping behaviour and drove a 7 per cent increase in revenues from Jan–June 2020. They then went on to invest in the setting up of 'digital talent hubs' in cities including Shanghai, London, Copenhagen and Billund.[10] LEGO are consistently named amongst the most innovative companies on the planet.

Agile transformation: the shift towards a 'think big, start small, scale fast' approach to change

The phrase 'think big, start small, scale fast' perfectly describes a definitive approach to agile transformation. Eric Ries, author of the Lean Startup, has used the phrase as a way to capture some of the key elements of a Lean product development approach,[11] and it has also popped up in the context of innovation[12] (specifically from McDonald's Ventures in 2006[13]). But the phrase is an excellent way to capture the key shifts in transformation process, organizational mindset, and working approaches that are inherent to greater business agility. It expresses the need to set a compelling direction for change, to begin establishing the foundational enablers that can support new ways of operating, to think boldly. Yet it also speaks to the need to be flexible and adaptive in our approach, to support more iterative strategy, and to change mindsets and not get stuck in traditional linear thinking. And it captures the need for continuous learning, focus, momentum and rapid growth.

Over the rest of the book I'm going to set out exactly what this means. A roadmap not just for agile transformation but for a whole new type of organization.

References

1 Walter, Gideon, Shanahan, Michael, Reeves, Martin and Goulet, Kaelin [accessed 25 October 2016] Why Transformation Needs a Second Chapter: Lean, but not yet mean, *Boston Consulting Group, Perspectives* [Online] https://www.bcgperspectives.com/content/articles/transformation_growth_why_transformation_needs_second_chapter_lean_not_yet_mean/ (archived at https://perma.cc/KSK7-GJB9)

2 Kotter Inc [accessed 10 April 2019] 8-Step Process [Online] https://www.kotterinc.com/8-steps-process-for-leading-change/ (archived at https://perma.cc/HYZ9-MZSH)

3 Co-op [accessed 10 April 2019] Developing Visual Design Across Co-op Products and Services, *Co-op Digital Team Blog* [Online] https://digitalblog. coop.co.uk/ (archived at https://perma.cc/4FYG-KNPT)

4 Andersen, Peter and Ross, Jeanne W [accessed 05 October 2022] Transforming the LEGO Group for the Digital Economy, MIT Sloan School of Management, Center for Information Systems Research, March 2016 [Online] https://ctl.mit. edu/sites/ctl.mit.edu/files/attachments/MIT_CISRwp407_TheLEGOGroup_ AndersenRoss_0.pdf (archived at https://perma.cc/NT7F-PFSJ)

5 McGrath, Rita Gunther [accessed 05 October 2022] How LEGO Used Agile Principles to Accelerate Innovation, August 2022 [Online] https://www. ritamcgrath.com/sparks/2022/08/how-lego-used-agile-principles-to-accelerate-innovation/ (archived at https://perma.cc/A48W-B88N)

6 Sommer, Anita Friis [accessed 05 October 2022] Agile Transformation at LEGO Group, October 2019 [Online] https://www.dockconsulting.nl/ wp-content/uploads/2021/03/Agile-at-Lego.pdf (archived at https://perma. cc/5AR5-FT9Q)

7 Roost, Lars and Kniberg, Henrik [accessed 05 October 2022] Is SAFe Evil?, GOTO 2015 [Online] https://youtu.be/TolNkqyvieE (archived at https://perma. cc/LX5Z-BUML)

8 Kniberg, Henrik and Brandsgård, Eik Thyrsted [accessed 05 October 2022] Planning as a Social Event, December 2016 [Online] https://crisp.se/wp-content/ uploads/2016/12/Agile@Lego.pdf (archived at https://perma.cc/8RFA-S5QL)

9 McGrath, Rita Gunther [accessed 05 October 2022] How LEGO Used Agile Principles to Accelerate Innovation, August 2022 [Online] https://www. ritamcgrath.com/sparks/2022/08/how-lego-used-agile-principles-to-accelerate-innovation/ (archived at https://perma.cc/8M2X-JGBY)

10 Mixson, Elizabeth [accessed 05 October 2022] A Look at Lego's Digital Revival, Intelligent Automation Network, January 2022 [Online] https://www. intelligentautomation.network/resiliency/articles/a-look-at-legos-digital-revival (archived at https://perma.cc/D8BD-AGYU)

11 Andreessen Horowitz [accessed 10 April 2019] a16z Podcast: Beyond Lean Startups with Eric Ries, November 2015 [Online] https://a16z.com/2015/11/08/ lean-startups/ (archived at https://perma.cc/SEK2-MXSG)

12 Carroll, Jim [accessed 10 April 2019] Innovation: Think Big, Start Small, Scale Fast!, May 2010 [Online] https://jimcarroll.com/2010/05/innovation-think-big-start-small-scale-fast/#.VqacZFN4aCQ (archived at https://perma.cc/ SAY6-4HMC)

13 Gubman, Ed and Russell, Steve [accessed 10 April 2019] 'Think Big, Start Small, Scale Fast': Growing customer innovation at McDonald's, *Questia* [Online] https://www.questia.com/library/journal/1G1-152641350/think-big-start-small-scale-fast-growing-customer (archived at https://perma.cc/3XLU-NKNQ)

05

Think big

The key elements of 'think big'

Thinking big is all about position, direction, context and foundations.

Visioning: capturing why the world has changed, the new contexts shaping a new environment, where the business is currently, developing a point of view on what the future looks like, creating a compelling vision, communicating that vision repeatedly, generating a positive urgency for change.

Bold, disruptive thinking: unlearning to relearn, thinking beyond incremental change, not looking at the new through the lens of the old, asking what is possible. Rather than always asking 'why?' perhaps we should more often be asking 'why not?'.

Foundation enablers: technology and data – core systems infrastructure that is scalable but flexible; a technology and data architecture and structure that empowers exceptional capability, agility, a higher cadence and a step change in experimentation; adept application of automation to drive efficiency and speed; adept application of human talent to higher value inputs.

Foundation enablers: culture and people – empowering a culture and leadership mindset to support agile approaches; high-velocity decision-making; balancing alignment with autonomy to move fast; governance of change; creating the space for experimentation and the new.

Context mapping: effective problem exploration; developing an understanding of the different contexts across the business, and where to DO Agile, and where to BE agile.

Visioning – setting a compelling direction for change

Generating a common language around 'agile' and 'digital'

Terms like 'agile' and 'digital' have rapidly become overused in businesses and yet there is rarely a common view on what each of these things really means. If you ask a room of 20 leaders this question you will often get 20 different answers (and definitions that often themselves are full of jargon). So it is essential that every business not only develops its own understanding of what agile and digital mean, but that those interpretations are widely understood.

With agile, a company may well develop its own version of Agile process, drawing from the most appropriate facets of different methodologies. That process needs to be well understood and socialized through the business, even with teams that are not 'doing' Agile. Beyond this, 'doing' Agile needs to be supported through a common approach to developing an agile culture and mindset right across the business.

With digital, it is useful to have a common frame of reference for what it means for the business. As an example, the team that originally led the digital transformation for the services provided by the UK Government (Government Digital Service, or GDS) have described how digital: 'is not a new function. It is not even a new way of running the existing functions of an organization... It is a new way of running organizations'.[1]

When the key members of that team went to the Co-op group to lead the transformation there, they created a definition that reflected a good combination of people plus technology, plus a need to change the way in which we work: 'Applying the culture, practices, processes and technologies of the internet era to respond to people's raised expectations' (Bracken, 2016).[2]

This common language helps support clarity and alignment, but also minimizes misunderstanding.

Creating a compelling vision for change

Company visions or missions are too often vague platitudes that could well apply to just about any business in any category. Saying that you will deliver exceptional value to your shareholders may sound good in an annual report but does little to inspire employees to go the extra mile. Saying that you will outperform your competitors won't become a reality if your employees don't understand how that will happen. Saying that you'll be the most customer-centric business in your category when everything that your customers and employees experience feels exactly the opposite serves only to undermine the purpose of having a vision in the first place.

Let's be clear. A compelling vision needs to be:

- inspirational enough to generate energy and excitement;
- distinctive enough to feel unique;
- simple enough to motivate with clarity;
- challenging enough to feel stretching;
- directional enough to express a point of view about the world/future;
- tangible enough to be a widely understood call to arms.

Netflix CEO Reed Hastings has talked about the importance of vision and focus in navigating the economic, emotive and resource challenges of a business that has reinvented itself multiple times (from mailing DVDs to content streaming to original content production).[3] Rather than spending too much time thinking about what the competition are doing, Netflix has a long-term point of view about what the future will look like, and is focused on servicing its customers in the best way possible on the journey towards realizing this vision. Following Andy Grove's famous maxim that 'only the paranoid survive',[4] he says, can easily distract you from your own path. Netflix famously publishes its long-term view of how it sees the market and where Netflix will focus.[5] Where you choose to focus your attention is a key determinant of organizational orientation. Many incumbents look at competitors and new entrants as they are now rather than envisaging what they could become as technology inevitably improves.

Hastings describes how focus can see a business through a challenging transition such as the one that Netflix underwent when it moved the entire business from DVDs to streaming. Developing an entirely new muscle as a business means that the transformation has to be positioned as essential to survival. You can't dabble in it. As previously mentioned, when the streaming part of Netflix started to take shape, Hastings deliberately created space between the two (competing) businesses and even went as far as separating the key management meetings to ensure that the streaming business should and could be built to stand on its own merits.

Stubborn on vision, flexible on details

If a compelling vision needs to be not only inspirational, challenging and distinctive but also simple, tangible and directional, how that vision is brought to life is just as critical in capitalizing on the power that it can have to be all of those things. The stories that grow up in a business through its life about times of success and struggle can be powerful influencers of cultural norms and behaviours in that company. The stories that an organization creates around its vision can be just as powerful in shaping changes in culture and practice.

A transformation vision needs to paint a picture of the positive future state for the business. It needs to connect with employees, partners and customers in ways that are emotional as well as rational. It needs to be something they can believe in. But a CEO standing up with a PowerPoint presentation is not going to transform a business. It also needs to be communicated repeatedly through the words and actions of the leadership team. German psychologist Hermann Ebbinghaus pioneered the study of memory and created the forgetting curve as a way of expressing the decline in the retention of memories over time. Put simply, information is lost over time unless it is frequently reinforced. Without any prompts to retain newly learned knowledge, its durability can decline rapidly. An example forgetting curve might look Figure 5.1.

FIGURE 5.1 The forgetting curve

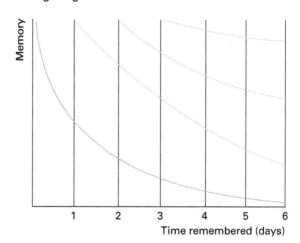

SOURCE Created by Icez and available in the public domain at https://commons.wikimedia.org/w/index.php?curid=2214107

The point is that a vision should be strongly directional, but it should also be repeated again and again, articulated, referenced and modelled at every opportunity by the leaders in the organization as a way to reinforce, embed, compel.

Earlier in the book I talked about how organizations become highly proficient at exploiting existing advantage and the inductive and deductive reasoning that comes with that, but are typically poor at abductive thinking, or imagining what the future advantage could look like. Abductive thinking often involves needing to work from incomplete information, but it can draw on creativity and intuition, and result in significant leaps forward (the 'shaping demand' jumps that we mentioned earlier). Yet abductive thinking is not divorced from scientific method or data. If we think about Einstein's work, for example, as much of it was informed by creative leaps of imagination and thought experiments as it was about deduction.

Too often businesses look at the new through the lens of the old. They use analogy and short cuts, which can lead to repurposing rather than reimagining. Asking yourself what the new proposition would look like if you built it from scratch is a good question to ask. Imagining what your business would look like if you launched it today is a good way to challenge your hidden, or toxic, assumptions. First principles thinking is the method of distilling a challenge down to its fundamental truths or atomic components before reasoning back from there in order to redefine what the solution is. It means that your start point gives you the optimal opportunity to create something fundamentally different, and solutions and visions are far more likely to be truly innovative and compelling rather than incremental versions of what went before.

Whilst the organizational and/or transformation vision needs to provide a clear direction that is likely to change only slowly, it shouldn't preclude the ability to adapt *how* we achieve that vision. Being agile and doing Agile is not an excuse not to have a plan.

Optimization is important but, just as you'll never reinvent your business through A/B testing, iteration without direction is foolish. So we need to balance direction with adaptation, conviction with flexibility. To paraphrase Jeff Bezos, we need to be stubborn on vision, but flexible on details.[6]

Problem exploration and definition

The ability to explore and define problems and contexts with confidence and proficiency is a critical organizational competency in complex adaptive environments. Problem definition frameworks such as the five whys (a technique drawn from the Toyota Production System that involves asking the question 'why' successively five times in order to get to the real route of the problem) are good for both problem solving and quality improvement, but perhaps are best suited for relatively simple or less complicated problems.

For truly complex problems and challenges, we need to be exploring in divergent ways in order to understand situations from different angles and imagine a full range of potential solutions before converging on the solution we believe to be the best.

The CIA's 'Phoenix Checklist'[7] is a useful problem definition approach used by the agency to enable their agents to understand challenges in a thorough, rounded, flexible and context-free way. The process involves isolating the problem you want to think about, committing yourself to finding an answer by a certain date, and using the checklist to dissect the challenge. The checklist defines a series of questions to aid understanding of the problem, followed by another series of questions to help shape the plan.

THE PROBLEM

- Why is it necessary to solve the problem?
- What benefits will you receive by solving the problem?
- What is the unknown?
- What is it you don't yet understand?
- What is the information you have?
- What isn't the problem?
- Is the information sufficient? Or is it insufficient? Or redundant? Or contradictory?
- Should you draw a diagram of the problem? A figure?
- Where are the boundaries of the problem?
- Can you separate the various parts of the problem? Can you write them down? What are the relationships of the parts of the problem? What are the constants of the problem?
- Have you seen this problem before?
- Have you seen this problem in a slightly different form? Do you know a related problem?
- Try to think of a familiar problem having the same or a similar unknown.

- Suppose you find a problem related to yours that has already been solved. Can you use it? Can you use its method?
- Can you restate your problem? How many different ways can you restate it? More general? More specific? Can the rules be changed?
- What are the best, worst and most probable cases you can imagine?

THE PLAN

- Can you solve the whole problem? Part of the problem?
- What would you like the resolution to be? Can you picture it?
- How much of the unknown can you determine?
- Can you derive something useful from the information you have?
- Have you used all the information?
- Have you taken into account all essential notions in the problem?
- Can you separate the steps in the problem-solving process? Can you determine the correctness of each step?
- What creative thinking techniques can you use to generate ideas? How many different techniques?
- Can you see the result? How many different kinds of results can you see?
- How many different ways have you tried to solve the problem?
- What have others done?
- Can you intuit the solution? Can you check the result?
- What should be done? How should it be done?
- Where should it be done?
- When should it be done?
- Who should do it?
- What do you need to do at this time?
- Who will be responsible for what?
- Can you use this problem to solve some other problem?
- What is the unique set of qualities that makes this problem what it is and none other?
- What milestones can best mark your progress?
- How will you know when you are successful?

The challenge of seeing into the future

Being able to anticipate what the future might look like can improve our competitive edge, minimize risk and identify opportunities. Having a point of view on the future can also inform our vision for what we need the organization of the future to be capable of, and the strategy for how we achieve that.

Yet forecasting the future with accuracy is notoriously tough. In 1987 psychologist Philip Tetlock was researching how social sciences might contribute to preventing a nuclear apocalypse and he became increasingly frustrated at the many contradictory positions taken by so-called experts, how stubborn these experts were in retaining their point of view even in the face of contradictory evidence, and how easy it was to justify even failed forecasts with excuses. So Tetlock decided to collect forecasts from hundreds of experts (he eventually accumulated 27,500) and establish some clearly defined questions that would enable him to clearly say whether they were wrong or right, and then he waited for 18 years.

The results, published in his book *Expert Political Judgment*[8], showed that most of these experts were terrible forecasters. But refusing to acknowledge that the world is simply too complex to forecast, Tetlock more recently set up a new research programme that aggregated thousands of quantifiable forecasts to show the potential of crowdsourced forecasting. In 2011, IARPA (Intelligence Advanced Research Projects Activity, the US intelligence community's equivalent to DARPA) began a competitive challenge to find cutting-edge methods to forecast geopolitical events. After four years, 500 questions and drawing on more than 1 million forecasts, Tetlock's Good Judgement Project won the challenge with forecasts that proved to be so accurate that they outperformed intelligence analysts that had access to classified data.[9]

The Good Judgement Project[10] draws on a broad variety of forecasters to produce better results, often putting forecasters into teams to enhance results further. Their experiments have shown that even brief training on how to put a probability on a forecast and correct for well-known biases also improves results. The project has shown that forecasting can work, and that some 'superforecasters' have the ability to predict events with a degree of accuracy far outstripping chance. They have found that the most successful forecasters were those who exhibited 'actively open-minded thinking' or in other words, those who were not afraid to change their minds in the face of fresh evidence, and are happy to seek out contrasting views.

One of the easiest ways to improve the accuracy of predictions is to use the Delphi Method, which draws from these ideas but in a vastly simplified way. Originally developed as a systematic forecasting technique and based on the principle that forecasts from a structured group of individuals are more accurate than those from unstructured groups, the method involves gathering relevant experts together and going through an estimate–talk–estimate process. The experts answer questionnaires in rounds and after each round a facilitator gives an anonymized summary of the outputs along with the reasons given for the predictions. The experts are then encouraged to revise their judgements in light of the other expert outputs. Undergoing this process with more than one round helps reduce divergence of prediction and convergence around a likely scenario. Median scores of the final round can be used to alight on a final result.

The Delphi Method has been shown to have advantages over other structured forecasting techniques such as prediction markets[11] but at its simplest level, the method speaks to the value that discussion and healthy debate amongst the experts within and outside of your business can have in determining the most likely future scenarios. Let's not also forget about the importance of avoiding bias and inflexibility through active open-minded thinking, seeking out contrasting views, and not being afraid to change one's mind when new evidence presents itself.

CASE STUDY
DBS Bank and the importance of focus

The transformation story of Asian bank DBS is an excellent example of how a singular, directional, well-articulated and well-communicated vision that is executed well can be a true catalyst for positive change. When Paul Cobban joined DBS in 2009 as Chief Operating Officer, it was a midsized Asian bank with around 22,000 employees that was performing poorly. It had the lowest customer satisfaction scores of any bank in Singapore. Cobban tells the story of how, when he got in a taxi on his first day in the job and told the driver that he worked at DBS, the reply was that DBS stood for 'damn bloody slow'.[12]

New CEO Piyush Gupta defined a refreshed core vision for the bank that was oriented around the concept of 'Asian Service'. One of the first steps in the digital transformation process was to define exactly what that meant in terms that were tangible and that everyone could easily grasp. This they expressed as respectful, easy to deal with and dependable, articulated as the acronym 'RED', which rapidly became part of the company's vocabulary. Cobban then focused the initial delivery of this vision through a focus on eliminating waste and reducing customer time and defined a singular metric for success – the customer hour. Cross-disciplinary working on customer journeys and process improvements managed to take out 250 million customer hours of waste per year and the bank went from the bottom of customer satisfaction scores to the top in only one year. In 2016 DBS was named by Euromoney as the world's best digital bank.[13]

Not content with that success, the bank underwent a broader, ongoing shift to customer-centred design to create a fundamental change towards working back from the customer. This customer-centric approach to transformation led to the realization that effective digital banking should enable customer transactions in as seamless a way as possible. In other words, banking services and the technology involved should largely be invisible. In keeping with an iterative approach to transformation Cobban identified a series of blockers to change and then ran experiments to remove them as barriers. One of these, for example, involved improving speed of decision-making by removing the practice of people seeking permission from their managers for decisions by e-mail, and replacing it with weekly decision-taking gatherings where employees could get immediate answers or approval on most issues.

This was supported with a fundamental technology reboot to establish a solid, common foundation of core systems that could be built upon. DBS Bank Chief Information Officer David Gledhill has described how he set a mission for the technology team to become the 'D' in GANDALF. The first letters of Google, Amazon, Netflix, Apple, LinkedIn and Facebook together spell GANALF, and this mission to be the missing D became one of the most impactful things for the organization:

> It had a bigger impact on our technology people and many other people in the organization than anything else we've done, because it started to make them think about what was possible. It got them to think, 'We're not acting like another bank, and here's how we really start to transform ourselves like a technology company.'[14]

Realizing the key role of culture and mindset in catalysing continuous innovation, leadership teams worked with startups in hackathons and the job of the innovation team shifted towards teaching the wider organization how to innovate. One outcome of this approach was the launch of Digibank, DBS's mobile-only bank in India, which uses AI and automation to efficiently deliver seamless banking services. Digibank acquired over a million customers in its first year of operations without any of them going into a branch and is projected to have 5 million customers by 2021.[15]

Between 2006 and 2017, DBS bank more than doubled in size, more than doubled its income and almost doubled its profit, and its market capitalization has tripled.

Applying bold, disruptive thinking

In order to think big, and continually generate new and exceptional value, senior teams need to recognize that in order to win big, the risk-to-reward ratio that might have worked for the company in the past needs to change.

Even some of the most innovative companies fail – think Google and its successive failures trying to enter the social networking space, or Amazon and the Fire Phone which reportedly cost the company more than US $170 million, and Webstore which was like a competitive service to Shopify. We can think big about our vision and direction, set a course founded in our belief about what the future looks like, and then mitigate as much risk as possible by starting small, experimenting, testing and validating. But we have to accept that if we're originating truly different and potentially disruptive ideas, we are in effect making a series of bets and plan for a risk profile that allows for that. As Jeff Bezos has said: 'You're still going to be wrong nine times out of ten. In business, every once in a while, when you step up to the plate, you can score 1,000 runs. This long-tailed distribution of returns is why it's important to be bold. Big winners pay for the many previous experiments.'[16]

The point is that in order to win big sometimes we need to lose, but the one thing we can't be is timid. And we need, of course, to learn from our failures – Google has adapted the technology developed for Google Glass in its self-driving cars, for example.

A good way to challenge teams to think big is to design around challenging customer, supplier or partner needs and use continually changing expectation as a reason to break open existing assumptions, timescales and targets with ambitious stretch goals.

CASE STUDY
Lemonade Insurance

Digital can disrupt, of course, by bringing the benefit of much greater efficiencies to the customer in ways that are hard for incumbent businesses with legacy systems, processes and thinking to do. But a good question to ask is what would a service or customer journey in the category look like if you could start all over again with a blank sheet of paper? Answering that question, welcoming the challenge of rising customer expectation, and working back from customer need can open up disproportionate advantage.

A good example of this is Lemonade Insurance, a renters and home insurance service centred around the promise of social good and a commitment to 'instant everything', that has used technology and customer-centric thinking to reinvent the insurance customer journey. Launched in 2015, its mission is to dramatically simplify the process of insurance and provide a mobile-first, exceptional and intuitive customer experience. Its promise is 90 seconds to get insured and three minutes to get paid. AI-powered chatbots help customers navigate processes like sign-up, cancelling old policies and making a claim. All unclaimed money is donated to good causes. In 2016 they set a world record by settling a claim within three seconds, and in 2017 introduced the world's first 'live' insurance policy, which enables customers to make changes to their coverage in real time from their phone. In 2017 they had US $10 million of policies across 19 US states and a year later they had more than 250,000 customers and were announcing plans to expand into Europe.[17]

Lemonade is an excellent exemplar of bold, new thinking and totally reinventing what good looks like in a sector.

Coming up with breakthrough ideas

Agile methods, principles and ways of working can be applied to both optimize existing processes, workflows and customer journeys but also to create and execute transformational ideas. In the latter scenario the need is often to break open existing assumptions and unlearn to relearn so that one can create new possibilities unburdened by the thinking from the past. Google have a way of deliberately encouraging teams to unlearn. One of their nine principles of innovation is to 'Think 10X' or in other words for a team to ask themselves, 'what is the ten times version of this idea?' Imagining this as a possibility forces a team to work from first principles and break open current assumptions about how problems can be solved, or even whether they are solving the right problem at all.

Astro Teller, the Director of Google X, the division of the company that focuses on truly breakout ideas, has described these 10X ideas as 'Moonshots'.[18] When combined with multiple short-term, incremental innovations which serve to consistently improve Google products (what they call 'roofshots'[19]) it can prove a powerful mix. The agile business needs both. Marginal innovation that brings incremental gain can be enormously valuable, particularly when compounded with many other marginal innovations. Yet it's arguably easier to work from existing thinking to look for how something can be done incrementally better, than it is to originate a truly breakthrough idea.

Elite sport can teach us a lot about the dynamics around breakthrough ideas. Incentives and expectations in legacy businesses can often be focused on relatively incremental innovation since it may be perceived as more realistic and achievable. Yet extrinsic and intrinsic incentives of this kind (from money and other tangible rewards to more intangible recognition as a reward) can have an unforeseen effect if not combined with incentives for larger, more groundbreaking ideas.

Sergey Bubka revolutionized the sport of pole-vaulting with his talent and athleticism which enabled him to use a heavier pole when competing and to hold it right at the end to gain extra leverage. Many athletes in the sport were initially not strong enough to mimic his technique but his ability to load more recoil into the pole and then combine this with a longer, faster run-up meant that he was able to push the boundaries of the sport and achieve heights that had never been reached before.

In 1983 at the age of 19 he won his first world championship, something he would go on to do a further six times. He pushed the world pole-vaulting record ever higher, from 5.83 metres to 6.14 metres, breaking the renowned 6 metre barrier and setting a new record an unbelievable 35 times. At the time sponsors typically gave win bonuses to the athletes that they sponsored but Bubka was so dominant that this kind of sponsorship proved elusive. Instead, Nike decided to incentivize him with a payment of up to $100,000 each time that he broke the world record. Some sports writers have noted since how Bubka then seemed to (rather smartly) set about breaking his own world records as incrementally and as often as he could.[20] As an example, he improved his previous record 14 times between 1991 and 1993 and it took 20 years for his final 6.14 metre record to be broken.

World records are often set when everything comes together for an elite athlete in a moment in time which enables a totally new level of performance that may be almost impossible to replicate. Bubka became one of the most successful athletes of all time by breaking his own record repeatedly. We'll never know whether he might have been able to achieve even greater heights but his achievements were second to none in the sport.

So many incentives in business are aligned towards incremental gain. These incentives set an expectation that can constrain thinking and focus effort towards marginal improvements or innovations. It's useful to consider how organizations might incentivize more breakthrough ideas alongside this and what this could mean for generating the kind of innovation that enables a jump, rather than a step, forwards.

Staying with elite athletes, we can learn a lot about the challenge of bringing breakthrough ideas to life through the story of high-jumper Dick Fosbury. Fosbury won the high jump gold medal at the 1968 Mexico City Olympic Games using a revolutionary new jumping technique that became known as the 'Fosbury Flop'. The athlete not only won an Olympic Gold Medal that year but changed how the sport was practised forever. By the time of the next Olympic games in 1972 the Fosbury Flop had become the dominant technique, with 28 out of 40 competitors using the method.

Yet rather than the ground-breaking technique originating from a light-bulb moment of inspiration, the story of how it came about can tell us a lot about how breakthrough ideas actually happen, and specifically the value of external perspectives, the right environmental factors, and the need to survive early criticism and misunderstanding.

Let's think first about the value of applying knowledge from outside of the immediate domain. Fosbury was an engineering student, and he cleverly used this expertise to come up with an entirely different way of tackling the challenge of how to get over the high bar without knocking it off. Prior to the Mexico games jumpers had for years used a straddle technique where the athletes face the bar as they approach it and then straddle it with their legs to get over it. As an engineer, Fosbury realized that if jumpers turned around and went over the bar backwards and head-first, they could arch their backs which would mean that the athlete's centre of gravity would pass below the bar even as their body sailed over it. It was this application of knowledge from outside of the sport that enabled the revolutionary leap forwards.

FIGURE 5.2 Centre of gravity

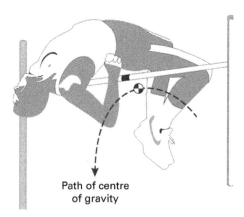

Path of centre
of gravity

It's worth also considering the environmental factors that helped the breakthrough to come about. When Fosbury first began practising high jump at high school in the early sixties the landing pits were typically sawdust or wood chips, which effectively meant that athletes had to land a certain way if they were to avoid injury. When a new foam pit was installed at Fosbury's school he was suddenly able to start experimenting safely with new techniques that involved landing backwards rather than forwards. The introduction of foam pits had enabled a few other athletes to also start experimenting with new methods (including Debbie Hill, who went on to become Canada's Commonwealth Games Champion) yet despite the wider availability of foam pits the vast majority of high jumpers were still following the old approaches. In business, the introduction of new enabling technologies can bring the potential for leaps forward in capability but teams need to be allowed to experiment. When new discoveries are made the rest of the organization needs to get behind new techniques and work hard to change entrenched behaviour.

The last lesson we can learn from Fosbury's brilliant innovation is the need to persist through early criticism. Many commentators were very cynical about the new technique. In fact one local newspaper at one point described him as the 'world's laziest high jumper'. Valery Brumel, the world high jump record holder at the time, initially called the method 'an aberration'. Yet Fosbury believed in his different approach and persisted with it until he won the Olympic Gold Medal in the sport. After the Mexico games Fosbury chose to pursue his career in engineering rather than a career as an elite athlete but he had already changed the sport forever and it would never go back. Revolutionary ideas always attract a degree of cynicism, backlash and dismissal but it is the belief and persistence of innovators that can push through this to realize truly big ideas.

Jeff Bezos has said that 90 per cent of the innovation at Amazon is incremental but that you also have to be willing to pursue big ideas. At the start of this book, I used a quote from him saying that this means that you need to be willing to be misunderstood, potentially for long periods of time. Yet if you have the vision and desire to invent frequently and sometimes to fail, you can generate breakthrough innovations without ever reaching the point where you are betting the whole company. 'Moonshots' are the visionary ideas. 'Roofshots' are the way in which these ideas can be pursued in a safe-to-fail manner.

Mapping your operating business contexts

Unknown unknowns

A simplistic view of transformation sees it simply as a linear transition from A to B, with one-size-fits-all solutions and ways of working and plenty of technology thrown in to facilitate the journey. An intelligent view of transformation takes a more nuanced view of the position of the business, the different contexts in which different areas of the business are operating in order to apply a more sophisticated understanding of the change needed and how we might apply different ways of working to those challenges.

A key method for understanding contexts in transformation better is to consider the level of knowledge that we have about situations and environments but also the level of uncertainty, risk and unpredictability involved. The 'unknown unknowns' framework is a simple differentiation that acknowledges that some risks are inherently unknowable, others are dependent on factors such as time, progress and response. The concept was popularized by US Secretary of Defense Donald Rumsfeld in 2002 who, in response to a question about Iraq's weapons of mass destruction at a Department of Defense briefing, said: 'Reports that say that something hasn't happened are always interesting to me, because as we know, there are known knowns; there are things we know we know. We also know there are known unknowns; that is to say we know there are some things we do not know.'[22]

A useful way of representing this idea is to characterize a quadrant of knowledge based on levels of identification and certainty (Figure 5.3).[23]

Understanding this balance between level of certainty and identification is key in helping a more sophisticated understanding of the type of response and problem solving that is required across the business and for different contexts. Domains and situations that are stable and well known, for example, are known knowns, suitable for processes and approaches that are concerned with exploiting and incrementally improving existing knowledge and experience. More complex, emergent areas and environments are characterized more by unknown unknowns. They are more likely to be moving fast, new territory, and so require approaches that can test and rapidly learn – you need to feel your way through.

FIGURE 5.3 Unknown unknowns

Certainty / Identification	Certain (known)	Certainty (unknown)
Identified (known)	Known known (Identified knowledge)	Known unknown (Identified risk)
Unidentified (unknown)	Unknown known (Untapped knowledge)	Unknown unknown (Unidentified risk)

Mapping position and movement

In *The Art of War*,[24] Sun Tzu set out five factors that define the competitive world and are needed to win any war:

- purpose or mission – shared vision, ideas and expectations;
- landscape – the understanding that we have of the terrain, our situation, opportunities and risks;
- climate – the environment, changes in climatic conditions;
- method – the doctrine, the logistics, rewards, discipline, measures;
- leadership – credibility, courage, intelligence.

Whilst several of these constants (like mission, leadership and method) are more evident and obvious in transformation programmes, the focus on landscape is perhaps less so. The need to understand the position from which we are moving and how the terrain and climate might change is often downplayed.

Researcher Simon Wardley (who also developed the pioneers, settlers, town planners concept that we mentioned earlier in the book) has written extensively about the importance of understanding position and movement in order to support strategy and change.[25] Hundreds of years ago, he says, Vikings would navigate by telling stories and the modern equivalent of this is the stories that get told within organizations, or the 'secrets of success' that allow the fallacy of strategy without positioning. We might set out to win a game of chess but it is the movement during the game that gives us learning as the game plays out, and a good understanding of our current context and position that allows us to apply that learning effectively.

So context-specific gameplay and situational awareness is important. Any half-decent military strategy has a good foundation formed by observation, an understanding of your context and position (your anchor), and therefore movement and the learning that comes from that movement. Most systems maps, business process maps, 'digital maps', and mind maps are not maps at all since whilst they may be visual, they have no representation of position or movement. It is the combination of strategy with execution, not either in isolation.

The S-curve chart that we featured in Chapter 3 of this book shows the progression of products and services from their genesis, through custom-built solutions through to ultimately becoming commoditized utilities (Figure 5.4).

In the same way that it's possible to map products and services, we might map components of those services such as practices, data and knowledge (Table 5.1).

FIGURE 5.4 Proposition evolution

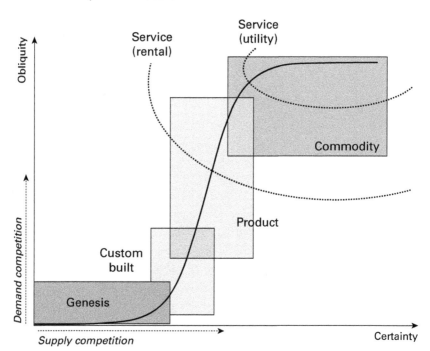

SOURCE Adapted from content created by Simon Wardley, available under Creative Commons Attribution-ShareAlike 4.0 International (CC BY-SA 4.0) https://medium.com/wardleymaps/anticipation-89692e9b0ced

TABLE 5.1 Service evolution components

Product/Service	Genesis	Custom built	Product	Commodity
Practices	Novel	Emerging	Good	Best
Data	Unmodelled	Divergent	Convergent	Modelled
Knowledge	Concept	Hypothesis	Theory	Accepted

FIGURE 5.5 Value chain mapping

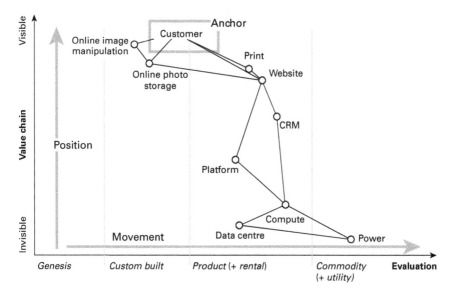

SOURCE Adapted from content created by Simon Wardley, available under Creative Commons Attribution-ShareAlike 4.0 International (CC BY-SA 4.0) https://medium.com/wardleymaps/anticipation-89692e9b0ced

An organization is complex but can be split into value chains. Value chains can be mapped against this evolution to show position and movement. In order to represent this properly we need to show position and movement relative to an anchor of some kind – if we are to work back from the customer, then the customer is the anchor. On the y-axis is the degree of visibility and proximity to the customer – this gives us position against the customer. The x-axis is plotted against the evolution of products and services based on the phases in the S-curve, and so gives us movement. Some elements of the value chain are naturally closer to the customer and some not, some are in the early stages of evolution and some are highly commoditized. Both customer needs and elements of the value chain may change position as they evolve to become more mature, for example, but the value chain can be linked together on the graph to form a map of position and movement (Figure 5.5).

FIGURE 5.6 Changing climatic conditions

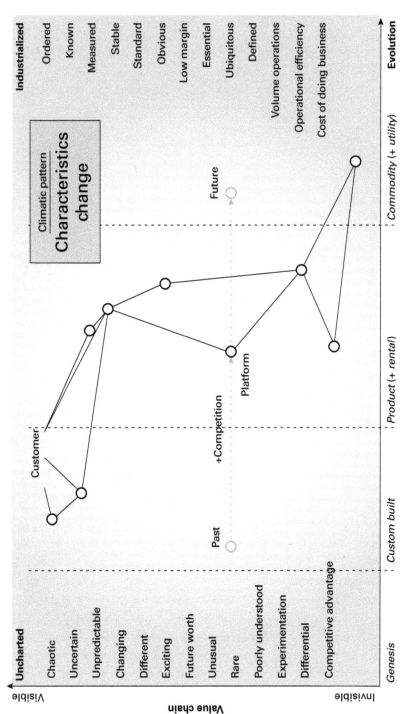

SOURCE Adapted from content created by Simon Wardley, available under Creative Commons Attribution-ShareAlike 4.0 International (CC BY-SA 4.0) https://medium.com/wardleymaps/anticipation-89692e9b0ced

Mapping in this way enables you to create a map of the landscape, which means that you can learn economic patterns that will influence outcomes (in other words climate, or the rules that influence the game). As we progress from genesis and custom built to commoditized and industrialized the characteristics change in key ways (Figure 5.6).

Early stages of maturity are characterized by relatively poor levels of understanding and higher levels of unpredictability. Latter stages are more ordered, stable and mature since we have greater experience and the market is mature. So given these different contexts there is no one-size-fits-all process – Agile and in-house is more likely to be used in uncertain environments in early stages of maturity; processes like Lean that are focused on learning and off-the-shelf services may be more utilized in the middle; and efficiency driving processes like Six Sigma and outsourcing may be used in highly commoditized contexts.

Having mapped the landscape and taken account of the climate (economic patterns) it is possible to create some doctrine, or approaches that are universal (such as a focus on user needs, using appropriate methodologies for different contexts, removing duplication, understanding what to in-house and what to outsource), and also to anticipate and even to manipulate. In order to do this we can use simple patterns such as how increased efficiency and stability can enable innovation since competition increases over time and pioneers can build out from services or use components that have become commoditized to create new value. Or the pattern that success breeds inertia. And higher order systems create new sources of worth.

Doctrine leads to leadership or deciding, or context-specific forms of gameplay like where we invest, what we make open-source, and so on. And then we act. 'Crossing the river by feeling the stones' (a phrase coined by Deng Xiaoping) means that as we move forwards into uncertainty we need to stay grounded, and feel our way incrementally and always be aware of our position and footing.

The three types of problem

Another similar but useful way of categorizing the different types of challenges and contexts that a business faces is considering the three types of problem in the world. Originally articulated in a paper on reform in the healthcare industry by Brenda Zimmerman of York University and Sholom Glouberman of the University of Toronto,[26] the framework differentiates between:

1 Simple problems – like baking a cake from a mix. There is a recipe.

2 Complicated problems – like sending a rocket to the moon. They can sometimes be broken down into a series of simple problems. But there is no straightforward recipe. Success frequently requires multiple people, often multiple teams, and specialized expertise. Unanticipated difficulties are frequent. Timing and coordination become serious concerns.

3 Complex problems – like raising a child. Once you learn how to send a rocket to the moon, you can repeat the process with other rockets and perfect it. One rocket is like another rocket. But not so with raising a child, the professors point out. Every child is unique. Although raising one child may provide experience, it does not guarantee success with the next child. Expertise is valuable but most certainly not sufficient. Indeed, the next child may require an entirely different approach from the previous one. And this brings up another feature of complex problems: their outcomes remain highly uncertain. Yet we all know that it is possible to raise a child well. It's complex, that's all.

Zimmerman and Glouberman go on to contend that it is often the case that complex problems are described as complicated ones, leading people to employ solutions wedded to rational planning approaches. These solutions serve only to miss aspects of complexity and so do not work. The sophistication of our language, theories and models may trick us into an illusion of clarity, ignoring the true complexity of a situation.

Yet there are even different shades of complexity. Complex adaptive problems are challenges where a good understanding of individual components or parts of a system does not automatically mean that a whole system is also understandable. This may be because they are dynamic networks of interactions, so the behaviour of the whole is not predicted by the behaviour of the components, and the individual component behaviour and collective behaviour can adapt in response to events. The term 'wicked problems' is sometimes used to denote particularly complex challenges that are very difficult to solve because of contradictory, incomplete information and/or changing requirements that may be tricky to recognize.

Again, the key is to understand how the different types of challenges map to your business and the types of response and process required to solve them well. More mature, well-understood, slower moving environments are likely to be characterized by relatively simple problems that can be solved with best-practice processes and checklists. More complicated contexts that are lesser known require expertise and the adept application of experience, learning and knowledge to navigate. Complex adaptive or 'wicked' challenges and environments such as those that might come from new, or rapidly developing and changing areas require emergent response characterized by experimentation and prototypical approaches. Given how critical it is to develop a more sophisticated understanding of how your contexts map across the business and the most appropriate response required, let's consider how these characteristics map across the 'explore, execute, extend and exploit' model.

Mapping your contexts

We've discussed how agile transformation involves an appreciation of the different types of approaches that we might use across the business for different contexts. It's worth repeating in this regard that unlike what many consultancy recommendations suggest, one size does not fit all. Just about every large business needs a much broader appreciation of agile thinking and ways of operating but Agile should not be the default process in the business. Questions about the scalability of agile processes run alongside questions about where we should apply them and, just as importantly, where we should

TABLE 5.2   Explore, execute, extend and exploit – organizational context and response

	Explore	Execute	Extend and Exploit
Environment	Uncertain, rapid change	Evolving	Certain, stable
Characteristics	Unknown unknowns	Known unknowns	Known knowns
Innovation Focus	Horizon 3 – Completely new	Horizon 2 – Adjacencies	Horizon 1 – Core
Problem Type	Complex	Complicated	Simple
Response	Emergent	Expertise	Best practice
Approach to Change	Embrace change, reduce cost of change	Learning, reduce waste	Reduce change
Capability Type	Pioneers	Settlers	Town planners
Orientation	Invention	Commercialization and rapid scaling	Operationalizing
Focus	Experiment/iterative	Test and learn	Efficiency, optimization
Working	Agile/Lean/Rapid prototyping	Agile/Lean/Process, Model adaptation	Six Sigma, Waterfall, Optimization

not. In order to determine the answers to these questions we need to take account of the different contexts and environments in which propositions, functions, tasks and areas of the business operate and apply appropriate methodologies, capability types, roles and ways of working. Context is everything.

The differences between the domains of explore, execute, extend and exploit define the organizational response (Table 5.2):

Explore: in areas and domains characterized by exploration, there are likely to be plenty of unknown unknowns, rapid change and high uncertainty. The problems that the business is trying to solve are complex, the context far newer, the response is emergent by necessity. Iterative and agile working is the only way of navigating this complexity and creating value in this ambiguous environment. This is new capability, future-facing ideas, exploration of entirely new propositions, the kinds of ideas that may disrupt the existing business or take it in a new direction. This is the domain of pioneers – lateral, creative or visionary thinkers who can visualize a different future.

Execute: execution is characterized by more certainty than exploration. The business can largely identify what it doesn't know (known unknowns) and set out to fill the gaps or to learn. The problems have more variables than areas that are concerned with exploitation and are complicated, so the response needs to be founded in developing and utilizing experience and expertise. The focus is more on test and learn, and iterative working to adapt existing capability, innovate in adjacencies, and commercialize and evolve ideas so that they can be scaled, but the rhythm is not necessarily as fast as domain three. This domain is suited to people who are great at developing models that work in the real world, who can define the operating model or revenue opportunity.

Extend and exploit: domains that are characterized by exploiting, extending and optimizing existing advantage; the contexts are typically defined by relatively stable slower-moving environments, higher degrees of certainty, and mature and well-established propositions. The challenges are there, but they are characterized more by 'known knowns'. The need is for common ways of doing things, scalability and best practice. There is value in innovation, but this is focused on innovating on core capability to drive incremental gain or to drive efficiencies and better ways of doing what you do now. This domain is well suited to those people who are exceptional at operationalizing, optimizing and institutionalizing.

The agile business needs to be good at all three domains. It needs to allocate sufficient resources to each one, and it needs to apply appropriate processes and thinking. New propositions in the business may mature from exploration to exploitation but as they progress the types of people whom we need working on them will shift, and the approaches and ways of working that should be applied will also likely evolve. But the different ways of operating need to coexist in the same business. One way of working should not suffocate the other. Agile is not just a process; it is a culture. Whilst key parts of the business will need to be DOING Agile, every part of the business will need to BE agile.

Foundational enablers for change

A word on technology and culture

As I'll discuss later in this section, agile transformation is people first, technology second. But that shouldn't diminish the significance of data and technology as enablers and catalysts for agility and change. Many organizations have made large investments now in technology systems that can take capability to a whole new level, but it remains for most a work in progress. Businesses need to think about their technology stacks and strategy not only in terms of the capabilities that they need now, but also those that they might need in the future. Technology architecture and procurement processes need to take greater account of flexibility, scalability and simplification to reduce complexity and future-proof their infrastructure. Organizations also need to develop forward-thinking data strategies alongside their investment in systems and resourcing. It's easy to get excited about the possibilities of so-called big data, algorithms, automation and machine learning, but if our data isn't structured, made available or interpreted in the right way, we will never realize the full potential. Alongside data and technology, we should also consider culture as a key enabler. The wrong culture can kill agile transformation before it has even started. But the right behaviours can catalyse lasting change.

This book is not designed to set out templates for technology architectures or data strategies, but whilst it's important to acknowledge the importance of these fundamental enablers, it's also key to understand the elemental role that people and culture play in actually creating the opportunity for real change to happen.

Why do we reject new technology?

The ability to adapt to and capitalize on the potential benefits of new technologies is clearly central to the modern transformation process and yet it can often be the case that bias can get in the way of successful technology adoption and change. This can even be true for technologies that can make our jobs easier owing to loss aversion (our tendency to prioritize avoiding losses over acquiring equivalent gains) and our awareness of switching costs (the outlay in time, effort or resource that it takes to switch to something new).

John Gourville of Harvard Business School has written about how these kinds of barriers can explain problems with the adoption of new innovations.[27] Their study of new products that are revolutionary to an existing product category or define an entirely new one found that this marketplace failure is two-sided, with consumers systematically undervaluing the innovation and businesses systematically overvaluing the innovation relative to what an objective analysis would show (they called this the 'curse of innovation'). On the consumer side, innovative new products will likely involve trade-offs relative to the existing solutions and they require a change in the way the consumers are doing things. On the company side, the degree of investment of time, energy and resource that has already been put into the new innovation means that companies are more likely to overvalue its appeal.

Reference dependence, one of the fundamental principles of behavioural economics, describes the tendency that people have to evaluate outcomes relative to a reference point and then to classify gains and losses against that position (Prospect Theory, Kahneman and Tversky, 1979[28]). Reference dependence can apply to any decision involving risk and uncertainty, but Gourville argues that the 'curse of innovation' arises because the consumers and the developers of an innovation have fundamentally different reference points. Since the consumers use the entrenched existing product as a reference point, loss aversion means that they overvalue the existing solution relative to the new one.

The company that came up with the innovative new product, however, uses the innovation itself as its reference point and so systematically overvalues it relative to the entrenched alternative:

> Having invested time, money, and energy in the development of these products, such innovations are no longer viewed as possibilities, but as realities. For developers, not having the features on which their innovation does better will feel like a shortcoming, or loss, and having the features on which the entrenched alternative does better will be nice to have, but not essential.[29]

This 'curse of innovation' therefore means that consumers often reject new innovations that may well objectively make them better off, and that the developers of the innovation systematically fail to anticipate this rejection. Hence, the innovation fails.

Beyond innovative new products we might apply these concepts more broadly to the adoption of new technologies, ways of working and even to how we approach risk in innovation and to organizational transformation itself. The 'curse of transformation' as we might call it, can mean that employees systematically overemphasize the trade-offs that they see in giving up the old way of doing things, and undervalue the benefits of the new solutions. Their reference point is the entrenched status quo, and loss aversion means that they are more keenly aware of what they will lose in the change process. Equally, executives leading the technology implementation or transformation have the new technology or vision for a reference point and so may well systematically fail to anticipate the challenges that they will face in embedding real behaviour change.

In effect, both sides here are subject to a kind of 'endowment effect' (Kahneman, Knetsch and Thaler, 1991[30]), a bias that happens when we overvalue something that we own regardless of its real market value (meaning, for example, that we can be overly reluctant to part with something for its cash equivalent). In the same way that we place greater value on things that we own (particularly things that have an emotional, experiential or symbolic meaning), we are likely to place greater value on ways of working that we have moulded to become our own, or those that we have contributed significant time and energy in creating meaning that we feel greater ownership and investment.

One example of this is the story of the first mercury thermometers. At the end of the 16th century Galileo Galilei invented the first device that could measure temperature variations – a rudimentary water thermometer. Around 120 years later Gabriel Fahrenheit came up with the first modern mercury thermometer. The Dutch physician Herman Boerhaave thought that the device had great potential and proposed that measurements using a thermometer could be used for diagnosis and to improve treatment.

Yet despite its evident utility it took over 100 years for use of the thermometer and the discipline of thermometry to become widespread. Prior to the mercury thermometer, doctors would largely use touch to determine whether the patient had a high temperature or was suffering from a fever. This qualitative approach was regarded as being able to capture a rich amount of information, more in depth than any tool could generate, and for many years was seen as a superior approach to using thermometry.

In spite of the prevailing inertia to adopting this new technology, a group of researchers persisted in attempting to turn the relatively idiosyncratic opinions and descriptions from doctors into reproducible laws, but it was not until 1871 that a breakthrough happened. In a transformation piece of work (published as *On the Temperature in Diseases: A manual of medical thermometry*[31]) Carl Reinhold Wunderlich recorded temperatures in 100,000 patient cases, and successfully established not only that the average human body temperature was 37 degrees Celsius, but also that a variation of one degree above this constituted a fever, which meant that the course of illness could be better predicted than by touch alone.

Thermometry represented a giant leap towards modern medical practice but it was not until this study became more widely known and understood that attitudes and patient expectation really started to change. By the 1880s it was considered medical incompetence *not* to use a thermometer, but until then the much more subjective method of touch remained dominant.

The original thermometers may have been large, cumbersome devices and the tool did develop over many iterations but the slow advance of the technology was more down to the challenge of shifting entrenched behaviour and expectation. It's easy to reject technology that we don't understand, or technology whose successes we've had nothing to do with, or which we fear will detract from our own utility. Andy Grove (of Intel) has called what I have been describing in this section as the '10×' rule, referring to the idea that a product must be at least 10 times better in order to overcome barriers to adoption and switching costs because people tend to underestimate the advantages of a new technology by a factor of 3 whilst simultaneously overestimating the disadvantages of giving up existing solutions by a factor of 3.

Yale physician Gina Siddiqui has described in the *Scientific American* how the subtlety in technology adoption is actually in how we combine the best of the old with the best of the new. She explains how a children's hospital in Philadelphia had used quantitative algorithms to identify particularly dangerous fevers. The algorithms proved better at picking out serious infections than the judgement of an experienced doctor. But when the two were combined it outperformed either in isolation: 'It's true that a doctor's eyes and hands are slower, less precise, and more biased than modern machines and algorithms. But these technologies can count only what they have been programmed to count: human perception is not so constrained.'[32]

Similarly, at the 2016 International Symposium of Biomedical Imaging in Prague, a Harvard team developed an AI that could detect cancer cells amongst breast tissue cells with 92 per cent accuracy, almost as good as the trained pathologists who could pick out 96 per cent of the biopsy samples with cancer cells. Yet when artificial and human intelligence were combined 99.5 per cent of cancerous biopsies were identified.

Transformation leaders underestimate the power of loss aversion and switching costs at their peril. Technological and organizational change rarely means forgetting all that we know. More often it is helpful to frame it in that thought of combining the best of the old with the best of the new since this helps people to understand a frame of reference that can help mitigate resistance to change.

Transformation is people first, technology second

A common problem with digital transformation is that it's called digital transformation when it is actually business transformation. The word 'digital' can sometimes lead to the practice of chasing shiny technology at the expense of the people side of change. One of my favourite studies that speaks to the need to invest in both the technology *and* people side of change comes from MIT Sloan and Cap Gemini.[33] They researched more than 400 large companies over two years looking at how they combined investment in technology-enabled initiatives with leadership capabilities, culture and process initiatives to support transformation.

The study found that companies that invested in both technology and people were not only more digitally mature but on average 26 per cent more profitable – an advantage that was repeated across different industries. What the research also showed, however, was that those businesses that pursued shiny new technologies without the underlying strategies, processes, team structures and cultures to exploit them effectively damaged their business performance and were on average 11 per cent less profitable. Transformation specialist Lucia Adams has articulated the imbalance that often characterizes the way that digital is perceived in businesses: 'Digital is 10 per cent tech and 90 per cent human. Organizations talk about digital as if it is 90 per cent tech and 10 per cent human.'[34]

With so much focus on new technology and on customer experience, employee experience is often the poor relation. And this is brought into even sharper focus when we consider the huge problem we already have in employee engagement worldwide. Gallup, which has long undertaken wide-ranging research in the area, conducted a data meta-analysis looking at the relationship between team performance and employee engagement.[35] The analysis covered 82,000 teams and 1.8 million employees in 230 organizations across 73 countries and 49 industries. Gallup made the point that whilst studies have long suggested a collective intelligence of teams that goes beyond the sum of the individual team members' abilities, it has always been difficult to find any reliable predictors for team performance. But the meta-analysis reveals that across a wide variation in industry, market and economic environment the relationship between employee engagement and performance is consistent across a set of factors that range from clarity of expectation, sense of belonging, autonomy, doing meaningful work, learning and progression.

When the researchers compared the performance metrics of teams that were engaged against those who were actively disengaged, they found that the top teams had four times the odds of success compared with the bottom teams. More than ever in transformation programmes employee engagement and team performance are absolutely critical: 10 per cent tech and 90 per cent human.

Mapping agile organizational culture

One of the crucial (yet often under-acknowledged) aspects of transformation is nurturing and enabling the organizational culture that can support greater agility. Teams working in agile ways but surrounded by the wrong kind of culture will encounter the kind of friction that can be potentially disastrous to progress. Trying to achieve greater organizational agility in an environment that does not support an agile mindset and approaches or at least acknowledge how important they are is doomed to fail.

One of the best ways of thinking about organizational culture comes from Edgar Schein (author of *Organizational Culture and Leadership*[36] and a former professor at MIT Sloan School of Management). Company culture might be defined in terms of the pattern of beliefs and behaviours that grows up around how the business has overcome challenges and prospered. Schein describes it as: 'a pattern of shared basic assumptions that the group learned as it solved its problems of external adaptation and internal integration, that has worked well enough to be considered valid and, therefore, to be taught to new members as the correct way to perceive, think, and feel in relation to those problems.'[37]

And he defines three key ways in which culture manifests within organizations: observable artefacts, espoused values and basic underlying assumptions:

- **Artefacts and behaviours:** visible behaviours and elements in an organization that might reveal what the company demonstrates as important, but might also be recognized by people who are not part of the culture. This might include physical surroundings and technologies but also language, jargon, stories, myths and practices. This might be thought of as the surface elements.

- **Espoused values:** qualities and rules of behaviour that are advocated by a company's leadership and management, and show how the organization might represent itself. This might include published things such as a code of conduct, public statements or specific events and material.

- **Basic assumptions:** less tangible, but powerful, underlying determinants of an organization's attitudes, thought processes and actions. These might include ingrained values and assumptions that are unquestioned, taken for granted, largely invisible and therefore hard to recognize from within.

All three of these areas are important to address when attempting to understand and evolve organizational culture.

One of my favourite ways to map organizational culture comes from William E Schneider.[38] Schneider wrote about how all organizations are like living, social organisms and so interventions and ideas that see companies as human systems see change as a process of adaptation and learning, and those that are tied to business strategy are more likely to succeed. Component-centred interventions, which are narrowly focused on one or a few elements of the system and are not tied to business strategy, will be more likely to fail.

Schneider describes research that indicates how each organization has a core culture and a dominant way that describes how the leadership believes things should be done and the organization realizes success. This core culture may be described by one of four main cultural archetypes:

1 **Control:** success is achieved primarily by gaining and retaining control. The key characteristics of controlling cultures would be stability, order, close monitoring of work, realism, conservative in nature, more predictable, but also high levels of clarity around expectation, unambiguous, decisive when it needs to be, a focus on what's working. In excess this core culture can lead to risk-aversion, lack of collaboration, inflexibility and rigidity, stifled possibility and innovation, internal politics.

2 **Collaboration:** the dominant motive is affiliation, with success coming from working together. The benefits of this core culture include open communication, strong people focus, good cohesion, high levels of trust, good synergy with team and customer needs, the ability to utilize talent

and capabilities well, integrated work. The potential downsides are that it may become too lenient at the expense of performance or accountability, or make it harder to implement tough decisions, or become too short term and lack direction or become too overcommitted.

3 **Competence:** this core culture is about success through cultivating the capability in the organization and a focus on achievement. The upside potentially comes from high performance standards and technical expertise, high levels of creativity and innovation, an emphasis on demonstrated performance and productivity, thorough decision-making. The potential downsides include lack of pragmatism, undervaluing generalism, a tendency to over-plan, unrealistic expectations on staff, stressed employees.

4 **Cultivation:** the key to this core culture is growth and potential. It values people, creativity, trust, individual talent, adaptation, inspiration, self-expression, self-actualization, social responsibility, empowerment. The potential risks here are lack of coordination, ignoring real problems, idealism, lack of attention to detail, failure to disengage from existing advantage when necessary.

FIGURE 5.7 Mapping organizational culture

SOURCE Adapted from William Schneider, *Re-engineering Alternative: A plan for making your current culture work*, Irwin Professional Publishing, May 1994 ISBN-10: 0786301201

Agile practitioner Michael Sahota has usefully described Schneider's archetypes as a two-by-two matrix, which positions people versus company-oriented businesses on the horizontal axis against reality versus possibility-oriented companies on the vertical axis (Figure 5.7).[39]

The key to utilizing the understanding of these archetypes, says Schneider, is in being aware of where your core culture is rooted and using the strengths of this to achieve success. Yet it is also useful in identifying the potential areas of conflict and tension likely to arise when attempting to become more agile. And also to identify those attributes that may be built upon.

For controlling cultures, high levels of clarity, expectation and decisiveness can really help agility. Conservatism, micromanagement, rigidity, inflexibility, risk-aversion can all badly get in the way. For collaboration cultures, open communication, trust, horizontal working, customer focus, good use of talent are all key to being and doing agile. Lack of accountability, lack of direction, too much over-commitment or short-termism can all kill it. For competence cultures we might want to dial-up on the focus on innovation, creativity, good technical expertise, demonstrated performance and high performance standards. We might want to dial-down on unrealistic expectations, being overly focused on specialist expertise, and the potential of over-burdening teams or employees. For cultivation cultures, the focus on people, trust, adaptation, self-expression and empowerment are all useful to amplify. The lack of attention to detail, lack of coordination, poor problem definition are all barriers. We can summarize these as cultural and behavioural attributes to amplify, and those to adapt (Table 5.3).

Developing a high level of awareness of where your organizational culture sits is key to understanding what you need to change, and what you don't need to change, to support agile transformation. Culture is far more than the visible signals (posters, words on walls, colourful cushions and ping-pong tables) that some seem to think it is. Whilst artefacts and behaviours might be thought of as more obvious, surface elements, it is the basic assumptions that are deeply embedded, often poorly recognized, and which are therefore powerful drivers of behaviour. We need to recognize what these are, focus on how to unlearn existing behaviours in order to relearn new ones, break existing habits, customs and routines in order to remake new ones. Assumptions and behaviours can either block change from happening at all, or they can be powerful enablers for transformation.

Ask yourself this – where is your core culture rooted? What behaviours might you therefore want to amplify and encourage, and what might you want to adapt or mitigate?

TABLE 5.3 Behaviour amplification and adaptation

	Control	Collaboration	Competence	Cultivation
Amplify	Focus on strengths, effective planning, clarity of expectation, decisiveness, well-organized	Open communication, trust, versatility, healthy conflict, cohesive horizontal working, customer focus, good use of talent	High performance standards, focus on innovation, ideas, creativity, future focused, good technical expertise, demonstrated performance	Focus on people, diversity, trust, optimism, adaptation, determination, self-expression and empowerment
Adapt	Conservatism, micromanagement, bureaucracy, conformity, rigidity, inflexibility, risk-aversion	Lack of accountability, lack of direction, too much over-commitment or short-termism, undervaluing individual commitment	Unrealistic expectations, over-planning, undervaluing generalism, over-burdening teams or employees	Inefficiency, poor problem definition, lack of attention to detail, lack of coordination

DEFINING DIGITAL AND AGILE CULTURE

Organizational culture is clearly key in enabling greater agility yet it is often ignored in transformation programmes or paid lip service, and can therefore act to stifle rather than catalyse effective change. Research conducted by McKinsey, based on a global survey of senior executives, amply demonstrates how powerful cultural and behavioural challenges can be in blocking digital progress.[40] When asked what the most significant challenges are to meeting digital priorities, culture and behaviour challenges was named by a third of all the respondents and came top, above a lack of understanding of digital trends, a lack of talent, a lack of IT infrastructure, the misalignment of organizational structure and a lack of senior support.

Selecting adjectives to describe the key characteristics of digital culture is arguably the easy part but since culture and behaviour so fundamentally inform, shape, and influence working practices, strategies, orientation, actions and values, it's worth summarizing the most important of these attributes to define what we mean when we talk about agile organization culture:

Flexible, responsive and adaptive: a willingness to change, pivot and flex, the kind of adaptability that builds resilience and momentum (antifragile), the environment to support greater fluidity, a good balance between vision and iteration, avoiding getting stuck in process or managing by proxies and losing sight of real customer need, greater manoeuvrability and responsiveness, an orientation towards greater experimentation, test and learn, a boldness and a less risk-averse culture, the ability to move quickly when necessary.

Customer-centric: customer-centricity is as wide as it is deep, and should be reflected in strategies, processes and structures but more than anything it should be embedded in the culture. It shapes outlook and informs every decision. It's one thing to develop fast-feedback loops and be characterized by data-driven decision-making but, as we've discussed, we also need to be data-informed. The latter may be good for incremental and continuous improvement but we also require vision, empathy and intuition. We need space to create the new, and a healthy balance between vision, creativity and feedback, and optimization. Data are critical but we should not be slaves to them.

Commercially focused: digital culture is results oriented, quick to explore, determine and assess opportunity, ready to disengage from existing advantage.

Visionary: characterized by a compelling common purpose that is well understood.

Technology-literate: a culture that is founded on comprehensive technology literacy whilst supporting an optimal balance of generalist and specialist expertise, technology as enabler, greater trust and flexibility in technology.

Networked: flow of fresh perspectives into the organization, flow of data through APIs, openness to utilize external resources and build off external capabilities, willingness and ability to capitalize on platform business economics.

Exploring and curious: agile culture is externally facing, inquisitive, lateral thinking, quick to explore technology and customer behaviour trends.

Entrepreneurial and innovative: bias to action, restless, continuous and systematic rather than episodic innovation.

Open and transparent: a working environment characterized by high levels of trust, a growth mindset, productive informality, psychological safety and openness.

Collaboration and learning: a culture that supports knowledge flow and ease of multidisciplinary and horizontal collaboration, embedded reflection and retrospective, continuous and rapid learning from successes and failure.

Autonomy and empowerment: less rigid hierarchy, empowered teams that can move fast, a culture of ownership, a good balance between alignment and autonomy.

The McKinsey research goes further than simply demonstrating how significant a potential barrier culture and behaviour can be to digital progress. It showed clearly that cultural factors, such as risk-aversion, siloed mindsets and behaviours, correlate clearly with negative economic performance.

Waiting for culture to change organically is simply too slow, Leadership teams need to actively engage in culture transformation, and proactively challenge, promote, reward, mentor, coach, demonstrate and recognize the attributes that can support it.

CASE STUDY
Culture at Stripe

Stripe is the hugely successful online payments infrastructure system that in January 2019 landed a US $100 million investment that valued the company at over US $22 billion.[41] Co-founder Patrick Collison has summarized the key attributes that they actively seek in the people that they hire: 'I think the three that really stand out to me are this rigour and clarity of thought, this hunger, appetite, wilfulness, determination, and this... warmth and desire to make people around them better off.'[42]

He describes how they look for clarity of thought and willingness to think the unthinkable and to be misunderstood. Often, he says, companies look for the easiest path, for 'smoothness' in transactions, to reduce friction. And yet there is value in ruffling a few feathers.

Consensus-driven decision-making, or the need to get every stakeholder aligned before you can move forwards, is often a problem in businesses that have become large and bureaucratic. It slows everything down. Whilst some decisions may be what Richard Branson has called an irreversible 'one-way door' decision, many others are more lightweight choices where it is better to move quickly and course correct than it is to deliberate or water-down the original proposal. Whilst 'gold-plating' every decision can be a real problem when trying to create a truly agile business, a culture that can move fast is one that combines high levels of trust, psychological safety and comfort with dissent.

At Stripe they look for people who can combine a determination to run against the status quo and willingness to 'push against the expected trajectory of non-existence' with qualities that actually make them nice to work with ('interpersonal warmth and a desire to make others around them better and just a degree of caring for others'[43]). They're deliberately prioritizing an ability to push through disruptive, big ideas that can protect the future of the business, without being sociopathic about how you do it.

Trust is one of those undervalued attributes in organizational culture, but so is the ability for people to be bold, determined and to really feel that they can say what they really think in that environment. It is often these kinds of soft qualities that can really enable a company to have the kind of culture that will truly support being bold but also agile.

The role of trust and transparency

High levels of trust within an operating environment are critical to moving fast. A lack of trust acts as a catalyst to internal politics and an overly hier-archical way of making progress. When every decision has to go up the hierarchy, across functions or teams, and down the hierarchy again in order to get anything done, the whole business slows down. The ability to work more horizontally depends on greater trust. The ability to make decisions quickly, not just in situations of crisis but also in everyday working, depends on trust.

It's easy to put words like 'innovation', 'creativity' and 'collaboration' in big letters on the wall of the office but they remain empty words if the culture and behaviours that infuse the working environment don't reflect these attributes as real priorities. If it's hard to move fast and be adaptive in climates that don't support trust we need to actively support and encourage the behavioural aspects that can enable it. A team that is able to support open and frank conversations and be comfortable with healthy conflict will have better ideas and get to solutions quicker. A team that sweeps failures under the metaphorical carpet rather than using them as an opportunity for learning will progress faster and further. A team that ignores feedback and seeks to apportion blame rather than evolve and make headway will slow up and become stuck.

Social network theorist Dr Karen Stephenson has developed what she calls the 'Quantum Theory of Trust' as a way of expressing the direct cogni-tive link that exists between amount of trust in an organization and the ability of staff to deploy tacit knowledge together.[44] If we have a conversa-tion with someone whom we trust, we are more likely to remember significant details about that conversation and can more readily pick up from where we left off and immediately build from that exchange. If there is a lack of trust, we might only remember vague details. This triggering of resurgence in mutual memory in high-trust environments immediately opens the potential for new learning and so networks of trust can empower significant cognitive capability. Similarly, social scientists argue that groups with high social capital – good interpersonal relationships characterized by shared understanding, identity, values and norms along with high levels of trust, reciprocity and cooperation – have significant advantage over those that don't since the transaction costs are lower.

Yet trust is lacking in so many corporate environments. A 2016 global study by EY that surveyed almost 10,000 employees and over 3,000 soon-to-be employees found that less than half of global professionals have a 'great deal of trust' in their current employers, boss or team/colleagues.[45] Interestingly, the top five factors that were contributing to respondents' lack of trust in their employers were: unfair employee compensation; unequal opportunity for pay and promotion; lack of leadership; high employee turn-over; and a work environment not conducive to collaboration. When participants were asked about the most important factors in determining the level of trust to place in their employers, delivering on promises came out top, followed by job security, fair compensation, open and transparent communication, and equal opportunities.

Alongside all the critical policy standards around diversity, equal opportunities and fair compensation, transparency in particular can play a key role in promoting greater trust since open communication breeds more open communication, which supports better information flow and productive relationships. It's a positive compounding loop. Too much self-orientation, however, or the feeling that another person or team is being closed or hidden, or the concern that the person or team lack reliability in delivering what they say they will, does not support effective cross-disciplinary or inter-team working.

A number of fast-growing businesses have recognized the importance of transparency and put it front and centre of their cultural values. Social and content marketing technology business Buffer, for example, has transparency as one of its nine key values on which it bases its culture:[46]

- Always choose positivity and happiness.
- Default to transparency.
- Have a focus on self-improvement.
- Be a 'no ego' doer.

- Listen first, then listen more.
- Have a bias towards clarity.
- Make time to reflect.
- Live smarter, not harder.
- Show gratitude.

Again, it's very easy to write down a bunch of values but it is how the business lives and breathes them that really make them work. The cultural values should be reflected in some key areas:

1 The visible behaviours of the leadership team and employees.
2 What the leaders pay attention to, and select to measure.
3 The response of leadership to significant challenges.
4 The priorities and choices that the business chooses to make, and how resources are allocated.
5 How staff are rewarded, incentivized and recognized.
6 The behaviours that support status within the organization.
7 The routines, expectations, habits and rituals of the business.
8 The stories that have grown up with the business.
9 The formal statements, releases, documentation.
10 The design and feel of the physical working environment.

Buffer, for example, has moved to make revenues, user numbers and performance completely open as a way of supporting its 'default to transparency' mantra. It publishes its investor update and monthly performance reports on its blog. It has also made efforts to encourage transparency in e-mail communication (every e-mail sent can be seen by team mates) and in personal development. More controversially, it also initiated an 'open salary' concept based on a formula that made remuneration for employees completely transparent.[47] Buffer has even created a 'transparency dashboard' that aggregates information on the equity formula, details of fundraising, salaries, real-time revenues, pricing and how the money is spent, diversity information, open source code, an open product roadmap, content plans, and even the books that the team is reading.[48]

Co-founder Joel Gascoigne has written about how sticking to radical transparency has probably been one of the most frightening but exciting things that the company has done. But it has shown unique potential to empower and inspire the team, to drastically break down barriers since every idea or new direction is shared early, even before it's completely formed. As he describes it, transparency is such a powerful value for Buffer for a particular reason: 'Transparency breeds trust, and trust is the foundation of great teamwork.'[49]

This kind of approach to transparency is a supremely confident thing to do. And there's nothing like confidence for inspiring belief. But it also dramatically improves the ability of the organization to move and develop fast, and to adapt and learn at scale.

CASE STUDY
Monzo and transparency

In a very similar way to Buffer, challenger bank brand Monzo has placed transparency at the heart of its cultural and strategic values. The fact that Monzo is a financial institution operating in a highly regulated environment makes this even more challenging but inspiring. Monzo's approach is echoed by other fast-growing fintech businesses like Lemonade Insurance whom I mentioned earlier in the book and whose 'transparency chronicles' openly describe the highs and lows involved with its rapid growth.[50]

Like Buffer, Monzo says that its aim is to 'default to transparency', and says that this must mean that the company puts in place policies and practices that bring information out into the open as often as possible: 'Over time, transparency becomes the norm, and we create a "burden of secrecy": an argument must be made to keep something secret, rather than to make it open – a very different approach to most organizations.'[51]

Monzo describes how transparency builds trust, and how a lack of trust can lead to unhappy, unproductive teams and poor employee retention. Transparency also helps build trust externally with customers, which is critical in ensuring that Monzo is seen as a reliable, safe place to bank: 'Being internally transparent forces our external transparency to also be genuine.'

Transparency, says Monzo, also helps teams make decisions independently and so empowers autonomy. Success comes from hiring people who are smarter than you and then letting them get on with their tasks, making decisions independently whilst adhering to company goals and policies, and this can only happen when teams have the full range of information to hand.

Being transparent by default also helps remote workers to keep up to speed, and onboard new team members effectively and speedily by having all relevant documentation open and available to read. It also supports personal development by giving everyone an unfiltered view of both the good and the bad stories involved with building a rapidly growing business.

Monzo supports this default to transparency in a number of key ways. Meetings are open for anyone from the company to join and anyone can put anything on the agenda for the weekly all-hands. Every team updates the rest of the business weekly on progress and challenges. Like Buffer, every e-mail sent can be read by anyone in the company by default. This applies to even hastily written replies or forgotten attachments, as a way to avoid employees feeling like they need to present a sanitized or corporate version of themselves (a phenomenon known as the 'Chilling Effect', which describes the tendency people have in social network sites to constrain the self they present online due to peer-to-peer surveillance[52]). Employees are also encouraged to use open Slack channels to communicate wherever possible. Whilst critically sensitive information such as specific customer or employee details is not made completely open, the default is always to be transparent.

Like Buffer, Monzo has created a transparency dashboard that openly brings together information on investment ethics, funding, user community suggestions, financial performance and an open product roadmap. In September 2018, Monzo hit 1 million customers, little more than three years after launching.[53]

For years, companies have believed in advantage through secrecy and closed firewalls but companies like Monzo have taken a very different and quite radical approach to openness and inclusiveness with their customers. Whilst confidentiality remains important in select, critical areas, the default to transparency exhibited by companies like Monzo, Buffer and Stripe is helping to support an unprecedented level of trust within the businesses that choose to adopt it and enabling them to be truly agile, and gain culture advantage, not just competitive advantage.

High-velocity decision-making

The way in which a company makes decisions is a powerful but underappreciated potential barrier to everyday agility. In many businesses this is typically characterized by one-size-fits-all decision-making and lengthy business case documentation or PowerPoint presentations filled with extensive projections based on very little. Copious executive hours are spent crafting PowerPoint presentations to present at internal meetings or e-mail around. Approvals take multiple meetings to secure everyone's approval before anyone can move forwards. Discussions go back and forth; decisions get delayed; progress is slow. It's a painful, broken process.

Many leaders make decisions in much the same way regardless of the context of what the decision is for. Sir Richard Branson has pointed out that not every decision is the same and has described the difference between what he calls 'one-way door' and 'two-way door' decisions. A one-way door decision is the type that is irreversible, where detailed consideration, consultation and discussion may be necessary. Once you go through a one-way door you are committed so you need to be sure that this is the right thing to do. Yet these types of choices are actually few and far between. Many other decisions will be a two-way door, where it is better to make the decision quickly in order to make faster progress: 'Even if they seem definite, they are actually reversible. You can walk through the door, see how it feels, and walk back through to the other side if it isn't working.'[54]

For a business trying to be innovative and nimble, says Sir Richard, the leadership team will need to make plenty of two-way door decisions. Jeff Bezos, in his 2016 annual Amazon shareholders letter described this difference as 70 per cent and 90 per cent decisions. He also notes how many larger, well-established enterprises make high-quality decisions, but make them slowly, adopting a one-size-fits-all approach to decision-making, which is typically characterized by waiting until you have 90 per cent of the information you need before making your choice. In many cases, he says, many less complex or easily adapted decisions can be made with around 70 per cent of the information you wish you had. But it's more advantageous to make the decision and course-correct if necessary than it is to slow everything down.

Similarly, a culture of consensus-driven decision-making where all stakeholders need to be aligned before you move forwards with something can also slow the company down. Amazon uses a phrase 'disagree and commit' as a useful way of acknowledging disagreement whilst enabling the project to progress rapidly. Bezos gives the example of when he disagreed with an Amazon Studios investment in an original content production project that he believed to be too complicated and not interesting enough. The team were all aligned that they wanted to move forwards with it though and so Bezos wrote back immediately saying: 'I disagree and commit and hope it becomes the most watched thing we've ever made.' His point is that if the team had had to convince him rather than just getting his commitment the decision-making process would have been a lot slower.

The Amazon approach to business case generation and approval is also instructive. Bezos famously banned PowerPoint (as long ago as 2004) as a way of presenting a case, saying: 'The traditional kind of corporate meeting starts with a presentation. Somebody gets up in front of the room and presents with a PowerPoint presentation, some type of slide show. In our view you get very little information, you get bullet points. This is easy for the presenter, but difficult for the audience.'[55]

Instead, Amazon meetings are structured around a six-page explanatory 'narrative' pitch (shortened for less in-depth decisions). The first 20 minutes of a team meeting is spent in silence reading the pitch, after which the presenter fields questions and a decision is made. Says Bezos: 'The reason writing a 4-page memo is harder than "writing" a 20-page PowerPoint is because the narrative structure of a good memo forces better thought and better understanding of what's more important than what, and how things are related.'[56]

These 'working backwards' documents (as we discussed earlier in the book) are always structured in the same way, giving the context or question, the approaches to answer the question (by whom, by which method, and their conclusions), why this attempt at answering the question is different from previous approaches, and what's in it for the customer and the company. The approach allows for deeper thinking, better decision-making, better use of time, and also reduces the role and influence of politics in the process.

Many large businesses are choked with PowerPoint presentations. The 'narrative' approach is a simple way to make better decisions faster. But beyond this, this kind of high-velocity decision-making enables larger companies to act and behave like much smaller ones.

The role of autonomy, mastery, purpose

When our job is to empower change and bring people on the journey with us it's critical to recognize the power of intrinsic motivators in creating the kind of environment that can support engaged, motivated employees who are doing their best work. In his book *Drive: The surprising truth about what motivates us,*[57] Dan Pink makes a compelling case (supported by plenty of academic studies) for the limitation of money as a motivating factor in the workplace and instead for the power of three key intrinsic motivators:

Autonomy: the ability to make decisions in the areas that we are responsible for that can make a difference.

Mastery: the ability to learn, continually improve, to see and be rewarded for progress.

Purpose: doing meaningful work that is important to use, working towards a vision or purpose that we believe in.

This intuitively makes a lot of sense but it's remarkable how many high-performing, agile organizations that I have worked with have these three attributes running through their DNA. They typically have cultures that are characterized by high levels of empowerment and ownership. They have processes and expectations that support continuous learning, and ways of connecting employees to the impact of their work and the progress that is being made. And the organization has a clear, well-understood mission that its staff really believe in. Leadership teams often focus on extrinsic motivators and rewards as drivers of change, yet these powerful intrinsic motivators should be front and centre of any cultural and agile change programme.

Creating meaningful work

There is great potential in making people's work meaningful, just as there is great detriment in employees feeling as though what they are doing every day has little or no purpose. When staff are connected with the impact that they are making, when they can feel that they are generating real, tangible value in what they do, when they can see visible progress in their learning and their outputs, employees feel more motivated, are more productive, and are happier in their work.

Yet there are a surprising number of people who actually do believe that the work that they are performing lacks any contributive value. A 2015 YouGov poll in the UK, for example, found that 37 per cent of British workers think that their jobs make no meaningful contribution to the world.[58] And one conducted by Dutch firm Schouten & Nelissen found that out of 1,900 workers surveyed 40 per cent did not think that their work was useful.[59]

These kinds of roles, where the people doing them feel that they are largely pointless and that they don't seem, at least to the outsider, to really accomplish very much or make any discernible difference in the world, are what author David Graeber has termed 'bullsh*t jobs'.[60] Graeber's definition of a 'bullsh*t job' is: 'a form of paid employment that is so completely pointless, unnecessary, or pernicious that even the employee cannot justify its existence even though, as part of the conditions of employment, the employee feels obliged to pretend that this is not the case.'[61]

This is, he believes, a great tragedy. A situation that generates resentment and even quiet rage amongst the notable numbers of people (he believes around two-fifths of jobs in the developed world) who work harder than they should at jobs that they secretly believe should not exist. 'Huge swathes of people, in Europe and North America in particular, spend their entire working lives performing tasks they secretly believe do not really need to be performed. The moral and spiritual damage that comes from this situation is profound. It is a scar across our collective soul. Yet virtually no one talks about it.'[62]

Graeber's assertion that it seems to be a general rule in our society that the more obviously someone's work benefits other people, the less likely they are to be paid well for it seems to hold some weight (think teachers, nurses, police for a start). But even if there is little research to show exactly how many people in more office and factory-based working societies feel this way, it is certainly intuitively right that large swathes of working people feel relatively unengaged, uninspired or, worse, frustrated by their jobs.

A well-known 2013 global Gallup survey of more than 230,000 workers found that only 13 per cent of workers feel engaged by their jobs (this was described as being psychologically committed to their jobs and likely to be making positive contributions). A further 63 per cent are 'not engaged' (which is characterized as lacking motivation and putting less effort in, especially when it comes to discretionary effort towards organizational goals. And 24 per cent are 'actively disengaged' (that is, unhappy, unproductive and liable to spread negativity). Gallup believes that this equates to roughly 900 million not engaged and 340 million actively disengaged workers around the world.

Notwithstanding how tragic this picture is, businesses are allowing themselves to be significantly disadvantaged by underengaged and underperforming employees, by failing to create meaning in the work that staff are undertaking, and connecting their input to visible outputs, improved company performance, progress and learning. The businesses that can fully engage their staff and can create that connection can benefit from the kind of enthusiasm and motivation that will create genuine advantage, better ideas and more creative and productive outputs.

And enthusiasm is surely one of the most underrated attributes employees can have. Enthusiasm is what encourages them to go further in search of working solutions to problems, to think harder about challenges, to work better with peers. The difference between an average team and a high-performing one in terms of productivity and outputs is often down to the discretionary effort of the team members. The work that people could put in above and beyond the minimum required. The difference between what people might want to do if they believe in the value of what they are doing, and what they have to do if they don't. You cannot expect to get discretionary effort when people feel disconnected from their job and that the work contributes little anyway.

Simple principles that sit at the heart of agile working, when done well, can help alleviate this disconnection. Having a clear sense of direction and meaningful vision. Being able to make decisions in the areas that you are responsible for and feeling that your opinion matters. Being part of a small team that is communicating well and producing regular delivery of value. Finding ways to tangibly enable team members to see that value and progress that they are creating and positively reinforce the good work. Not overburdening the team through sensible de-prioritization. Being able to take a step back and reflect on what's working and what's not, and the feeling that you are continually learning. These may feel like minor working procedures but are actually fundamental to connecting people with meaningful and highly productive work.

The power of purpose-driven

I have discussed the importance of creating meaning for employees in the work that they do, and organizational direction and a higher organizational purpose can play a key role in getting the kind of engagement that can lead to fulfilling roles for staff but also exceptional performance, discretionary effort and forward momentum.

A higher organizational purpose is different from a company mission or vision. A great example of this is the diversified energy business DTE Energy and how they recovered from a financial crisis point in 2008 to triple their stock price in under 10 years and not only survive but achieve some quite spectacular results. Robert Quinn and Anjan Thakor (authors of *The Economics of Higher Purpose*,[63] and from the University of Michigan and Washington University respectively) have defined this higher purpose as going beyond economic exchanges: 'It reflects something more aspirational. It explains how the people involved with an organization are making a difference, gives them a sense of meaning, and draws their support.'[64]

When DTE was hit hard by the 2008 recession, new CEO Gerry Anderson knew that he had to get more from his employees if the company was to survive. Earlier surveys had shown that the staff lacked engagement. They were stuck in old behaviours and not applying the full potential of their creativity, intuition and understanding. Previous initiatives around incentives, supervision and training had failed to really address the challenge.

Inspired by a visit to a USAA call centre in which he had observed truly committed employees going about their work with enthusiasm and positivity Anderson sought to apply the lessons he had learned. The USAA staff had undergone an intensive orientation programme designed to really connect them with both the purpose of the organization and their own purpose. This was then continually reinforced through all-hands meetings and other staff forums that enabled people to ask questions and share ideas.

Anderson framed a new purpose for DTE Energy based on the contribution and value that the company brought to its end-customers and the well-being of the wider community: 'We serve with our energy, the lifeblood of communities and the engine of progress.'[65] Anderson brought this to life with a video that showed customers of DTE including teachers and doctors and the impact of the work that DTE staff were doing. This contribution had never been acknowledged before and it had a profound emotional impact on the staff. Anderson framed the challenge that the company was facing with honesty and in ways that demonstrated his belief not only in the potential of discretionary energy but also of his employees' ability to deliver it:

> We went to our people and told them that this was a very big event we were
> facing. We couldn't promise how it would turn out, but we would promise one
> thing. We promised that the last lever we would pull to protect the integrity
> of the company would be a layoff. That we'd do everything in our power to
> prevent it. But in return, we said there's something we need to ask of you. You
> need to go to bat for this company with an energy level and an intensity and a
> level of creativity that you never have before.[66]

Anderson's point is that we only really give our extra energy to things that we really care about and believe in. It was only by turning people's energy outwards and generating meaningful aspiration about the purpose that the company was fulfilling in the wider community that that extra energy could be empowered. Authors Robert Quinn and Anjan Thakor describe how every decision that the company makes should be played through the lens of this purpose in order to make it truly authentic, and how goals should be framed as contributive goals rather than ego-driven goals, so that staff know exactly what the work they are doing is contributing.

Author Dan Pink has explained this as how we should think about purpose not only in terms of the grand, visionary purpose that a business might set out to establish a compelling direction (Purpose with a capital 'P') but also the importance of purpose (with a small 'p') in the sense of employees knowing and feeling that they are making a valuable daily contribution.[67]

In other words: to personalize purpose. Timely and salient feedback on what they are doing in the context of that purpose is one way of achieving this. But one of the simplest ways is to put your people in front of customers and for them to actually talk to customers rather than read about them in research reports or observe them remotely from behind a screen in a focus group lab. That opportunity to hear directly about the impact (good and bad) of what you're doing creates the kind of unique connection with the work that can't come from anywhere else.

It's worth noting that for every positive there is a negative and purpose is no different. Nokia is an example of how a negative, fear-driven sense of urgency can lead directly to a company's downturn. Research conducted by Quy Huy, a professor of strategic management at INSEAD, and Timo Vuori, assistant professor at Aalto University in Finland,[68] reveals that during their decline a climate of fear inside the organization made it hard for managers to pass bad news back up the line and froze coordination between senior and middle management. Rather than catalyse motivation, stretch targets actually generated inertia as communication between layers of management broke down, with executives not wishing to be told they were not ambitious enough or were failing to perform, and competition for resources increased. The researchers conclude by saying that leaders of transformation need to develop a collective 'emotional capability' in their companies and be sensitive to the impact that emotion can have on culture and performance.

Contributive goals. Not ego or fear-driven urgency. That's what catalyses discretionary energy and effort and drives real change and performance. People want to believe. They want to do work that means something: work that matters. That's why, when it's done right, it is properly transformative.

Creating the space

One of the critical challenges in transitioning to a truly ambidextrous, bimodal organization is creating the space to try new things, be more experimental, and continuously develop the new whilst still managing the current. As I mentioned before, this is like trying to change the wheels on the car as you're driving along. But without creating space for the new to emerge, nothing will really change.

We need this to happen at both a strategic, organizational level and an everyday operational level. The former requires support from the very top, and clear enablement through structures and process. The latter requires management and employee empowerment, and a culture that supports it.

There are three clear ways in which we can start to free-up space within the organization to allow more resourcing, focus and time to be put towards generating emerging models and ways of working:

1 **Ruthless and systematic de-prioritization:** most companies are terrible at de-prioritization. It's a lot easier to be consistently additive – to expect your employees to do what they did before whilst also taking on new projects and initiatives. It's a lot harder to ask what we're going to stop doing in order to free-up time and space to take on new tasks. But there's no getting away from the fact that without some level of de-prioritization it is extremely hard to consistently create the kind of space that an agile, bimodal organization needs. Freeing-up space is a continuous process – we need to build-in ways to systematically disengage and de-prioritize as much as we do for originating and developing new propositions.

One of the principles of sprint wo-rking in Agile is that you don't overload the team. If short-term tasks come in, wherever possible the team prioritizes them into the next sprint backlog. If they have to take it into the sprint, then they de-prioritize something else. This is a fundamentally sensible principle that has much broader potential application. Short-term priorities are inevitable, but they are also no excuse for overloading our employees. Work overload is not good for employee well-being, but it also doesn't help people to do their best work, be their most productive, keep their focus, or minimize time on superfluous communication.

At an organizational level, there is a need to get better at disengaging from existing propositions that are declining in advantage, and to create structures that enable an unencumbered focus on experimentation and the generation of new value. So it makes sense to create a system of regular reviews to identify propositions that are due to be retired and a process to manage disengagement.

The duplication of initiatives or work is a surprisingly common waste of effort and time in large organizations, as multiple projects are initiated in separate areas that partially or entirely cross over. Senior leaders are often entirely unaware of it. So it helps to periodically audit projects being run across the business, remove duplication and prioritize based on alignment with organizational purpose and vision, potential impact, time, cost and urgency. Ironically, it's often the case that senior teams that are most risk-averse have the larger number of projects on the go – they want to hedge their bets. But in doing so they are opening up the potential for greater dilution and duplication of effort and resources. Better to have clarity of focus on the big but broad areas of opportunity and then align resources around experimentation and rapid learning in those areas.

2 **Challenge the defaults:** at an operational level, one of the most powerful ways to free-up time and resource is to challenge embedded assumptions about how things should work day to day. One of my favourite examples of this is a powerful way to change the defaults around meetings that was originated by leading content marketing technology business Percolate. The company has created 'six rules of meetings', which are designed to maximize the usefulness of all gatherings in the business. Employees should question whether they need a meeting at all, ensure there are no unnecessary attendees or spectators, state the purpose of the meeting upfront, assign tasks, and avoid bringing computers and phones along.[69]

One of the rules is that meetings should be 15 minutes by default. Most meetings in businesses are scheduled in blocks of an hour (this is what Silicon Valley startup mentor Paul Graham called the 'manager's schedule'[70]) and somehow, they always expand to fill that time whether they really need to or not. Parkinson's law is the famous adage that: 'work expands so as to fill the time available for its completion'.[71] As organizations become larger and more complex this seems to somehow become truer. Executives' diaries fill up with hour or two-hour meetings so that they end up going from one to the next to the next and arrive at the end of the day wondering when they can get started on the real work. Imagine the power of making every meeting throughout a business 15 minutes by default. Fine if it needed to be longer, but just changing the default will ensure meetings are run more efficiently and free-up countless hours of executive and employee time.

Another default that is often worth challenging is reporting. It is another common area of duplication and unnecessary or low-value work. Staff often spend long hours populating detailed reports to send to executives when a far more focused summary would suffice. Our tendency when reporting upwards is to over-deliver in our enthusiasm to impress or to ensure everything is covered. Managers don't correct the over-delivery since there is comfort in comprehensive information, just in case. One company that I consulted with had a real problem with freeing-up employee time, so we conducted an audit of reporting through the business and found that there was one team spending two days out of every five producing a weekly report that few if any executives actually read.

So challenge the default. If you suspect that there is an unnecessary level of detail in the reporting mutually agree to cut it out. If you suspect that no one is reading the information you are providing, then stop providing it. Colleagues will soon shout if it is still needed, but that gives you an opportunity to revisit how much information is really necessary. Ask for forgiveness, not permission.

3 **Starting small:** there are a number of widely cited examples of businesses that give their employees dedicated time to explore and develop new propositions. We've all heard of Google 20 per cent time, or 3M's 'Time to Think' or Facebook's regular 24-hour hackathons. These approaches are extremely useful in creating the space to nurture early-stage ideas, but are relatively rare. Yet in the absence of structured programmes there is much that can come from an approach that everyone can adopt – starting small in creating more space in the operational day to day. Just as great things can come from small empowered teams, so amazing outputs can come from small segments of time that are integrated into the fabric of the working week.

Here's an example. Scientists Andrei Geim and Kostya Novoselov won the Nobel Prize for Physics in 2010 for their creation of graphene, which has been described as the scientific find of the century.[72] Graphene is the 'wonder material' comprised of a single layer of carbon atoms and is the thinnest and strongest substance known to science. It is about 200 times stronger than the strongest steel and it already has an almost limitless number of applications.

But the creation of graphene didn't come from a structured long-term research programme. It came from mucking about in the lab. Geim and Novoselov ran 'Friday night experiments', a small amount of free time on Friday afternoons when lab staff could work on scientific experiments not related to their day job. In one such session they were playing around with sticky Scotch tape, using it to peel off layers of graphite flakes until they were only a few atoms thick. They realized that they could actually use this method to get down to the thinnest possible layer, just one atom thick, and create a material with completely unique properties.

My challenge is this: if Andrei Geim and Kostya Novoselov can win the Nobel Prize from a small amount of time on a Friday afternoon, surely every team can find an hour a week to experiment and learn. When they won their Nobel Prize, the Nobel committee noted the way in which the scientists used playfulness in the way that they work together. There should be more space for playfulness in business. Without it, we might never come up with the breakthrough ideas and concepts that can not only enable creative leaps forwards, but can quite possibly save our business.

Fixed and growth mindsets in leadership

Stanford Psychologist Carol Dweck's concept of fixed and growth mindsets is an excellent way of expressing some of the key leadership attributes that are most essential in modern, agile businesses. There are, says Carol (in *Mindset: The new psychology of success*[73]), key differences in how we view our personality.

A 'fixed' mindset is founded in the view that your intelligence, character and creative ability are static and so cannot change in meaningful ways. Success is an affirmation of those inherent attributes that compare favourably to other fixed standards. Avoiding failure and striving for success become critical ways to maintain the feeling of being skilled, smart or accomplished, and so pursued at all costs. In contrast, a 'growth' mindset relishes challenges and sees them as an opportunity to learn, and failure as an opportunity to grow and improve.

The context of Dweck's research is mainly focused on children, students and how they learn but there are strong parallels to defining what successful organizational cultures and leadership should look like in the modern world. In her research, children with fixed and growth mindsets demonstrated very different approaches and goals. Those with the latter recognized the need for effort, work and practice in order to improve. Their goal was to learn at all times and at all costs. Conversely, those students with fixed mindsets were afraid to try new things in case it made them look dumb. Their goal was to look smart at all costs and to avoid tasks that might show deficiency.

More than this, there was a key dynamic in the relationship between ability and effort. Those with fixed mindsets believed that if you have the inherent ability then you don't need to put in the real effort. Any setbacks simply reveal their limitations and so they try to avoid deficiencies or failure at all costs, and have no way to effectively handle real difficulty. Growth mindset children, however, believe in improvement through effort and practice, and relish hard challenges as an opportunity to learn.

Dweck says that this difference is a fundamental reason behind so many students not reaching their full potential. And with the universal need for continuous improvement and more than ever for rapid and constant learning, these different mindsets and cultures are also a fundamental reason why so many organizations fail to reach their full potential. An organizational mindset that rewards leaders for looking smart and never admitting when they don't know the answer or have made a mistake is a culture that will not support learning. A business that is too focused on outputs to the detriment of how those results will be achieved is one that will struggle to find new and potentially exceptional alternatives.

Dweck has shown that these mindsets can be transmitted through words and actions. So in order to embed a culture of continuous learning in an organization leaders need to be very attuned to the behaviours that they support and those that they discourage. With children, Dweck has shown that praising intelligence rather than effort encourages a fixed mindset from a very early age. It can turn students off from learning. Instead, praising the process, the strategies or the effort leads to a desire to persist, to experiment and to learn at all times. We need to take the same approaches with our teams.

Taking these themes, we might classify the key attributes of fixed and growth leadership (Table 5.4).

As Guy Kawasaki has put it: 'There are two kinds of people and organizations in the world: eaters and bakers. Eaters want a bigger slice of an existing pie; bakers want to make a bigger pie. Eaters think that if they win, you lose, and if you win, they lose. Bakers think that everyone can win with a bigger pie.'[74]

TABLE 5.4 Fixed and growth leadership

	Fixed Leadership	Growth Leadership
Challenges	Views challenges as a potential to fail, so tries to avoid where possible	Views challenges as a potential to learn so embraces them
Feedback	Ignores feedback that is useful but negative, or sees it as personal criticism	Values critical judgement and useful feedback negative or positive
Effort	Sees effort as something needed when you're not good	Inputs lead to outputs and learning
Capabilities	Inherent and fixed, intelligence is static	Can be developed and cultivated
Mistakes	Avoid at all costs, discouraged by setbacks	An opportunity to learn and improve, views setbacks as a wake-up call
Collaboration	I win when you lose .	Win–win works best
Weaknesses	Hides at all costs	Confident and open about acknowledging deficiencies
Success	Threatened by others' success, turns down offers of help	Celebrates having smarter people working for them, seeks help when needed, inspired by others' success

These behaviours are very subtle and yet the value systems that we create within organizations are hugely powerful determinants of success and failure. In the modern world we need to regard every initiative as an opportunity to learn and we need to recognize the importance of behaviours that support a growth mindset and culture.

Givers and Takers

Building on the idea of a fixed and growth leadership mindset, we can link these types of attributes to creating a high-performing culture. In his book *Give and Take: Why helping others drives our success*,[75] organizational psychologist Adam Grant draws on extensive research to demonstrate that there are three basic kinds of people in the workplace, 'Givers', 'Takers' and 'Matchers', and that the difference between these approaches can be fundamental to our success or lack of it. Conventional wisdom has us believe that success is down to a combination of motivation, ability and opportunity, but there is a fourth, critical but often neglected, ingredient – how we choose to interact with other people: 'Every time we interact with another person at work, we have a choice to make: do we try to claim as much value as we can, or contribute value without worrying about what we receive in return?'[76]

According to Grant's research, Takers are cautious, self-protective, see the world as a competitive place and so like to get more than they give. Givers, on the other hand are generous, sharing, helping others without being as concerned about reward or personal cost: 'They tilt reciprocity in the other direction, preferring to give more than they get. Whereas takers tend to be self-focused, evaluating what other people can offer them, givers are other-focused, paying more attention to what other people need from them.'[77]

In the workplace many of us are not pure Givers and Takers, but instead what Grant calls Matchers, who operate on a principle of fairness, and strive to preserve an equal balance of giving and getting. We may adopt different styles according to different situations but typically each of us will develop a dominant style for social interaction and behaviour.

When Grant looked at the degree of success that people with the different reciprocity styles had achieved he found something interesting. Givers tended to be at the bottom of the pile, but they were also right at the top of the ladder as the most successful people in the study. Takers and Matchers fell in the middle. So if Givers were both the worst and the best performers, what made the difference? It turned out that successful Givers were absolutely as ambitious as Takers or Matchers, but they made smart choices in their interactions with others. Put simply, the Givers who excel are those who are willing to ask for help when they need it.

Moreover, when Givers do succeed, it has a cascading effect. When Takers win, there may well be someone else who loses, but when Givers win there is far more likely to be widespread support for them, creating a kind of ripple effect that enhances the success of people around them. People are envious of successful Takers. People root for successful Givers. Giver success, says Grant, creates value instead of just claiming it.

Organizational culture has a critical influence over the dominant patterns of behaviour within a business. Cultures that recognize and support Givers create their own cascades of success that builds the foundation for exceptional performance.

Why modern leaders need to be sculptors as well as painters

Michelangelo said this about the art of sculpture: 'Every block of stone has a statue inside it and it is the task of the sculptor to discover it. I saw the angel in the marble and carved until I set him free.'

This quote has been used in multiple contexts. Social psychologist Eli Finkel has used it in the context of successful marriage between two people, and how a great marriage can bring out the best of what's already inherent within both partners and enable them both to flourish.[78] His concept of the all-or-nothing marriage describes how our expectations around marriage have changed to such an extent that a marriage that would have been acceptable to us in the 1950s would likely be a disappointment to us today, but also how the flip side of this is that with investment and work modern marriages can be more amazing than ever.[79]

Editor and screenwriter Nils Parker uses the quote as a metaphor for the process of editing manuscripts:

> Before they get to me, most manuscripts are essentially a collection of strong ideas and great stories that have been suffocated by authorial self-doubt, insecurity, and bias. My job, as the editor, is to clear all of that away and expose the greater truths that sit at the core of these stories. I shape the words around the mould created by their intent so that the ideas may come to life like they already do in the minds of their creators. The process is very much like a sculptor's – an artist in an artisan's body, chipping away at the rock diligently and purposefully until the image reveals itself.[80]

For Michelangelo, says Parker, the idea is already there inside the hunk of stone, and the eyes and hands of the sculptor are merely vessels through which it can be brought into the physical world. Nils has also referenced Michelangelo's thoughts on the differences between sculpture as an art form and that of painting: 'By sculpture I mean that which is fashioned by the effort of cutting away, that which is fashioned by the method of building up being like unto painting.'[81]

In building high-performing teams we too often think of a leader's job as being like the painter. We think of our job as building and adding layers (of competency, knowledge or capability).

Instead, we need to think about how leaders can be more like sculptors. So many things in the corporate environment can get in the way of people doing their best work – internal politics, being uncomfortable with disagreement, micromanagement. If teams are to move fast it's so important that team members have the confidence to take ownership, and the encouragement to say what they really think.

Stripping away the things that can get in the way of enabling people to be their true and best selves is one of the best ways in which a leader can create the culture a team needs to move rapidly and with confidence. And to enable team members to do the best work that they've ever done.

References

1   Greenway, A, Terett, B, Bracken, M and Loosemore, T (2018) *Digital Transformation at Scale: Why the strategy is delivery*, London Publishing Partnership

2   Bracken, Mike [accessed 10 April 2019] What We Mean When We Say Digital, Co-op digital blog [Online] https://digital.blogs.coop/2016/06/14/what-we-mean-when-we-say-digital/ (archived at https://perma.cc/KW7N-VNFT)

3   Andreessen Horowitz [accessed 30 March 2019] a16z Podcast: Tech and Entertainment in the 'Era of Mass Customization' [Online] https://a16z.com/2017/02/25/reedhastings-netflix-entertainment-internet-streaming-content/ (archived at https://perma.cc/RYF8-TMHS)

4   Grove, A (1999) *Only the Paranoid Survive: How to exploit the crisis points that challenge every company*, Crown Business

5   Netflix Investors [accessed 30 March 2019] Long-Term View [Online] https://www.netflixinvestor.com/ir-overview/long-term-view/default.aspx (archived at https://perma.cc/EN2C-X2VM)

6   Forbes [accessed 30 March 2019] 5 Time Tested Success Tips From Amazon
       Founder Jeff Bezos, April 2013 [Online] https://www.forbes.com/sites/
       johngreathouse/2013/04/30/5-time-tested-success-tips-from-amazon-founder-
       jeff-bezos/#45e2c3e5370c (archived at https://perma.cc/3NQH-P2DR)

7   BBH Labs [accessed 30 March 2019] How The CIA Define Problems and Plan
       Solutions: The Phoenix Checklist [Online]: http://bbh-labs.com/how-the-cia-
       define-problems-plan-solutions-the-phoenix-checklist/ (archived at https://
       perma.cc/MWC9-R2Y2)

8   Tetlock, P (2017) *Expert Political Judgment: How good is it? How can we
       know?*, Princeton University Press

9   Good Judgement [accessed 30 March 2019] About web page [Online] https://
       goodjudgment.com/about/ (archived at https://perma.cc/5K64-G69G)

10 The Good Judgement Project [accessed 30 March 2019] [Online] https://www.
       gjopen.com/ (archived at https://perma.cc/ZT4Y-S8KS)

11 Green, KC, Armstrong, JS and Graefe, A (2007) Methods to Elicit Forecasts
       from Groups: Delphi and prediction markets compared, *Foresight: The
       International Journal of Applied Forecasting*, Issue 8

12 Bloomberg, Jason [accessed 30 March 2019] How DBS Bank Became the Best
       Digital Bank in the World By Becoming Invisible, *Forbes*, December 2016
       [Online] https://www.forbes.com/sites/jasonbloomberg/2016/12/23/how-dbs-
       bank-became-the-best-digital-bank-in-the-world-by-becoming-
       invisible/#6b0a54ce3061 (archived at https://perma.cc/6BLC-M8F8)

13 Euromoney [accessed 28 March 2019] World's Best Digital Bank 2016
       [Online] http://www.euromoney.com/Article/3566974/Worlds-best-digital-
       bank-2016-DBS.html (archived at https://perma.cc/CDC3-NMRR)

14 Gledhill, David [accessed 1 April 2019] Transforming a Bank by Becoming
       Digital to the Core, *McKinsey & Company*, April 2018 [Online] https://www.
       mckinsey.com/industries/financial-services/our-insights/transforming-a-bank-
       by-becoming-digital-to-the-core (archived at https://perma.cc/UWT9-SPKQ)

15 DBS [accessed 1 April 2019] Banking Without Branches, DBS Digibank India
       Gains 1m Customers in a Year, June 2017 [Online] https://www.dbs.com/
       innovation/dbs-innovates/banking-without-branches-dbs-digibank-india-gains-
       1m-customers-in-a-year.html (archived at https://perma.cc/7ZB2-L7R8)

16 Collins, Bryan [accessed 8 March 2019] Jeff Bezos Says Successful People
       Make These Two Types of Decision, *Forbes*, March 2019 [Online] https://
       www.forbes.com/sites/bryancollinseurope/2019/03/07/jeff-bezos-says-
       successful-people-make-these-two-types-of-decisions/#6effa9ef63bf (archived
       at https://perma.cc/NE8E-WK7E)

17 Schreiber, Daniel [accessed 8 March 2019] Two Years of Lemonade: A Super
       Transparency Chronicle, *Lemonade Blog*, September 2018 [Online] https://
       www.lemonade.com/blog/two-years-transparency/ (archived at https://perma.
       cc/DHF2-D64P)

18 X-company [accessed 20 August 2022] Astro Teller [Online] available at https://x.company/team/astroteller/ (archived at https://perma.cc/G8VL-7MLR)

19 Google Rework [accessed 20 August 2022] The Roofshot Manifesto, July 2016 [Online] https://rework.withgoogle.com/blog/the-roofshot-manifesto/ (archived at https://perma.cc/XNL7-3GNF)

20 Gibson, Paul [accessed 20 August 2022] The Strange Evolution of the Pole Vault World Record: from Bubka to Lavillenie, *The Guardian*, February 2015 [Online] https://www.theguardian.com/sport/the-balls-of-wrath/2015/feb/16/strange-evolution-pole-vault-world-record-bubka-lavillenie (archived at https://perma.cc/Q4NQ-8ZX8)

21 Fosbury flop image [accessed 20 August 2022] [Online] https://commons.wikimedia.org/wiki/File:Fosbury_Flop_English.gif (archived at https://perma.cc/W5AC-Y4KR)

22 US Department of Defense [accessed 10 April 2019] DoD News Briefing – Secretary Rumsfeld and Gen Myers, Feb 2002 [Online] http://archive.defense.gov/Transcripts/Transcript.aspx?TranscriptID=2636 (archived at https://perma.cc/6YZP-KB9Q)

23 Project Management Institute [accessed 10 April 2019] Characterizing Unknown Unknowns, October 2012 [Online] https://www.pmi.org/learning/library/characterizing-unknown-unknowns-6077 (archived at https://perma.cc/W2VV-5SJU)

24 Sun Tzu [accessed 10 April 2019] The Art of War, Classic short story, *Wikisource* [Online] https://en.wikisource.org/wiki/The_Art_of_War_(Sun) (archived at https://perma.cc/WGH2-LNMB)

25 Wardley, Simon [accessed 10 April 2019] Wardley Mapping [Online]https://medium.com/wardleymaps (archived at https://perma.cc/9ARL-327F)

26 Glouberman, Sholom and Zimmerman, Brenda [accessed 24 October 2016] Complicated and Complex Systems: What Would Successful Reform of Medicare Look Like? *Government of Canada*, July 2002 [Online]http://publications.gc.ca/collections/Collection/CP32-79-8-2002E.pdf (archived at https://perma.cc/4GD9-Q4PR)

27 HBS Marketing Research Paper, The Curse of Innovation: A Theory of Why Innovative New Products Fail in the Marketplace, August 2005, [Online] https://papers.ssrn.com/sol3/papers.cfm?abstract_id=777644 (archived at https://perma.cc/L8C3-Y537) [accessed 15 March 2019]

28 Kahneman, D and Tversky, A (1979) Prospect theory: An analysis of decision under risk, *Econometrica*, **47**, 263–291

29 Gourville, John T [accessed 15 March 2019] The Curse of Innovation: A Theory of Why Innovative New Products Fail in the Marketplace, *HBS Marketing Research Paper*, August 2005 [Online] https://papers.ssrn.com/sol3/papers.cfm?abstract_id=777644 (archived at https://perma.cc/L8C3-Y537)

30 Kahneman, D, Knetsch, J and Thaler, R (1991) Anomalies: The endowment effect, loss aversion, and status quo bias, *Journal of Economic Perspectives*, 5 (1), pp 193–206

31 Wunderlich, CA (2019) *On the Temperature in Diseases: A manual of medical thermometry* (Classic Reprint – original 1871) Forgotten Books

32 Siddiqui, Gina [accessed 15 March 2019] Why Doctors Reject Tools That Make Their Jobs Easier, *Scientific American*, October 2018 [Online] https://blogs.scientificamerican.com/observations/why-doctors-reject-tools-that-make-their-jobs-easier/ (archived at https://perma.cc/9Y5Q-B3J4)

33 Capgemini Consulting/MIT Sloan [accessed 10 April 2019] The Digital Advantage: How Digital Leaders Outperform their Peers in Every Industry, *Capgemini* [Online] http://www.capgemini.com/resources/the-digital-advantage-how-digital-leaders-outperform-their-peers-in-every-industry (archived at https://perma.cc/39DF-FEC7)

34 Adams, Lucia [accessed 10 April 2019] My Love-Hate Relationship With 'Digital Transformation' [Online] https://medium.com/@lucia_adams/my-love-hate-relationship-with-the-term-digital-transformation-db27bec0cde (archived at https://perma.cc/G9WG-37T8)

35 Harter, J [accessed 10 April 2019] Moneyball for Business: Employee Engagement Meta-Analysis, *Gallup*, May 2016 [Online] https://www.gallup.com/workplace/236468/moneyball-business-employee-engagement-meta-analysis.aspx (archived at https://perma.cc/WR3Q-2SHJ)

36 Schein, EH (2010) *Organizational Culture and Leadership*, 4th edn, Jossey-Bass

37 Schein, EH (2010) *Organizational Culture and Leadership*, 4th edn, Jossey-Bass

38 Schneider, WE (1994) *Reengineering Alternative: A plan for making your current culture work*, Irwin Professional Publishing

39 Sahota, Michael [accessed 25 October 2016] An Agile Adoption and Transformation Survival Guide, *Info Q* [Online] https://www.infoq.com/minibooks/agile-adoption-transformation (archived at https://perma.cc/5KEL-T9UL)

40 Goran, Julie, LaBerge, Laura and Srinivasan, Ramesh [accessed 15 March 2019] Culture for a Digital Age, *McKinsey Digital*, July 2017 [Online] https://www.mckinsey.com/business-functions/digital-mckinsey/our-insights/culture-for-a-digital-age (archived at https://perma.cc/MRW9-Y96Y)

41 Pymnts.com [accessed 14 March 2019] Stripe Raises $100m on a $22.5Bn Valuation, January 2019 [Online] https://www.pymnts.com/news/investment-tracker/2019/stripe-venture-capital-funding-valuation/ (archived at https://perma.cc/VS56-84BP)

42 Parrish, Shane [accessed 14 March 2019] Patrick Collison on the Culture of Stripe and How to Hire, May 2018 [Online] https://medium.com/swlh/patrick-collison-on-the-culture-of-stripe-and-how-to-hire-b0a14033e154 (archived at https://perma.cc/Q7QT-GZ3N)

43 Parrish, Shane [accessed 14 March 2019] Patrick Collison on the Culture of Stripe and How to Hire, May 2018 [Online] https://medium.com/swlh/patrick-collison-on-the-culture-of-stripe-and-how-to-hire-b0a14033e154 (archived at https://perma.cc/Q7QT-GZ3N)

44 Kleiner, Art [accessed 14 March 2019] Karen Stephenson's Quantum Theory of Trust, *Strategy and Business* [Online] https://www.strategy-business.com/article/20964?gko=8942e (archived at https://perma.cc/FM8N-Q7BK)

45 EY [accessed 14 March 2019] Global Study on Trust in the Workplace, 2016 [Online] https://www.ey.com/gl/en/about-us/our-people-and-culture/ey-global-study-trust-in-the-workplace (archived at https://perma.cc/4XRE-DC2G)

46 The Buffer Culture [accessed 14 March 2019] SlideShare presentation, July 2013 [Online] https://www.slideshare.net/Bufferapp/buffer-culture-03 (archived at https://perma.cc/84X3-F3AM)

47 Buffer Salary Formula [accessed 14 March 2019] [Online] https://open.buffer.com/salary-formula/ (archived at https://perma.cc/Q7NC-F7TY)

48 Buffer Transparency Dashboard [accessed 14 March 2019] [Online]https://buffer.com/transparency (archived at https://perma.cc/BP4W-ZLA9)

49 Gascoigne, Joel [accessed 14 March 2019] Introducing Open Salaries at Buffer, originally published December 2013, updated August 2018 [Online] https://open.buffer.com/introducing-open-salaries-at-buffer-including-our-transparent-formula-and-all-individual-salaries/ (archived at https://perma.cc/BR7A-W6XA)

50 Lemonade Insurance [accessed 14 March 2019] Transparency Chronicles [Online]: https://www.lemonade.com/transparency (archived at https://perma.cc/B6EB-53MF)

51 Monzo [accessed 14 March 2019] Transparency By Default, March 2017 [Online] https://monzo.com/blog/2017/03/10/transparent-by-default/ (archived at https://perma.cc/AM3F-RPAN)

52 Marder, Ben, Shankar, Avi, Joinson, Adam N and Houghton, David [accessed 14 March 2019] The Extended 'Chilling' Effect of Facebook: The cold reality of ubiquitous social networking, ResearchGate, July 2016 [Online] https://www.researchgate.net/publication/296637938_The_extended_'chilling'_effect_of_Facebook_The_cold_reality_of_ubiquitous_social_networking (archived at https://perma.cc/W8B6-XWK4)

53 Monzo blog [accessed 14 March 2019] 1 Million People Are Now Using Monzo [Online] https://monzo.com/blog/2018/09/24/one-million-monzo-customers/ (archived at https://perma.cc/BV4X-CR3H)

54 Branson, Richard [accessed 14 March 2019] Two-Way Door Decisions, Virgin, February 2018 [Online] https://www.virgin.com/richard-branson/two-way-door-decisions (archived at https://perma.cc/W7B4-2P9W)

55 Neill, Conor [accessed 14 March 2019] Amazon Staff Meetings 'No PowerPoint', November 2012 [Online] https://conorneill.com/2012/11/30/amazon-staff-meetings-no-powerpoint/ (archived at https://perma.cc/QPH5-X66D)

56 Stone, Madeline [accessed 14 March 2019] A 2004 Email From Jeff Bezos Explains Why PowerPoint Presentations Aren't Allowed at Amazon, *Business Insider*, July 2015 [Online] https://www.businessinsider.com.au/jeff-bezos-email-against-powerpoint-presentations-2015-7#ckRYd1lzAweoLcIQ.99 (archived at https://perma.cc/W27W-LUAH)

57 Pink, DH (2011) *Drive: The surprising truth about what motivates us*, Canongate Books

58 Dahlgreen, Will [accessed 13 March 2019] 37% of British Workers Think Their Jobs Are Meaningless, *YouGov*, August 2015 [Online] https://yougov.co.uk/topics/lifestyle/articles-reports/2015/08/12/british-jobs-meaningless (archived at https://perma.cc/LC8H-9429)

59 Schouten and Nelissen [accessed 13 March 2019] 4 Out of 10 Employees Do Not Find Their Work Useful, March 2017 [Online] https://www.sn.nl/nieuws/4-op-de-10-medewerkers-vinden-hun-werk-niet-zinvol/ (archived at https://perma.cc/RE2E-MRVU)

60 Graeber, David [accessed 13 March 2019] On the Phenomenon of Bullshit Jobs: A work rant, *Strike!*, August 2013 [Online] http://strikemag.org/bullshit-jobs/ (archived at https://perma.cc/FWM2-GAMJ)

61 Graeber, D (2018) *Bullshit Jobs: A theory*, Simon & Schuster

62 Graeber, D (2018) *Bullshit Jobs: A theory*, Simon & Schuster

63 Quinn, RE and Thakor, AV (2019) *The Economics of Higher Purpose: Eight counterintuitive steps for creating a purpose-driven organization*, Berrett-Koehler Publishers

64 Quinn, Robert E and Thakor, Anjan V [accessed 13 March 2019] Creating a Purpose-Driven Organization, *Harvard Business Review*, August 2018 [Online] https://hbr.org/2018/07/creating-a-purpose-driven-organization (archived at https://perma.cc/2X4T-UT9G)

65 Quinn, Robert E and Thakor, Anjan V [accessed 13 March 2019] Creating a Purpose-Driven Organization, *Harvard Business Review*, August 2018 [Online] https://hbr.org/2018/07/creating-a-purpose-driven-organization (archived at https://perma.cc/2X4T-UT9G)

66 HBR Ideacast podcast [accessed 13 March 2019] Turning Purpose Into Performance, July 2018 [Online] https://hbr.org/ideacast/2018/07/turning-purpose-into-performance (archived at https://perma.cc/8J3B-43RH)

67 Daisley, Bruce [accessed 13 March 2019] Dan Pink on the Secret of Drive, *EatSleepWorkRepeat*, September 2018 [Online] https://eatsleepworkrepeat.fm/dan-pink-on-the-secret-of-drive/ (archived at https://perma.cc/4L5M-LA2X)

68 Huy, Quy and Vuori, Timo [accessed 25 October 2016] Who Killed Nokia? Nokia Did, *INSEAD Alumni Magazine: Salamander* [Online]http:// alumnimagazine.insead.edu/who-killed-nokia-nokia-did/ (archived at https:// perma.cc/3YUL-AFLU)

69 Brier, Noah [accessed 8 February 2019] The 6 Meeting Rules of Percolate, Percolate [Online] https://blog.percolate.com/2014/06/6-meeting-rules-of-percolate/ (archived at https://perma.cc/8QR4-VMUP)

70 Graham, Paul [accessed 8 February 2019] Maker's Schedule, Manager's Schedule [Online] http://www.paulgraham.com/makersschedule.html (archived at https://perma.cc/2JWP-2Z42)

71 Parrish, Shane [accessed 9 February 2019] The Original Parkinson's Law and the Law of Triviality, Farnam Street [Online] https://fs.blog/2013/12/parkinsons-law/ (archived at https://perma.cc/9JVB-3KYY)

72 Connor, Steve [accessed 9 February 2019] The Graphene Story: How Andrei Geim and Kostya Novoselov hit on a scientific breakthrough that changed the world... by playing with sticky tape, The Independent [Online] https://www. independent.co.uk/news/science/the-graphene-story-how-andrei-geim-and-kostya-novoselov-hit-on-a-scientific-breakthrough-that-8539743.html (archived at https://perma.cc/8DTV-LSSJ)

73 Dweck, CS (2007) Mindset: The new psychology of success, Ballantine Books

74 Kawasaki, G (2011) Enchantment: The art of changing hearts, minds and actions, Portfolio Penguin

75 Grant, A (2014) Give and Take: Why helping others drives our success, Penguin Books

76 Grant, A (2014) Give and Take: Why helping others drives our success, Penguin Books

77 Grant, A (2014) Give and Take: Why helping others drives our success, Penguin Books

78 NPR [accessed 12 March 2019] When Did Marriage Become So Hard? Hidden Brain, February 2018 [Online] https://www.npr.org/2018/02/12/584531641/when-did-marriage-become-so-hard (archived at https://perma.cc/H92N-NE8Z)

79 Finkel, E (2018) The All or Nothing Marriage: How the best marriages work, Dutton

80 Parker, Nils [accessed 12 March 2019] The Angel in the Marble, July 2013 [Online] https://medium.com/@nilsaparker/the-angel-in-the-marble-f7aa43f333dc (archived at https://perma.cc/J75W-HJ53)

81 Parker, Nils [accessed 12 March 2019] The Angel in the Marble, July 2013 [Online] https://medium.com/@nilsaparker/the-angel-in-the-marble-f7aa43f333dc (archived at https://perma.cc/J75W-HJ53)

06

Start small

Why start small?

As we've already discussed, small, empowered teams can not only move faster, but can also generate disproportionate impact and change. Agile principles applied judiciously at scale in an organization can create heightened levels of responsiveness for the whole company. A company that learns fast is a company that is building resilience in a complex adaptive world. So, we shouldn't be linear and waterfall about how we become more adaptive as an organization. In other words, we need to be agile about how we become more agile.

There is no single blueprint for success. No set roadmap to follow. But there is an approach that can enable every business to find its own unique way to success.

Starting small allows a company to mitigate risk, not bet the entire company but instead to learn fast what will work for its unique contexts. Starting small enables a company to find its own way, stay close to changing contexts whilst driving change. Starting small enables business ambidexterity – the capability to manage business as usual whilst also creating the business of the future, to change the wheels on the car as it is driving along.

Starting small ensures that a business can get past being 'stuck'.

The key elements of starting small

Starting small is about piloting new approaches that can catalyse learning and enable a more informed approach to rapid scaling:

Focus: selecting the right projects, initiatives, areas or objectives on which to pilot new ways of working.

Setting the teams up for success: getting the right people, creating the optimal chance that the teams will thrive, and mitigating the inevitable tensions that will arise between old and new.

Mindset: acknowledging some of the key mindset shifts involved with start small, and why they can be so difficult to embed.

Achieving ambidexterity

Running a large business today means delivering to shareholder value whilst simultaneously inventing the business of the future. So the business of today and tomorrow needs to be structured in a way that creates a steady stream of new value as easily as possible. It needs to be well-managed enough to ensure exceptional efficiency and continuous optimization of known components, whilst also having the desire, discipline and space to experiment and find profit in new paradigms.

Hierarchy enables governance, vertically focused productivity, optimization and efficiency. Networked small teams enable experimentation, rapid development of value, adaptability and exploration. We need both but we need a balance between the two. That balance is likely to shift over time, so we need to be flexible in how we resource both sides. The inherent risk is that we create separation between the two sides and so we need to ensure there are strong links between them but also the right kind of links that do not hamper agility. And every organization and its contexts are different.

Starting small to scale fast

The key to achieving the right balance is to think big, start small and scale fast. We need to have the vision for the change that we want to make and the senior commitment to establish infrastructure and culture enablers, but then we can start small with a few small, multidisciplinary teams or squads aligned to key challenges or opportunities and then scale the number of teams rapidly as new opportunities emerge. I may be using the term 'dual operating system' here but in reality, small squads may be aligned to a variety of different objectives that may be focused on exploration, execution or even extension and exploitation. Typical alignment for teams might include:

- **Strategic challenges:** high-level or more specific challenges that the business is facing. A small agile team or squad can explore the territory to better define the challenge, understand its components or influences, and even start to develop solutions.

- **Innovation and new opportunity:** any new proposition can be developed and tested rapidly in order to generate new value, emergent areas and markets can be explored.
- **Service design and transformation:** small squads can be aligned to redesigning or improving specific services.
- **Customer journey:** teams might be aligned to end-to-end customer journeys or improving specific areas of customer engagement.
- **Process, network or relationship optimization:** the improvement of processes, driving efficiencies, working smarter with suppliers and partners, optimizing ecosystems.
- **Technology development and implementation:** the building and integration of new technologies and systems.

Teams that are aligned to innovation, generating new value, understanding and defining strategic challenges operate in the explore domain. Squads that are working on commercializing and scaling innovations or looking to create opportunity through adjacencies operate in the execute domain. Teams that are focused on optimization, reapplying existing capabilities in new ways, creating reusable components from them, driving efficiencies, protecting advantage, operate in the extend and exploit domain.

An example start small to scale fast may be the organization that begins by defining several key business challenges that it needs to solve and aligns a squad to explore each challenge. Those teams work iteratively to turn those high-level business challenges into more defined challenges or even into customer problems to solve. A larger number of teams then work iteratively to solve those problems, which in turn generates further opportunity.

In order to succeed, teams need a definitive objective that can be captured in one sentence. This is the reason that the team exists and its north star. Where possible this should reflect customer and business need. It should be up on the wall where the team is co-located. The team needs the combination of skills in the team that can achieve the outputs required, and no more. Once the objective is set, a small basket of measures may be specified upfront that will provide a way of monitoring progress and delivery of value. The team needs logical but wide guard rails that define its domain of authority – enough autonomy to be able to move fast and make whatever changes that it needs to make to optimize outcomes against its objective, but not so loose that a critical business system may be taken offline by its activity. An example of this is giving a squad end-to-end responsibility for a customer journey. Doing this generates real opportunity to create exceptional customer experience since the team has the ability to work on whichever part of the customer journey needs fixing, to prioritize well, and create a truly seamless journey. Having one or more parts of a customer journey not within its domain or authority could result in a disjointed or poor experience.

Separation and integration

There are a number of key ways in which the dual operating system can take shape, but the key watch-out is the integration challenges that can get in the way of scalability or hamper the adoption of new ways of working. We might consider there to be three key approaches to catalyse agile adoption:

- **Independent units:** with this approach, a new unit is established that has a good degree of separation from the main hierarchical organization. The unit might be a startup within the mother organization but could well be housed in a different building or location. The separation creates the space for new ways of working to embed more easily and it also allows organizations to build propositions that can exist in the market on their own merits. The clear downside to this approach is that whilst it may be an excellent way to launch new digital-native brands, there is limited learning that comes back into the organization and the disconnection limits the transformational impact at the core. There is a danger that change becomes compartmentalized and the wider organization does not feel that it is relevant to them.

- **Pirate within:** a new team, market or brand is positioned as a catalyst for change and given the freedom to adopt new operating models and processes. There is still a degree of separation between the traditional and new ways of working but the new team will likely not be in a separate building and may well use many of the essential capabilities of the wider organization whilst having greater flexibility to look outside. The advantage here is that learning is more easily scaled more widely across the business and there is an obvious exemplar for change. The potential challenge is that there is not enough space between the old and the new and so the latter becomes stifled, or that there is too much space, which makes it difficult to scale. An innovation lab, for example, may originate great concepts but on its own will not save your company – for that you need execution and scaling.

- **Integrated:** in a more integrated approach, small teams may be aligned to different areas, markets and different objectives as a catalyst for change.

They are not aligned to a specific function, brand or proposition area within the business but seek to drive change by demonstrating in close proximity how things can be done differently. The advantage comes from that proximity, and the ability to rapidly scale, drive change from within and socialize new approaches easily. The challenge also comes from that proximity, and the danger of the new being misunderstood, or suffocated, or tissue rejection kicking in.

Different approaches suit different contexts, and might involve different strategies including acquisition, working with external partners in new ways, startup incubators and accelerators.

The key point is that leaders need to always be aware of the challenges and opportunities created by proximity and work to mitigate those risks and capitalize on the benefits. There will always need to be enough space and support to allow new ways of working to flourish, but in order to catalyse transformation in a larger organization there also needs to be enough integration to enable scalability.

CASE STUDY
Vodafone's transformation

Vodafone has undergone a significant long-term transformation that has put culture, people and technology at the heart of a comprehensive agile change programme. Historically a largely decentralized business, the company took some decisions at the beginning of a decade-long process to centralize some key facets of its technology capability that would enable change and provide a common infrastructure platform. The company also underwent a programme to capitalize on the huge opportunity for unified communication and shared learning, upgrading communications technology and the approaches around it to embed new behaviours in everyday working. It also invested in systems to enable automated testing and continuous deployment, which enabled digital releases to be reduced from a frequency of six-months to one week and then daily. Digital skills were brought in-house changing the business from being 97 per cent outsourced to one which was 95 per cent in-house, enabling greater control, lowering costs and improving time to market.[1]

Yet alongside this technology transformation there was a powerful focus on how the company could bring its people on the journey with it. A new vision around what it really meant to be a 'digital telco' ran through the business as a way of capturing a step change in expectation around both customer and employee experience and aligning the external brand with the internal employee value proposition. This vision was expressed in an approach to digital-native working that Vodafone framed as 'The Digital Vodafone Way', which acted as a signal to the business of the importance of new ways of working but which created common approaches whilst allowing enough flexibility for successful localization.[2]

A key part in this shift was the widespread adoption of agile thinking and principles right through the business. The board spent time in Silicon Valley being immersed in digital-native approaches and ways of working, and thousands of senior leaders went through an immersive programme that reset expectation but also supported much broader understanding of agile culture and principles. A series of hackathons, town halls and communications helped socialize this understanding. The introduction of the 'Digital Ninjas' for the top 250 leaders connected young digitally savvy employees to key directors.[3]

The business worked to move beyond approaches characterized by discipline silos, large builds and long lead times through giving staff greater autonomy and empowering them to respond faster to changing customer needs. A 'Build it, Ship it, Love it' code amongst the engineering teams encouraged a sense of ownership and pride in the work that they were doing. Engineering talent shortages were addressed through university partnerships and apprenticeships, and a programme called 'Code Ready' gave frontline retail and contact centre staff the opportunity to retrain as developers in 16 weeks.[4]

Alongside this culture and behaviour change Vodafone underwent an operating model shift, adopting an approach that scaled agile working rapidly and created a series of small, multidisciplinary squads in each operating market focused on specific objectives. These pilot squads were fully supported with new tools, process support and working environment change. In 12 months, this approach scaled across 16 different countries, 200 squads and 2,000 people, with an ambition to take this much further.[5]

Selection criteria for early projects

When beginning a transformation process or starting to shape new ways of working, the selection criteria for early projects can make a real difference in determining early success or failure. New projects or initiatives can be an excellent catalyst for new ways of working within a large organization, as long as this 'start small' is then followed expeditiously with a rapid scaling and learning. It's important to look for quick wins, to buy time, to create early exemplars that help to socialize a new way of working, but it's also important to scale quickly to things that have significant impact.

The team that led the transformation at the UK Government Digital Service have written about how the first challenge for a team that is working on digital transformation is to prove to those watching that the team can deliver something that really works a whole order of magnitude faster, better and of more value than the organization has ever been able to do before: 'The strategy for your first project, like all that follow, should be delivery.'[6]

That same team identified four key questions that can inform the selection criteria for early projects – questions that enable a balance to be struck between delivering maximum impact and value to users, whilst mitigating political risk that might get in the way (the questions are paraphrased here):

1 **How many people will benefit, and how much?** A good strategy is small noticeable improvement for a large number of people (they give the example of a search query that millions of people ask every year – when is the next national holiday? – and creating a simple page to answer it).

2 **Is solving this a common problem?** Often organizations solve problems many times over in different places, so early projects should focus on creating services that can be reused and repurposed by other teams.

3 **How institutionally complex is it?** Earlier in the book I talked about the challenges brought by architectural and radical innovation that challenges existing organization structures. Having multiple departments involved in a project does more than anything else to hamper agility and quick delivery so it's important wherever possible to pick projects that have clear institutional boundaries, and which are entirely owned within the organization.

4 **Is it greenfield or brownfield?** Greenfield projects are those that are built to meet a user need that is new (or at least newly defined). This is fresh territory, unencumbered with embedded assumptions. Brownfield projects naturally come with layers of expectation, political baggage and potential restrictions in technology or process.

It can be so important when starting small to give yourself maximum chance of success. They can be the catalyst for new ways of working at a much more scaled level, but early projects will need to disprove the cynics, and demonstrate clearly the benefits that agile teams can bring. So pick your projects with care.

Selecting the right teams – missionaries not mercenaries

Agile teams typically combine a broad triumvirate of three areas of skill/experience/expertise: business, creative and technology. You need people and roles (like product managers, delivery managers, user researchers) that can link the team's activity back to commercial impact and the wider needs of both users and the business. You need people who have creative skills (like designers or content designers) or are creative problem-solvers. And you need people who are skilled with technology (like developers) and have high technology literacy.

Beyond skills and aptitude, you need the right attitude. In the early stages of implementing different ways of operating in the business, it's critical to have people that really *believe* in the change actually *enacting* the change. We need missionaries, not mercenaries. Missionaries will continue to push forwards even when they are surrounded by resistance. Mercenaries (people who are there because they've been told to be there, or are a part of the project purely for compensation) will always be weighing up whether the effort is actually worth the reward. Missionaries will be passionate enough to sweep people up in their enthusiasm and bring people on the journey with them. Mercenaries will be motivated by self-gain. Missionaries are willing to challenge precedent and convention for reasons that support positive change. Mercenaries challenge rules out of self-interest.

Missionaries lead. Mercenaries manage. Management is a brilliant invention since it enables organizations to scale in orderly, predictable, stable and aligned ways. But management is not leadership. Leadership is about empowering a direction that people want to follow, and enabling the circumstances that enable people to realize that vision. Real leadership doesn't only reside at the top of an organization. It can exist anywhere that there are passionate people who want to make a difference.

Transforming a legacy business can be a gruelling, bruising experience. You're forging a new path, asking the challenging questions, doing things differently. So you need resilience. Transformation is as much a personal challenge and journey as it is a corporate one. That's why you need missionaries. People who can see the change that's needed and have the passion and enthusiasm to advocate it and bring it to life. People who are willing to go against the flow. We need to empower our missionaries, and celebrate our mavericks.

CASE STUDY
Nasa's Pirates

John Muratore, a young engineer fresh out of the US Air Force, joined NASA's Johnson Space Center in 1983. When he began he was surprised to discover that the shuttle mission control centre still ran on an old, basic mainframe system from the Apollo era. The system lacked the capability to handle more than a limited number of simultaneous calculations and updates to functionality could take months. The system might have worked well for past missions, but with growing complexity to the Space Shuttle missions and NASA's ambitions for a new International Space Station, it was in danger of being overwhelmed.

Alongside a group of other newly recruited engineers, Muratore made the case that the system needed to be upgraded to one that was more modern, scalable, flexible and open to incorporate new as yet unrealized technologies. Yet their pleas were dismissed by leaders who remained confident in their outdated system. As Muratore has described it: 'It was a constant battle because the mainframe community wanted to bring all the workstations and the applications there underneath the mainframe complex, and we wanted to have the power and flexibility of distributed computing.'[7]

Undeterred, the group of engineers (who would later become known as the 'Pirates' in reference to their renegade approach) set out to show how improved and upgraded technology could benefit mission control. Making use of off-the-shelf and borrowed hardware, code that they wrote themselves, a small budget that they acquired from a new technology fund, and hundreds of hours of time outside of their core responsibilities, they created Real-Time Data Systems (RTDS), an upgraded system that had much improved capabilities, was more robust and enabled flight controllers to make better decisions, faster. When its capabilities became clear, the new system won senior support and it began to replace the outdated mainframe technology, transforming Space Shuttle mission control.[8]

After this success, Muratore was given the task of upgrading the mission control system for the upcoming International Space Station (ISS). Realizing that they needed to operate differently from established NASA ways of working in order to achieve their objective, Muratore and his team created a 'Pirate Paradigm' to switch the risk equation to show that there was greater risk to not changing than there was of just doing the wrong thing: 'This got me in a lot of trouble eventually, but the idea behind the Pirate Paradigm was to switch the way we looked at the problem from "this is a big facility and it's our job to protect it" to "if we don't make radical change, everything's going to go away".'[9]

The team realized the need to challenge the existing culture if they were ever to succeed in the task they had been set. So the paradigm celebrated values such as continuous improvement, frequent experimentation, short-milestones, testing and learning, a focus on results and cutting through bureaucracy, emphasizing ownership and accountability but also challenging convention. Their 'build a little, test a little, fix a little' approach involved breaking down big problems into smaller elements, creating solutions to those smaller components that users could use immediately, learning and iterating to then add on new pieces, and making the solutions universal enough to come together to solve the bigger problem.

Research from a team of academics from Warwick Business School showed that a key part of the Pirate Paradigm was the 'Pirate Code', which reads like an early version of the agile manifesto:[10]

- Don't wait to be told to do something; figure it out for yourself.
- Challenge everything, and steel yourself for the inevitable cynicism, opposition, rumours, false reporting, innuendos and slander.
- Break the rules, not the law.
- Take risks as a rule, not as the exception.
- Cut out unnecessary timelines, schedules, processes, reviews and bureaucracy.
- Just get started; fix problems as you go along.
- Build a product, not an organization; outsource as much as possible.

Muratore's team were a group of mavericks not afraid to challenge the norms and champion new ways of working within a rules-bound, strictly hierarchical organization. It shows the transformational impact that a small team with a big ambition can have. They were able to affect real change, win senior support, and eventually deliver huge cost savings to the programme through improved, enhanced technology.

People who are determined enough to go up against long-standing, entrenched practices and culture in order to drive change in an environment that doesn't want it are rare but valuable. We need to celebrate these astute renegades, allow them the space to challenge and the consideration to give them the time, space and opportunity to prove the potential of their ideas. In a truly agile business, they can be transformational.

Setting your teams up for success

When still in the foothills of agile transformation it is critical that the first teams are given as much chance to succeed as possible. Above all this means that wherever possible sponsorship for what the teams are working on comes from the highest level possible in business. It can certainly be possible to begin under the radar with a 'ask forgiveness, not permission' approach, but pretty soon more senior buy-in will become essential. The people in the teams need to be as focused as possible on delivery, and that means that this senior sponsorship will be key in providing cover and removing the teams from the kind of political wrangling that gets in the way of shipping outputs fast. The danger will always be tissue rejection by the large bureaucratic areas of the business. Good gatekeeping will also be needed on an ongoing basis to prevent the teams from getting swamped with low-value, short-term priorities from the business. The product team plays a key role in this, ensuring that the business strategy is mapped to a clear product strategy, and development is more proactive than it is reactive.

Companies like to make big announcements about new initiatives but far better to break cover when the teams have something good to show, and to build credibility and reputation through delivery. As the UK Government Digital Team put it: 'Good digital work is a million silent nods of approval, not one loud round of applause.'[11]

Once delivery is well in progress the teams should be able to move forwards with focus and speed. Early successes can move swiftly into something integral to what the organization does on a daily basis. Focus should then shift to scaling fast – transforming the small proportion of propositions or services that account for the majority of impact/user interaction/revenue and profit.

Defining a new way of working

Why, in order to scale, sometimes you need to do things that don't scale

The challenge of starting small is often that the mindset of a large organization is so wrapped up in linear, waterfall approaches that it can be extremely difficult to suggest anything else. Ideas need to have big investment, returns need to be sizeable and realized early, programmes and projects need to work immediately and robustly across large numbers of employees or customers.

But what happens when you need to start small, learn and scale from there? And what happens when you need to do something that doesn't scale? Airbnb co-founder Brian Chesky tells a story from the earliest days of the service when they were still part of the programme in Y-Combinator, the Silicon Valley seed accelerator. Paul Graham (founder of Y-Combinator) had asked him where they were getting traction with their idea. Brian told him that they didn't actually have a lot of traction at the time, but they did have a few people in New York who had started using the service:

Graham: 'So your users are in New York and you're still in Mountain View.'

Chesky: 'Yeah.'

Graham: 'What are you still doing here?'

Chesky: 'What do you mean?'

Graham: 'Go to your users. Get to know them. Get your customers one by one.'

Chesky: 'But that won't scale. If we're huge and we have millions of customers we can't meet every customer.'

Graham: 'That's exactly why you should do it now because this is the only time you'll ever be small enough that you can meet all your customers, get to know them, and make something directly for them.'[12]

So the Airbnb founders literally commuted from Mountain View to New York, and went door to door, meeting their hosts in person. To give them a reason for visiting they personally offered to photograph the host places for the site. When they'd talk to the hosts they would get direct feedback that enabled them to start designing touchpoint by touchpoint in order to hand-craft the user experience and feed directly into their product roadmap. Brian Chesky describes how this roadmap often exists in the minds of the users that you're designing for.

Almost all of the early features that would become critical to Airbnb's success came from that early feedback. As Airbnb grew, that habit of hand-crafting the user experience stayed with them as they visualized what a truly exceptional experience might look like in order to challenge thinking, and work back from the customer to deliver a service that is truly remarkable. The core thesis, says Chesky, is that: 'if you want to build a massively successful company, you need to build something that people love so much they tell each other. Which means that you must build something worth talking about.'[13]

It's too easy in large organizations to dismiss doing things that don't scale. Like talking face to face with your earliest users to craft remarkable experiences. It's too common for leaders, as they progress higher up the hierarchy, to become more and more distant from actual customers. We need to challenge these conventions. And that's as much about culture and mindset as it is about process and practice.

Building high-performing teams

What truly distinguishes high-performing teams from those that might be otherwise? It's a question that is worth exploring not only because every business chases high performance, but also because there is a good potential for misinterpretation and a poor understanding of what truly makes a difference. The point in looking at the research behind this question is that creating an environment that supports high performance is critical to any business that wants to be more agile, and yet incentives and rewards are so often positioned around the wrong things.

Some of the best, and most comprehensive, research into team performance has been done by Google, whose comprehensive multiyear studies, aligned to academic research findings and conducted across hundreds of teams, have shown that many of the factors that we traditionally associate with significantly influencing team performance (team longevity, background, personality or skills of team members) make little difference.

Instead, a study that considered more than 250 attributes of over 180 active Google teams demonstrated that there were five key dynamics that characterized high performance:[14]

1 **Psychological safety:** the ability to say what we really mean, and take risks in the team environment without feeling insecure.
2 **Dependability:** being able to rely on other team members to do high-quality work on time.
3 **Structure & clarity:** ensuring that goals, execution plans and roles of individual team members are clear.
4 **Meaning of work:** the work that is being done is personally important.
5 **Impact of work:** the feeling that the work being done actually matters.

The idea of psychological safety and the group norms on the team (or what Charles Duhigg calls 'the traditions, behavioural standards and unwritten rules that govern how we function when we gather'[15]) proved to be far and away the most important factor. Professor Amy Edmondson from Harvard Business School has defined psychological safety as a 'shared belief held by members of a team that the team is safe for interpersonal risk-taking'.[16] Psychological safety should enable team members to say what they really mean, feel that they are working in an environment of high trust, healthy debate and respect. Analyst Ben Thompson has described a culture of true collaboration as being one that is able to combine mutual trust and respect and comfort with dissent.[17] These are the building blocks for collaboration, and a culture that can move fast.

What most people miss about high-performing teams is that, rather than focus all your attention on perfecting skills and composition, what is more critical is how the team communicates and works together. In other words, the 'softer elements' are key.

FIGURE 6.1 Psychological safety

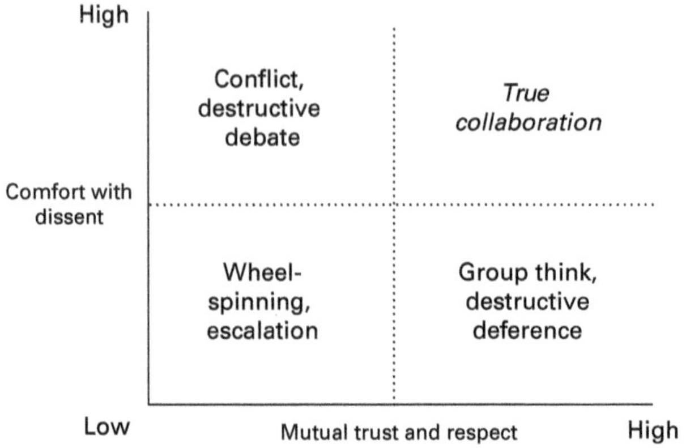

SOURCE Adapted from Ben Thompson, The Uncanny Valley of a Functional Organization, July 2013
https://stratechery.com/2013/the-uncanny-valley-of-a-functional-organization/

This is supported by extensive research conducted by MIT's Human Dynamics Laboratory, which shows that even above the individual talent included in the team, it is the manner in which a team communicates that directly impacts how successful they will be. In fact, they showed that patterns of communication was the single most important predictor of a team's success.

Research across a wide set of industries that had similar teams with varying performance demonstrated remarkable consistency in the 'data signatures' from the research on the factors that can predict team performance. Successful teams share several common factors around how they communicate.[18] There is equality on how much everyone on the team talks and listens, and contributions are kept short and sweet. When they speak team members face each other, connect directly and with energy. Side or back channel conversations complement team discussion, and team members actively explore outside of the team to bring useful information back. In particular, there were three key aspects of team communication that really mattered:

1 **Energy:** the number and nature of exchanges between team members – face-to-face communication is more valuable than e-mail, for example.

2 **Engagement:** a more even distribution of energy amongst team members.

3 **Exploration:** the energy and communication between team members and other teams – high-performing teams, especially those focused on creativity or innovation, seek more outside connections.

Relatively simple things, including the number of face-to-face exchanges, a team's engagement outside of formal meetings, how they socialize together in breaks, really makes a difference. The MIT research shows that ideal team players are what they call 'charismatic connectors' – people who:

> circulate actively, engaging people in short, high-energy conversations... are democratic with their time, communicating with everyone equally... listen as much as or more than they talk and are usually very engaged with whomever they're listening to... connect their teammates with one another and spread ideas around... are appropriately exploratory.[19]

Amy Edmondson has defined three key strategies that leaders can adopt in order to create an environment of psychological safety:[20]

1 **Framing work as learning problems, rather than execution problems:** each team member's input has value in helping to solve challenges and navigate uncertainty.

2 **Acknowledging fallibility:** creating permission for input from others, using statements and questions that show that the leader does not have all the answers.

3 **Model curiosity by asking a lot of questions:** encouraging people to have a voice through questions, creating the need to generate answers.

Yet Edmondson also recognizes the need for psychological safety to be combined with accountability. Too much accountability without the environment

FIGURE 6.2 Psychological safety and accountability

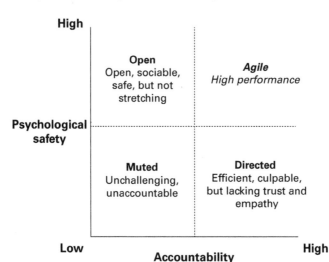

to enable questions and good discussion creates anxiety and mistakes; an overly open and safe culture with little accountability can lead to complacency and staying with comfort zones.

Team performance is increasingly the critical differentiator between businesses that can compete well in rapidly changing contexts, and those that get left behind. As the best research into high-performing teams demonstrates we give a disproportionately high degree of focus to individual skill and team composition, and far too little attention to group norms and patterns of communication. The smart, agile business redresses that balance.

The challenges and tensions

FIST – Fast, Inexpensive, Simple, Tiny

One of the key mindset challenges around starting small to scale fast often lies in undoing years (decades) of waterfall thinking, which has typically been characterized by comprehensive inputs and gold-plated approaches, and instead learning to take far more iterative approaches to solving problems. 'Death Star IT', for example, happens when a large, expensive, proprietary software system is seen as the answer to a business challenge. Ironically, big businesses often seem to feel more comfortable making big decisions about big spends on big solutions than they do about adopting a more open approach that can lead to greater flexibility in the future.

Yet tying yourself into a multiyear, single-solution IT programme creates far greater long-term risk than creating more malleable technology stack solutions that can adapt to changing contexts over time. Significant technology debt can occur when large, inflexible technology systems are customized repeatedly over time to try to cope with inevitable change. This endless patching up and adaptation for jobs that they were not really designed to do simply serves to reduce agility and build up operational risk over time. It's far easier to be additive with projects, to see future possibilities, to add features, widen the scope, take comfort in building something grand and expensive. Far harder to be reductive, to focus first on the key problem you're trying to solve, to test assumptions and validate hypotheses as you go, to start small and scale fast.

Dan Ward, an author and specialist in defence acquisition, has captured this approach in the acronym FIST, which stands for 'Fast, Inexpensive, Simple and Tiny'.[21] He developed this framework to describe a new approach for acquisitions and system development building on an original concept from NASA. In the 1990s NASA saw great success with their 'Faster, Better, Cheaper' (FBC) series of missions that set out to redefine time, cost and output expectations of their work and included the wildly successful Mars Pathfinder mission (which for the first time ever put a rover on another planet at a fraction of the cost and time of the earlier Viking mission) and the Near Earth Asteroid Rendezvous (NEAR) mission (which collected 10 times more data about the asteroid Eros than expected yet was under budget by tens of millions of dollars).[22] FIST defines an approach that uses a small team of talented people working with tight time and resource constraints adhering to a particular set of principles and practices.

Like most great concepts, FIST has much broader application and lots in common, of course, with Lean and Agile. Yet the concept of starting small remains challenging in environments that are used to big upfront investments. The term 'Minimum Viable Product' (or MVP) originated in Lean Startup to describe the version of a new product that 'allows a team to collect the maximum amount of validated learning about customers with the least effort'.[23] In effect, it is a first version of a proposition that has just enough features to satisfy early customers, but which can provide useful feedback for development. It's become another of those terms that are overused yet often poorly understood and applied. The real challenge with MVP and other start small approaches is that they are anathema to organizational practice steeped in comprehensive inputs, business case forecasts and significant upfront investment. Consequently, teams can find that approaches are misunderstood or questioned, and they can easily drift back to more comfortable ways of working. So a prototype becomes a piece of market research (assessing claimed behaviour rather than real behaviour), teams are forced to forecast future outcomes (which restricts learning and means they are back in a linear approach), small becomes quite big (leading to the risk of wasted investment). Starting small then, is a mindset that needs to be appreciated far beyond product and innovation teams. It needs to be understood from the very top of the organization.

CASE STUDY
Amazon Prime Now

Amazon Prime, the paid subscription service through which Amazon bundles access to premium services including fast delivery and content streaming services, has rapidly grown from its launch in 2005 to become a critical revenue generator for the company. In April 2018 Amazon reported that Prime had more than 100 million subscribers globally.[24] Yet the idea for Prime did not come from one of Amazon's senior executives, but from a software engineer in the company called Charlie Ward who put the idea onto an ideas platform on the internal company website called the Ideas Tool.[25] When Jeff Bezos saw the idea, he liked it, and proceeded towards putting Amazon's full weight behind making it happen.

In 2014, with shopping delivery services such as Instacart having begun to offer a sometimes-same-day grocery delivery service, Amazon decided to launch Prime Now as a way to allow customers to have products delivered to them within one hour for a fee, or two hours for no additional cost. But instead of investing heavily in a nationwide service launch they took an MVP approach and built a basic prototype in 100 days that could be launched in a few parts of New York City. This enabled them to build a low-cost version of the service to test its appeal, learn better how it could work, and limit potentially unnecessary spend.

The first prototype of Prime Now involved a screen within a distribution centre that showed orders coming in via the service. A bell would then ring to alert staff and put into action a group of delivery bikes and riders that were waiting to take the packages straight out for delivery. The MVP worked, and gave Amazon critical learning about how they could deploy it successfully. Less than two years later, Prime Now had expanded to 11 US cities and also to the UK, Germany, Italy, France, Spain, Japan and Singapore. As of 2018, almost a million products were available through the service across more than 50 global markets.[26]

Operational and business rhythm tensions

Since more traditional linear ways of operating and iterative working like Agile and Lean Startup run at different rhythms, there are inevitable tensions that arise between them when both are running in the same business. These cadence tensions are often under-acknowledged and not planned for but they have the potential to suffocate newer working cultures and practices before they've even become established.

The 'Buxton index', originated by Professor John Buxton at Warwick University and brought to wider attention by pioneering computer scientist Edsger W Dijkstra, is a lesser-known business concept that defines the length of the period over which an entity makes its plans. Different entities have different planning horizons that they are fundamentally working towards. For a politician seeking re-election it may be the period of government but for a manager striving to reach a quarterly target it will be much shorter. Significant cooperation is required between entities operating to different Buxton indices.

Problems therefore arise when there is poor understanding and empathy of divergent requirements and dependencies between teams operating to different indices or horizons. This has to be acknowledged upfront and worked through. Cadence tensions can also occur on a more regular and even day-to-day basis. An agile team might be looking to gain fast customer feedback but be hampered by slow technology release cycles. A finance department might be frustrated that a development team is proposing budgeting cycles or investment methods that are counterintuitive to existing and well-established processes. These tensions also need to be recognized and worked through.

Author Stewart Brand described the concept of pace layering in his book *The Clock of the Long Now*.[27] Pace layering acknowledges the different cadence to which elements of society (fashion, commerce, infrastructure, governance, culture) operate. Gartner used this concept to capture the different rhythms to which layers of technology work – from fastest to slowest: systems of innovation (characterized by experimentation); systems of differentiation (supporting processes that are different from competitors); systems of record (supporting core processes that may not be unique).[28] The concept of pace layering is therefore a useful way of expressing the different needs of various areas of the business. Teams that are closer to customers, making use using systems of innovation and differentiation, needing to iterate and adapt (in other words in the Explore or Execute domains) are likely to be operating at a higher cadence and to shorter horizons. Teams that are focused on incremental improvement of existing, mature propositions and capabilities, using systems of record, or working towards longer-term survival and gain are likely to be operating to a longer Buxton index.

In an era when horizontal collaboration within organizations and across entities is critical for advantage and adaptability, recognizing and mitigating these inevitable tensions is key. A heightened appreciation of the differences and the flexibility needed can lead to a deeper understanding of motivations and so aid better collaboration.

Dealing with dependencies

As agile begins to scale beyond a few teams, the need to manage interdependencies between teams and also establish ways of operating that can mitigate the kinds of tensions that I mention in the previous section, becomes critical. One of the benefits of Spotify's Squads, Chapters, Tribes model that I discuss in the next section is that the Tribes group Squads together into logical areas of commonality that helps support more unified working, but also that the Tribe leads can play a key role in managing interdependencies between Squads and also between Tribes. The need to do this is another under-acknowledged but inevitable and critical challenge that will need to be navigated. As are the interrelation and working processes between agile and non-agile teams.

When small teams are likely to have need for multiple different inputs at various stages of the development process the temptation is to bloat the team with people whose skills will be needed only infrequently. Avoid this at all costs. A better way to ensure that agile teams remain small whilst still retaining access to required support and input is to create a structured approach and clear lines to communication. The Agile team onion model, originated by Agile expert and coach Emily Webber, is one way of doing this, and it enables a flow of inputs between the hierarchical, functionally driven part of the business, and the small, agile team.[29]

In the model, the core delivery team is kept small and co-located, with very frequent communication between team members. Depending on the outputs required of the team there will likely be developers, a scrum master, designers, perhaps marketing and/or data and analytics. The collaborators can input specialist knowledge and expertise as and when required to support the agile team. These are point people that might sit in a hierarchical function (like HR, Finance, Compliance) and/or be aligned across a number of agile teams but they are there to give support and answers, and

FIGURE 6.3 Team onions

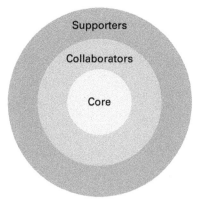

SOURCE Reproduced with kind permission. The Team Onion © Copyright Emily Webber tacit.pub/teamonion

to remove barriers to keeping the agile team/s moving fast. The communication is likely to be regular and they may even attend some agile team meetings or standups, or be in the team a day a week. In some cases, they may be supplier representatives. The supporters are likely to be senior leaders who are overseeing the direction of the team/s (but not telling the team/s what to do), staying informed of progress, ensuring that teams are doing work that feeds in to broader organizational priorities. They may be updated via demos, and communication is regular but less frequent. Since collaborators and supporters may work across multiple teams, it may be possible to create overlapping team onions.

Alongside collaborators and supporters, the product owners or managers are the other key conduit of communication between the hierarchical side and the agile teams. Their job is to help prioritize and evaluate the work that the agile team does (but again, they don't issue direct orders), align and interpret organizational needs for the benefit of the team, retain and communicate the vision for what the agile team is working on. They play a key role in turning the business strategy into a product strategy.

References

1 Price, Chris [accessed 29 April 2019] Digitisation Continues to Compel Businesses to Adapt and Evolve, *Daily Telegraph*, March 2019 [Online] https://www.telegraph.co.uk/business/digital-transformation-forum/manchester-event/ (archived at https://perma.cc/K8S2-XSAM)

2 Doherty, Sharon [accessed 29 April 2019] Living Through the Shift: How to survive and thrive in the age of digital transformation, *London Business School*, March 2019, https://www.london.edu/lbsr/living-through-the-shift?dm_i=2SVQ%2CV51B%2C2XYF1G%2C38DAK%2C1 (archived at https://perma.cc/A66W-QSB6)

3 Doherty, Sharon [accessed 29 April 2019] End of an Era at Vodafone, *LinkedIn*, March 2019 [Online] https://www.linkedin.com/pulse/end-era-vodafone-my-top-5-highlights-sharon-doherty/ (archived at https://perma.cc/35DP-RVZ8)

4 Petty, Scott [accessed 29 April 2019] Empowering People Is Key to Digital Transformation, *CIO* [Online] https://www.cio.co.uk/it-strategy/empowering-people-is-key-digital-transformation-3690087/ (archived at https://perma.cc/AN2A-5FLV)

5 Muller-Heyndyk, Rachel [accessed 29 April 2019] HR and Digital Transformation at Vodafone, *HR Magazine*, October 2018 [Online] https://www.hrmagazine.co.uk/article-details/hr-and-digital-transformation-at-vodafone (archived at https://perma.cc/9UG3-QWXG)

6 Greenway, A, Terett, B, Bracken, M and Loosemore, T (2018) *Digital Transformation at Scale: Why the strategy is delivery*, London Publishing Partnership

7 NASA History Portal [accessed 6 April 2019] [Online] https://historycollection. jsc.nasa.gov/JSCHistoryPortal/history/oral_histories/SSP/MuratoreJF_5-14-08. htm (archived at https://perma.cc/3NAW-8PWD)

8 Heracleous, Loizos, Wawarta, Christina, Gonzalez, Steven and Paroutis, Sotirios [accessed 6 April 2019] How a Group of NASA Renegades Transformed Mission Control, *MIT Sloan Management Review*, April 2019 [Online] https://sloanreview.mit.edu/article/how-a-group-of-nasa-renegades-transformed-mission-control/ (archived at https://perma.cc/KK5E-9T8F)

9 NASA History Portal [accessed 6 April 2019] [Online] https://historycollection. jsc.nasa.gov/JSCHistoryPortal/history/oral_histories/SSP/MuratoreJF_5-14-08. htm (archived at https://perma.cc/3NAW-8PWD)

10 Heracleous, Loizos, Wawarta, Christina, Gonzalez, Steven and Paroutis, Sotirios [accessed 6 April 2019] How a Group of NASA Renegades Transformed Mission Control, *MIT Sloan Management Review*, April 2019 [Online] https://sloanreview.mit.edu/article/how-a-group-of-nasa-renegades-transformed-mission-control/ (archived at https://perma.cc/KK5E-9T8F)

11 Greenway, A, Terett, B, Bracken, M and Loosemore, T (2018) *Digital Transformation at Scale: Why the strategy is delivery*, London Publishing Partnership

12 Hoffman, Reid [accessed 6 April 2019] Masters of Scale, Brian Chesky interview [Online] https://mastersofscale.com/brian-chesky-handcrafted/ (archived at https://perma.cc/9SAJ-7CWJ)

13 Hoffman, Reid [accessed 6 April 2019] Masters of Scale, Brian Chesky interview [Online] https://mastersofscale.com/brian-chesky-handcrafted/ (archived at https://perma.cc/9SAJ-7CWJ)

14 Rozovsky, Julia [accessed 10 March 2019] Five Keys to a Successful Google Team, *Google*, November 2015 [Online] https://rework.withgoogle.com/blog/five-keys-to-a-successful-google-team/ (archived at https://perma.cc/4X4S-2Z7D)

15 Duhigg, Charles [accessed 10 March 2019] What Google Learned From Its Quest to Build the Perfect Team, *The New York Times Magazine*, February 2016 [Online] https://www.nytimes.com/2016/02/28/magazine/what-google-learned-from-its-quest-to-build-the-perfect-team.html (archived at https://perma.cc/5NCJ-QRA6)

16 Edmondson, Amy [accessed 10 March 2019] Psychological Safety and Learning Behaviour in Work Teams, *Administrative Science Quarterly*, June 1999 [Online] https://journals.sagepub.com/doi/abs/10.2307/2666999 (archived at https://perma.cc/348Q-9DW3)

17 Turner, Joe [accessed 10 April 2019] The Building Blocks of Real
Collaboration, *Medium*, April 2016 [Online] https://medium.com/@joeturner/
the-building-blocks-of-real-collaboration-450d1b115041#.xt7eoqk2t (archived
at https://perma.cc/FS6E-VZL2)

18 Pentland, Alex [accessed 10 March 2019] The New Science of Building Great
Teams, *Harvard Business Review*, April 2012 [Online] https://hbr.org/2012/04/
the-new-science-of-building-great-teams (archived at https://perma.cc/A8RT-
BEQ4)

19 Pentland, Alex [accessed 10 March 2019] The New Science of Building Great
Teams, *Harvard Business Review*, April 2012 [Online] https://hbr.org/2012/04/
the-new-science-of-building-great-teams (archived at https://perma.cc/A8RT-
BEQ4)

20 Lebowitz, Shana [accessed 10 April 2019] Google Considers This to be the
Most Critical Trait of Successful Teams, *Business Insider*, November 2015
[Online] http://uk.businessinsider.com/amy-edmondson-on-psychological-
safety-2015-11 (archived at https://perma.cc/5QDL-M5UC)

21 Ward, D (2014) *FIRE: How Fast, Inexpensive, Restrained, and Elegant
Methods Ignite Innovation*, HarperBusiness

22 Ward, Dan [accessed 10 April 2019] Faster Better Cheaper: Lessons Defense
Could Learn From NASA, *Breaking Defense*, May 2013 [Online]
https://breakingdefense.com/2013/05/faster-better-cheaper-lessons-defense-
could-learn-from-nasa/ (archived at https://perma.cc/69CT-2238)

23 Ries, Eric [accessed 10 April 2019] Minimum Viable Product – A Guide,
Startup Lessons Learned, August 2009 [Online] http://www.
startuplessonslearned.com/2009/08/minimum-viable-product-guide.html
(archived at https://perma.cc/96NH-8G9U)

24 Alvarez, Edgar [accessed 16 January 2019] Amazon Has 100 Million Prime
Members, *Engadget*, April 2018 [Online] https://www.engadget.com/
amp/2018/04/18/amazon-100-million-prime-members/ (archived at https://
perma.cc/Q6F8-9PVE)

25 Cheever, Charlie [accessed 16 January 2019] Who Invented Amazon Prime?
Quora [Online] https://www.quora.com/Who-invented-Amazon-Prime
(archived at https://perma.cc/FRQ2-H7H9)

26 ScrapeHero [accessed 8 March 2019] How Many Products Does Amazon
Prime Now Sell? June 2018 [Online] https://www.scrapehero.com/number-of-
products-amazon-prime-now-june-2018/ (archived at https://perma.cc/
F2RJ-GFX8)

27 Brand, S (2000) *The Clock of the Long Now: Time and responsibility – the
ideas behind the world's slowest computer*, Basic Books

28 Gartner newsroom [accessed 25 October 2016] Gartner Says Adopting a Pace-Layered Application Strategy Can Accelerate Innovation, *Gartner* [Online] http://www.gartner.com/newsroom/id/1923014 (archived at https://perma.cc/AD88-BXC6)

29 Webber, Emily [accessed 25 October 2016] The Agile Team Onion. How many pizzas does it really take to feed your team?, *Emily Webber* [Online] http://emilywebber.co.uk/agile-team-onion-many-pizzas-really-take-feed-team/ (archived at https://perma.cc/8Q22-NJ4F)

07

Scale fast

Applying agile principles at scale

The key elements of 'scaling fast'

Scaling fast is all about capitalizing on continuous learning to scale change and agility more widely through the business:

Scaling agile structures: growing beyond a small number of agile teams to create a more networked organization, understanding the key stages of growth.

Building momentum for change through strategy and execution: creating growth through standards, spend controls and linking strategy to execution. Balancing alignment and direction with autonomy.

Building momentum for change through leadership mindset: enabling the behaviours and culture to embed agile transformation.

Building momentum for change through adaptive strategy: navigating with data, avoiding bias, agile governance.

Agile structures at scale

Scaling beyond a few agile teams requires a more defined approach to structure, alignment and interdependencies. A popular approach to scaling agile (but not the only one, of course) is to apply learning from Spotify's model of Squads, Chapters, Tribes and Guilds (Figure 7.1):

- **Squads:** small, multidisciplinary teams (of no more than 10 people) are the basic units of development at Spotify. Squads are co-located, often self-organizing, but focused on particular areas of the product or service, a specific customer need or interface. They work iteratively in sprints and have highly focused KPIs relating to their area of responsibility. Teams comprise all the skillsets needed to achieve the desired outputs from design, to development, to testing, release and production.

- **Tribes:** Squads are grouped together by business area. No more than 150 people in a Tribe. Environments that support intra-squad contact and regular gatherings for show and tell, shared learning. The Tribe leader is responsible for coordination across the different Squads and with other Tribes, managing resourcing, budgets and inter-dependencies, establishing priorities.

- **Chapters and Guilds:** these link Squads together horizontally, enabling inter-team knowledge sharing and wider organizational best practice. Chapters are the groups of functional experts who do similar work (like UX, for example) within a Tribe. The Chapter lead is a Squad member but is likely to be the line manager for other functional experts in that Tribe, and is responsible for performance review and people development, functional meet-ups to support learning. The Guilds are looser, more wide-reaching communities of practice or interest that can stretch across the whole company, enabling better knowledge, practice and tool sharing across the wider group.

FIGURE 7.1 Squads; Chapters; Tribes

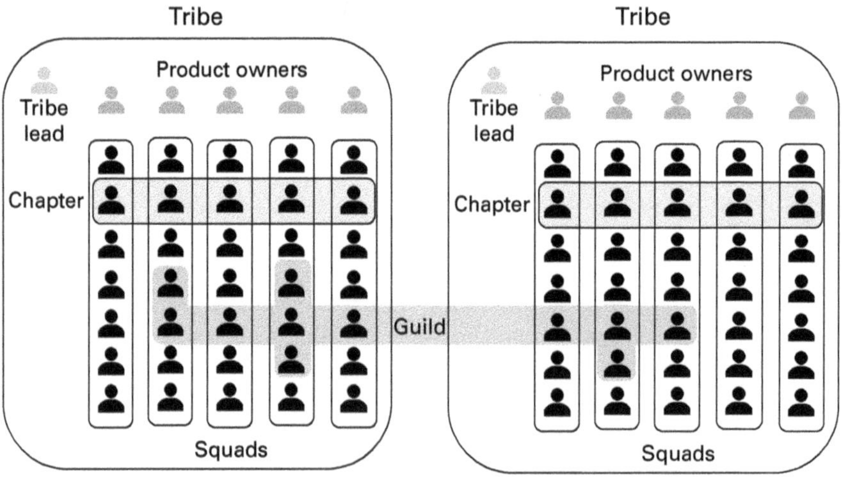

SOURCE Adapted from Henrik Kniberg and Anders Ivarsson, October 2012, Scaling Agile @ Spotify, with Tribes, Squads, Chapters and Guilds: https://blog.crisp.se/wp-content/uploads/2012/11/SpotifyScaling.pdf

Agile and organizational coaches at Spotify Henrik Kniberg and Anders Ivarsson, who originally wrote about the model, described it as like a matrix organization but one that is weighted towards delivery.[1] Rather than being primarily organized around functional efficiency and responsibility, the structure fundamentally starts with the product and the customer and works backwards from there. The product owners, for example, work with each Squad to capture and articulate the vision for what they are doing, support prioritization of the backlog, and ensure that outputs are fulfilling customer needs but the teams have the autonomy to decide how best to do the work.

This model has become more widely known and copied but it is important to recognize that there is no one-size-fits-all solution to what a good agile structure looks like. Spotify, like every other organization that has implemented agile structures, iterated its way towards this model, learning as it went. There are, however, some essential rules of thumb for agile structures that are key to bear in mind:

- **Keep the core team small:** some teams may be dealing with high levels of complexity but it is critical that no agile team gets beyond the 'two pizza' rule that I mentioned earlier in the book. No more than 10 people in a team.

- **Group together Squads into logical areas:** once the numbers of Squads increase beyond a few, grouping them together helps mitigate challenges around alignment, coordination and interdependencies. Spotify groups Squads into Tribes but no Tribe gets larger than around 150 people. There is some scientific basis for why this should be the maximum – anthropologist Robin Dunbar has proposed that there is a cognitive limit to the number of people with whom a person can maintain stable social relationships of around 150 (known as the Dunbar Number). Agile teams may be grouped together into areas defined by product (as with Spotify), other propositions (customer journeys), job-to-be-done (teams working on strategic challenges, teams working on innovation, teams working on product), or even types of work (explore, execute, extend and exploit).

- **Manage resourcing in a fluid way:** as the work that teams do evolves, it may well be necessary to swap people in and out of teams as the need arises to ensure that there are the most appropriate people working on outputs. This requires a much greater degree of fluidity around resourcing than would happen in a hierarchical environment, and adept management of talent.

- **Manage interdependencies:** as the number of teams scale, managing the interdependencies between the work that the teams are doing is critical – setting up technology infrastructure and testing processes that enable multiple teams to be working concurrently on product without interfering with what the other teams are doing. Leadership and oversight, documentation and key meeting frequency also all help.

- **Establish productive links with the rest of the business:** in the early stages of introducing agile teams the key job will be to create enough space to enable a different way of working, and to protect the new culture. As agile teams are scaled, the need to integrate the two sides of the dual operating system takes on more significance. I'll discuss this more in the next section.

CASE STUDY
Scaling Agile at ING Bank

ING has reinvented its organization at group headquarters in the Netherlands (comprising 3,500 staff) from the ground up, moving from a traditional organizational model featuring functional departments such as marketing, IT and Product Management, to a completely agile model that shares much in common with the Spotify example. ING started with the group headquarters to show that you could begin with the core and set an example to the rest of the business. It was a transformation that took place over a multiyear period but instead of organizing around functional departments ING staff are now organized into about 350 nine-person Squads and 13 Tribes.

The Squads are small multidisciplinary teams (no more than nine people) that are co-located and operate with a high degree of autonomy. Each Squad is focused on a specific client-related objective for which it has end-to-end responsibility (for example, an end-to-end customer journey) and may include marketing, data and analytics, design, UX, product and technology expertise. A product owner is responsible for coordinating the activities of the Squad and managing the backlog and priorities, but the product owner is a squad member rather than leader. As the mission evolves, the team and the functions that are represented evolve with it. As the mission is completed, the team is dissolved.

Squads that have interconnected missions or related business and customer propositions (for example, all Squads focused on mortgages) are grouped together into Tribes, and these tend not to exceed 100 to 150 people. A Tribe lead helps coordinate priorities, budgets, manage interdependencies and is the interface with other Tribes to ensure alignment and knowledge sharing. Each Tribe also has an Agile coach to support high performance. Functional expertise and learning is supported through cross-squad Chapters, and a Chapter lead effectively represents hierarchy for the Chapter, particularly in terms of performance management, staffing and personal development.

This approach has not only improved time-to-market, but increased productivity and employee engagement. Apart from the level of exceptional commitment to agile working and resourcing, there are a number of aspects of this that are particularly notable:[2]

1   When ING began the transformation there was no financial imperative to do so since the company was actually doing well at the time, but ING recognized that changing consumer behaviours and expectation could soon create significant challenges if it didn't become more agile.

2   ING recognized that it was not a linear transition, but about becoming a different type of organization that is itself characterized by continuous change. As Chief Operating Officer Bart Schlatmann has said: 'Transformation is not just moving an organization from A to B, because once you hit B, you need to move to C, and when you arrive at C, you probably have to start thinking about D.'[3]

3   The reorganization is focused on minimizing obvious barriers to agility like bureaucracy and functional handovers but also on greater empowerment and autonomy to enable teams to move fast. Technology was organized around more frequent release cycles of two to three weeks rather than five or six times a year.

4   The fact that each Squad is focused end to end on a particular customer objective, a common definition of success and includes all the key functions needed to create value means that this is a structure that is genuinely customer-centric.

5   The new organization is supported by a new agile performance-management model. Instead of a manager's salary and status being based on how much resource he or she controls, it is now focused far more on how the manager deals with knowledge and delivers outputs.

6   There was a staged approach to the reorganization – it began with a compelling vision about what the business could be, and drew learnings from a pilot incorporating five or six Squads. Implementation involved a revamp of the working environment to support better meeting spaces, retrospectives, larger gatherings and whiteboards.

7 Support functions such as HR, finance, call centres, IT infrastructure and risk have not initially been included in the Squads but have instead adopted agile working practices in different ways.

8 ING has been focused as much on getting the culture right as it has on the structure, spending a lot of time and energy focused on role-modelling the right behaviours (customer-centricity, empowerment, ownership) to support change. One example of this is a complete revamp of the onboarding programme, which not only involves new employees moving around the business to generate informal networks and learning, but every employee spending a week in the call centre taking customer calls.

9 Meeting structure and governance – most meetings are informal, with formal ones kept to a minimum. Each Squad has a clear written purpose for what it is working on, and an agreed way to measure the impact it has on customers, but has autonomy to prioritize and manage its daily activities. Mechanisms such as portfolio wall planning, scrums and standups ensure that the product owners within each Tribe keep the Squads aligned. Quarterly Business Reviews (QBR) involve each Tribe notating what it achieved over the quarter, its biggest learning (from both successes and failures), its objectives for the next quarter and what it will need from other Tribes. These QBR documents are openly available to support transparency.

The new structure has enabled ING to dramatically improve speed-to-market through more frequent releases and increase the rate of innovation to help position it as the primary mobile bank in the Netherlands.

But it is the level of commitment to agile resourcing that is truly impressive, avoiding the common trap of adopting some agile attributes but not letting go of legacy structures, processes or governance. Bart Schlatmann (who was the COO throughout the transformation) talks of the importance of having a clear vision for the agile transformation, and being clear about what you are willing to give up:

It requires sacrifices and a willingness to give up fundamental parts of your current way of working – starting with the leaders. We gave up traditional hierarchy, formal meetings, over-engineering, detailed planning, and excessive 'input steering' in exchange for empowered teams, informal networks, and 'output steering'. You need to look beyond your own industry and allow yourself to make mistakes and learn. The prize will be an organization ready to face any challenge.[4]

A great example of real agile transformation.

Scaling stages

As I've mentioned there is no one end result to agile transformation. No one blueprint for an agile organizational structure. No one roadmap for change. It's notable that ING took an iterative, staged approach to its transformation and the secret really is to *be* agile about how you *become* more agile and learn and iterate. But we can draw out some key structural stages that organizations are most likely to pass through on their journey towards becoming truly agile:

1 **Stage one:** start small by aligning a few small, agile teams to new challenges, propositions, or customer-focused objectives. The objective of this stage should be to learn as much as possible about what works and what is right for the contexts of your organization. Teams might be aligned to strategic problems, innovation tasks or customer journeys but the leadership team needs to understand the context for how small teams can best support real change. Teams will be staffed by change agents and pioneers. Fluidity and adaptability are key since teams may need to be realigned, but look for learnings that can support scalability. An appropriate leader/team of senior leaders (with a strong connection to the board) oversee direction and progress and ensure that the networked agile teams are given the support, autonomy and space that they need, and that new ways of working are not suffocated (Figure 7.2).

FIGURE 7.2 Stage one – agile structures

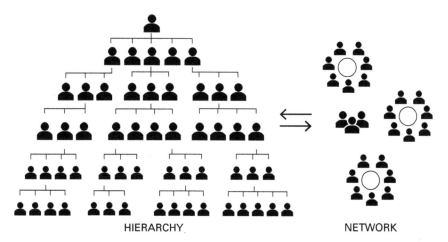

HIERARCHY   NETWORK

2 **Stage two:** by this stage, the business will have a better understanding of the opportunity to align and use small agile teams in service of strategic challenges and change, so this is about scaling in sensible ways. It might be, for example, that the business has understood the value of aligning agile teams to end-to-end customer journeys and can now scale that approach. The learning and adaptation do not stop, but a key part of the change at this point is ensuring that there is wider adoption and understanding of agile principles and culture right across the organization. It's also critical that as the networked side of the business scales it is not seen as entirely separate – there needs to be great communication and a good connection back to the business as usual so that the wider organization can learn, but also to ensure a flow of staff as needed from one side to the other (Figure 7.3).

3 **Stage three:** when the number of agile teams reaches the point when alignment becomes challenging, the Squads will need to be grouped together (for ease, we can call these groupings Tribes, but this does not have to follow the Spotify model). Tribes can be allocated Tribe leads, and work can be done to create the scaled infrastructure and process support that will mitigate interdependency issues (Figure 7.4).

It may well be that eventually there will be a stage four to this model, where the entire organization is structured into groups of small, agile squads but more likely there will remain some need for a more functional approach to some disciplines and managing business as usual. The proportions of the

FIGURE 7.3 Stage two – agile structures

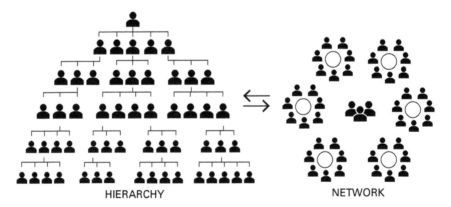

HIERARCHY   NETWORK

FIGURE 7.4 Stage three – agile structures

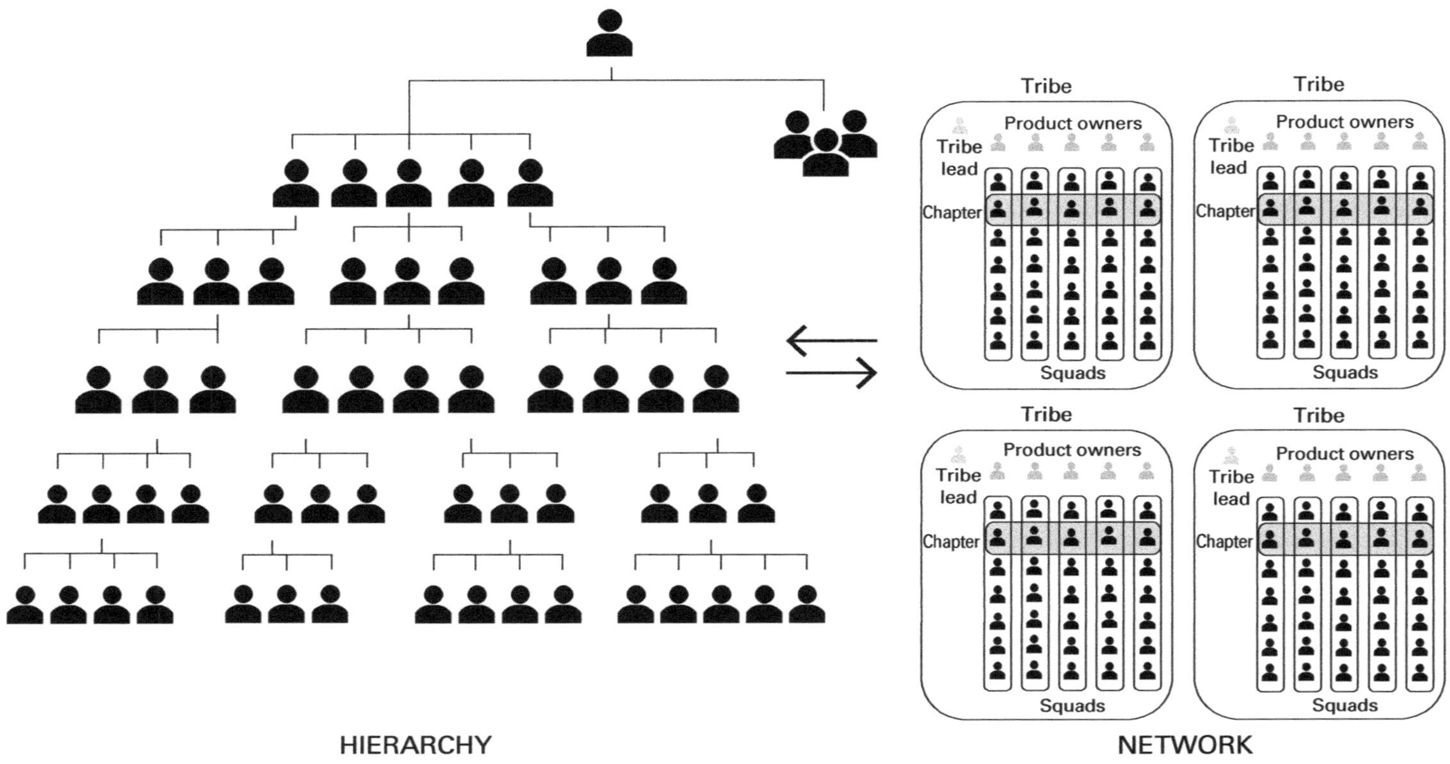

NETWORK

HIERARCHY

business that are hierarchical and networked will change over time – an example would be the business that begins as 95 per cent hierarchy and 5 per cent networked, but then shifts to become more like 80 per cent and 20 per cent, and then adjusts back slightly because of a short- to medium-term context before reverting back to a more even balance owing to the need to evolve rapidly. So it is critical to continue learning and continue to be flexible in achieving the right balance. The point is that through adopting this approach a business is able to scale agile approaches in a way that mitigates risk and best suits its unique contexts. It's the best way for the business to become truly ambidextrous and develop engines for exploration, execution, extension and exploitation.

Momentum for change (1): foundations and flywheels

Agile transformation is not simply a matter of setting out a linear progression for change. It is about building momentum through adaptation and creating a flywheel effect where change can empower more change. It is about enabling scalability through standards and alignment combined with the autonomy to move fast: speed and scalability.

Why momentum trumps speed alone

In Lewis Carroll's *Through the Looking-Glass*[5] the Red Queen's race sees Alice and the Queen running fast yet standing still. Alice decries the pointlessness of running without getting anywhere. In our country, she says, you run to get somewhere. 'Now, here, you see,' says the Queen, 'it takes all the running you can do, to keep in the same place. If you want to get somewhere else, you must run at least twice as fast as that!'

Many businesses are caught in the Red Queen's trap. In response to rapidly changing contexts they attempt to run faster and faster just to stay in the same spot. They demand longer working hours, make their people work harder, continuously shorten deadlines. But as long as you continue to work largely in the way that you have always worked, there will be a limit to the gains that you can make. Renowned management thinker Peter Drucker once wrote: 'There is surely nothing quite so useless as doing with great efficiency what should not be done at all.'[6]

Velocity is speed with direction. We might celebrate moving quickly but we need to move quickly in the right way. But we also need mass to create momentum. In physics, mass is both a property of a physical body and also a measure of its resistance to acceleration when a force is applied. So in order to create mass in transformation, we need to bring people on the journey with us, and create force for change through practice and cultural transformation, but we also need to reduce the drag on progress. We need to get the barriers and blockers to change out of the way. Once we have mass and velocity, we have speed, weight, direction, acceleration – we have momentum.

Colonel John Boyd was a military strategist and something of a maverick. His analysis of air combat situations in the Korean War led to the origination of the OODA loop, a way of representing the benefits that can come from not just speed and force, but greater manoeuvrability. His proposals ran counter to a lot of contemporary military strategic thinking, which believed that US fighter planes had to be bigger, and fly higher, further and faster than their opposition to win in combat. Boyd's Korean War analysis showed that the F-86 Sabre, which US pilots were flying, was disproportionately successful against the MiG15s being flown by the North Koreans, but also that the reason for this was not because the F-86 was a larger plane since it wasn't, or that it could fly higher, further, faster since it couldn't. The reason it won out was because it was more manoeuvrable.

The OODA loop stands for 'Observe, Orient, Decide, Act' and recognizes the need for those on the frontline to always be taking account of latest contexts and inputs in a rapidly changing environment like the battlefield. Observation collects the necessary data and information inputs. Orientation turns this into an appreciation and understanding of position. Decision is the determination of a course of action. Action is the resultant activity.

Boyd believed that intelligent organizations and organisms have a continuous cycle of interaction with their environment, which can enable adaptation. Advantage can come from moving through the cycle quicker than your opponent, thereby leaving him or her responding to dynamics that have already changed.

This is a good metaphor for modern competitive advantage. Success comes not only from making smarter decisions but also from responding faster to changing situations. If a business can operate to a faster tempo it can become far more manoeuvrable. It's no accident that sprint working using iterative methodologies like Agile can reduce time to market and improve speed of delivery, but we shouldn't forget that one of the key advantages of this type of working is the ability to have learning and adaptation built into the fabric of how we are working. If we can learn continuously and then successfully adapt and reprioritize on a frequent basis, we can embed not just speed, but greater manoeuvrability.

Creating an organizational 'flywheel'

In order to create real momentum for change we need to create a self-perpetuating organizational flywheel that adds to the momentum with every additional exemplar of a new way of working in the business. There are several key tools and approaches from network thinking that we can utilize.

POSITIVE FEEDBACK LOOPS

These are the kind of feedback loops where making a small change has a compounding effect. They enhance or amplify changes. A simple example of a positive feedback loop is a savings account that earns interest, which then generates interest on a larger amount. A startup may well look for positive feedback loops to support exponential rather than linear user growth through customer acquisition or engagement loops. A positive acquisition loop occurs, for example, when new users of a platform help to recruit other new users. A positive engagement loop can be triggered by mechanics that help ensure that user engagement promotes more user engagement, or in other words how customers' use of a platform can encourage a higher level of use from other customers, which in turn supports even more use from other users.

Similarly, positive feedback loops can also be created in innovation through the creation of a self-perpetuating innovation system where the efforts of one part of the business in the field empowers that of other groups, the wider business and even external operators. This is a key reason for teams to create reusable components and socialize their availability. Externalizing the good work that an organization is doing in an emerging field can make it more attractive for in-demand specialists to work there, which in turn can attract other specialists who want to learn and work with the best. In transformation we might also create positive feedback loops for behaviour in which small changes can create new habits that can generate real change in individuals but also wider groups.

NETWORK EFFECTS

I mentioned network effects in a couple of contexts earlier in the book. This is, of course, the principle that the value of a network is the square of the number of people on that network. Every additional user or node on the network increases the value of the whole network. This is valuable to understand since these effects can generate greater value for marginal increase in cost. In a supply and demand marketplace like Airbnb, for example, cross-side network effects can support growth since the more supply there is (interesting places to stay) the more demand that generates, and the more demand there is the more likely landlords and hosts are to list their place on Airbnb. Same-side network effects mean that if I use Airbnb for the first time and am so impressed I tell my friends about the experience, then they are more likely to use the service too. So we get positive feedback loops much like we discussed above. But every additional place to stay and user on the network is increasing the value of the whole network and therefore Airbnb itself.

In order to leverage network effects, we need to focus on network value, and how we can leverage mechanics that will increase that overall value. Network value is effectively the sum of the value to all users of the network, or the cost differential that would be there if the network didn't exist (for example, Airbnb users paying extra for hotel rooms that weren't located as conveniently, if Airbnb didn't exist). So if we are building new networks that might include employees, partners, suppliers and other contributors in exchanges of information, capability or other value we need to think about total network value, and how we can create mechanics whereby every additional user on the network increases its overall worth to all. Strategies can be determined by what will have the highest impact on network value, and since revenue and other benefits typically lag behind network value, we can develop a more sophisticated understanding of potential future value.

PLATFORM ECONOMICS

Platforms typically facilitate efficient value exchange between multiple groups of users and players in an ecosystem. An example would be Spotify, which facilitates a relationship between artists, record companies, music lovers, and a whole range of services that have integrated with Spotify's API. Platforms orchestrate and create shared common standards and might enable exchange of value between consumers and producers, or enable producers to create content that can be shared widely. The value comes from access, interaction and data but above all from learning. We might consider, for example, how we can externalize organizational capability through APIs and build platforms that can enable third parties to utilize services and capacity, thereby scaling our own learning.

Working together, these approaches can create a flywheel effect that can increase organizational momentum.

Scaling through standards

Once momentum has been created it's necessary to build on that forward energy by putting even more energy into the system and the change process. Charging agile teams with creating reusable components in the course of their work that can be used and repurposed by other teams and encouraging all teams to share code and other assets to minimize duplication of effort, is a simple way to allow agile teams to build off each other's capabilities and catalyse progress. Another way is to create standards, manuals, guides and playbooks that can enable a universal approach, help teams to answer questions quickly, and socialize the best and fastest procedures. It's one thing to move with speed. But we need to move fast with quality. Doing Agile doesn't mean that we open ourselves up for unnecessary risk.

A good set of standards can codify a way of working and scale positive behaviours fast. They are also key when people are moving from more traditional ways of working in helping the transition to be as smooth as possible. And they can help communicate to those teams that are not doing Agile what it really means and assure them that quality is embedded into the process. Standards can also help set performance at the right level. When the UK Government Digital Service created their 'digital-by-default' service standard and service manual in 2013 they (of course) put it online to make it universally accessible, but the objective of the standard was ultimately to make all government digital services so good that people would prefer to carry out the task online and each new service had to pass that simple standard.[7] Interestingly, they also then took down all other existing standards pages from intranets and the internet to minimize confusion and nobody noticed. No one looks at a complicated, poorly written or designed standards documents so they need to be as accessible and well designed as possible. Good, widely available and well-understood standards should serve to minimize questions and demands on agile teams from the rest of the business – whilst agile teams should be able to assist the rest of the business in useful ways, their job is delivery and so anything that frees-up time for more of that is a good thing.

One final thing on standards – avoid rule creep. It's very easy (and very typical) for a set of rules to expand over time as new concerns or situations arise. The intention of the business in doing this is a good one –to mitigate risk and make sure that every scenario is covered. But, of course, what happens is that no one ever takes any rules out and so you end up with an unwieldy set of standards that serve to lock teams down and restrict options rather than free them up to do their best work. The unacknowledged consequence of this is that assessment of new work against these standards then becomes an unnecessarily long process involving too many people and the whole thing slows down.

The importance of spend controls

A renewed process for sensible spend controls should run alongside simple, accessible standards to ensure that things are done right but also that time, money and resource are not wasted. Spend controls are not exactly the sexiest part of digital transformation and so are not often discussed, yet they are absolutely critical.

To begin with, it needs to be acknowledged that stopping projects that are not delivering is just as important in an agile business as starting new ones. This process needs to be freed from the blame, status and reputation impact that often goes with it. It's no wonder that leaders stick with projects far beyond the time that they should really have been stopped when they become so invested in their success and the prospect of failure could well be seen as detrimental to their career. So setting up a process to review technology spend in sensible ways, and having the necessary power to stop projects that are clearly wasting resource, is essential. The team that runs this process has to have the requisite level of seniority but also credibility. The level of technology literacy amongst many senior leadership teams is woefully low, so don't have people who have vested interests or particular agendas (favourite suppliers, for example) or who don't know what they're doing making critical decisions about critical capability.

Staying with the UK Government Digital Service, the efficiency programme that ran alongside the ground-up redesign of a succession of high-transaction volume services cumulatively saved £50 billion in five years, savings that were mostly made from the running costs of government. Large organizations are particularly susceptible to wasting resource on huge technology projects that take multiple years to implement and fail to deliver on user needs or worse, are cancelled outright after a lot of money has been spent. Public institutions are no exception. The NHS National Programme for IT – a £12 billion project and the biggest civilian IT project of its kind anywhere ever for an organization with the largest workforce in Europe – was scrapped in 2011. The UK's first e-Borders scheme which was started in 2003 set out to collect and analyse data on everyone travelling to and from the UK, but was cancelled after 11 years and an £830 million investment. When GDS was asked by the Cabinet Office to run a technology transformation programme the service set out a broad set of guiding principles that combine an inherent focus on user need with built-in long-term flexibility to enable adaptation:

- Start with user needs.
- Design with choice and flexibility in mind.
- Be transparent throughout.
- Architect loosely coupled services, not a single system.
- Favour short contracts.
- Bring the best of consumer technology to the enterprise.
- Make security as invisible as possible.
- Build a long-term capability.[8]

It's common practice in large organizations for extremely expensive, multi-year, locked-in contracts to be awarded to large technology consultancies but this is far from always being the best way. GDS framed the principles as 'technology at least as good as people have at home' – a gloriously simple way of expressing what the technology *really* needs to look like.

Where business meets customer need

I've talked a lot in this book about genuinely working back from the customer and creating fast customer feedback loops to inform iterative creation of value. But where does customer need meet the needs of the business? To execute well, a truly agile organization needs to map customer-focused problem solving and innovation to business and product strategy in seamless but adaptive ways. If we think of the business goals and strategy as top-down, the bottom-up will be customer inputs that help to execute well, refine, inform and even challenge (Figure 7.5).

The business vision and goals provide an overarching direction and are likely to change slowly. Out of that flows a business strategy that brings to life how the goals will be realized, and this can then be expressed through a product strategy. Out of the business and product strategy flow themes, areas of focus and initiatives – it is important not to overwhelm the business or create inefficiencies through too diverse a focus or with overlapping programmes (unless new initiatives are deliberately set up in competition with each other). Major projects and initiatives may well be managed

FIGURE 7.5 Business need meeting customer need in organizational strategy

through quarterly business reviews (QBRs), which can inform a backlog of Epics to be worked on by small, multidisciplinary Squads. The Squads create User Stories that express the Epics as customer value. Just as the strategy informs the themes and initiatives that in turn inform the Epics and User Stories, so the customer shapes the execution and informs the Epics, themes and strategy. One is top-down, the other is bottom-up, but they each flow up and down, informed by each other in order to deliver a business strategy in a customer-focused way.

Alignment and measuring progress

As the number of agile teams increases organizations need to guard against misalignment and also find ways to cascade strategy through the organization in inclusive, empowering ways that balance the need for team autonomy in moving fast with the need for everyone to go in the right direction. Having a strategy cascade that enables the happy confluence of organizational and customer strategy as we discussed in the previous section is key to this. Alignment should also come from governance and the oversight that the business creates for the agile teams whether that is through the Chief Digital Officer, the Tribe leads, or a 'Digital Board' that is comprised of senior directors and links oversight directly with the main board.

Another key way to support alignment through the business is to use frameworks such as Objectives and Key Results (or OKRs). These involve setting quarterly objectives that are specific and measurable at a company, team and individual level. These objectives are then supported by quantifiable key results, against which performance is measured. Systems like OKRs are useful since everyone in the business has them from the CEO down (often they are made transparent for everyone to see, as they are at Google), we can use them to assess progress and performance, and they can align strategy with execution and measurement all the way down through the company. OKRs also have the benefit of making strategy at every level very clear, and agile teams and the people in them can be aligned around very specific objectives and measures, which helps ensure that activity that supports strategic objectives is prioritized. This is key when needing to change behaviour and implement a new strategy that can support transformation.

Measuring progress can be tricky. There are typically many metrics that *could* be looked at but the challenge is deciding which ones *should* be looked at. To paraphrase the famous saying: not everything that can be counted counts. The measures that should count are those that are aligned to both user and business value. The UK Government Digital Service, for example, had four key measures aligned to the organization's primary strategic objectives: getting more people to use online government services; building services that worked first time; saving money; and meeting user needs. To track progress against these they focused on four performance metrics: digital take-up; completion rate; cost per transaction; user satisfaction.

Key metrics can be dashboarded to support transparency and access. GDS have public-facing dashboards covering 781 different government services and over a billion transactions a year.[9]

Empowering aligned autonomy

Greater autonomy, team and individual empowerment are powerful catalysts for adaptability. As I discussed earlier, high levels of autonomy mean faster decision-making, decisions being made closer to execution and customer feedback, and improved ability to pivot, respond quickly, or seize growth opportunities at speed. There is a high correlation between the degree of empowerment present in teams and how quickly the organization is able to make decisions and therefore its manoeuvrability.

In slow-moving environments, it might work to have most of the decision-making power centralized at the top of the company but amongst rapidly shifting contexts the old idea of all the power residing at the top of the business and all the decisions flowing downwards is no longer fit for purpose. Instead, distributing authority more widely through the organization, ensuring clarity about decision-making rights, setting clear expectations, deploying more agile forms of governance, and encouraging a culture of ownership can all support being more agile.

Autonomy can counteract overburdensome bureaucracy and overly hierarchical control. If small, multidisciplinary teams or squads can act as the engine for transformation and change, then they need autonomy to iterate value properly, and have the kind of working culture and practices that enable them to move fast and be truly adaptive.

The common challenge to this, though, is often focused around governance and alignment. If we have numbers of squads working with high levels of autonomy, how can we ensure they all go in the right direction? How can we make sure that interdependencies are managed properly? How can we make sure that they are working on the things that matter and avoid misdirection and poor governance? A fast-and-roughly-right mindset does not have to mean poor standards, inadequate quality, compromised requirements. Leaders need to let go, but they don't need to let go of everything.

The best framing for this is Spotify's concept of 'aligned autonomy' which seeks to strike the right balance between high levels of autonomy and flexibility, and the need to marshal progress to make it all go in the same direction.[10] Low autonomy and low alignment leads to misdirection and chaos. High autonomy but low alignment means that leadership is too removed from the work of the team. Low autonomy and high alignment results in leadership being too directive, and too much in the detail. Yet high autonomy combined with high alignment sets a clear direction and effectively frames the challenge to be addressed but facilitates velocity by enabling the team to decide how best to solve the problem.

As we described earlier, Spotify aligns multiple small, multidisciplinary teams into Tribes in an arrangement that they have described as 'loosely coupled, tightly aligned Squads'. The key is that there is a balance between the autonomy that the Squads need to move fast, and the alignment that is needed to ensure direction and governance. Working in agile, iterative ways need not mean a lack of either alignment or governance, but it does mean a shift in leadership style. Instead of hierarchically driven command and control style leadership, aligned autonomy requires leaders to frame the challenge in the way that teams can understand the problem/s that they need to solve. But the team decides how to solve the problem. This balance is key in achieving adaptiveness balanced with direction. Alignment enables true autonomy.

Momentum for change (2): culture and learning

Agile transformation is nothing if we don't bring our people on the journey. It will inevitably fail if we don't create the environment that empowers, engages and motivates as many employees as possible to think differently and get things done. We need to create an organizational engine for curiosity, progress and high-velocity decision-making.

Why, in transformation, the real battle is for hearts, not minds

Earlier in the book I discussed how employee experience is often the poor relation to customer experience and technology focus in many transformation programmes. In agile transformation, bringing people on the journey with you is absolutely critical. As part of that discussion I mentioned the work that Gallup has done, demonstrating the appallingly low levels of employee engagement that exist across many companies, industries and countries. Gallup's research shows that an amazing 87 per cent of employees worldwide are not engaged at work, but also that companies with highly engaged workforces outperform their peers by 147 per cent in earnings per share.[11]

Lack of engagement can kill momentum for change just as surely as a directive from the CEO. You can't expect change programmes to change anything if you don't bring your people on the journey with you. Happy staff in touch with their end-users create exceptional customer experiences. Great employee engagement brings dividends in productivity and performance. The Gallup meta-analysis that I mentioned earlier in the book (covering more than 82,000 business units in 73 countries across 49 industries) found that for those business units that were in the top quartile of engagements, scores were 17 per cent more productive and 21 per cent more profitable than those in the bottom quartile. And yet we pay so little attention to it.

Dan Cable, Professor of Organizational Behaviour at London Business School (and author of the book *Alive at Work*[12]) has conducted extensive research focusing on the power of work environments that enable employees to bring their 'best selves' to work. People, he says, bring different things into the workplace. Some bring hands to do the work (where leaders write the script and come up with the game plan). Some bring brains (innovation, trying new things, emergent value). The heart (empathy, passion, desire to make a difference) is perhaps the most difficult, yet is more important than ever – the ability to empathize well with customer need, to take risks to try new things, to be authentic when dealing with clients, is difficult to do when you're not feeling it yourself. So it's more critical than ever that we feel able to bring our whole self into the work environment.

Yet this clearly isn't happening in many workplaces. Dan quotes another stark statistic from an older Gallup survey that covered 1.7 million employees across 63 countries and 101 companies and which found that 80 per cent of people go to work to 'shut off' (in other words they hide their true selves).[13] Many of our working norms and practices come from an industrial age where standardization and replicability was what was required. In a modern era where creativity, problem solving and invention play a much bigger role, we need people to apply their unique strengths to tasks and problems, and we need them to feel like they don't have to pretend to be something they're not as soon as they get to work. We need more personalization of work.

In the context of leadership, traditional hierarchically driven ideas about answers only existing at the seniormost levels of the organization gives way to leaders who are able to nurture the kind of environments in which answers can emerge. As Dan says: 'The leader doesn't have to have all the answers... you have to engage people to find the answers'.[14]

In the context of change, modern transformation should be less about the idea of fear-driven change from a 'burning platform', and more about missionaries and volunteers who can really catalyse positive change. Scripted calls to arms and motivation through fear creates rigidity. And in an age when adaptability is so key, investing in people who are truly able to be their best selves allows for the kind of flexibility needed to thrive. There are two dominant systems within our brains – the fear system and the seeking system. The former is based on cortisol and the response that we have to stressful situations, the latter is based on dopamine and is more a response to exploration, curiosity and play. When organizations create fear, that fear comes from within the group and so, just at the point when we most need different thinking and ideas, our response is to want to conform. Conformity is fine when you have the right rules but as Dan says: 'there is no more important time to stimulate the right answer than when we don't know the right answer'.[15] It's all too easy for fear to dominate, and stifle the kind of creativity, exploration and energy we need to find those right answers and survive and thrive.

There are some simple hacks that Dan talks about as ways to encourage people to bring their whole selves to work including changing the onboarding process. He gives the example of some research they did with Wipro where enabling new employees to describe examples of when they've done their very best work made them 57 per cent less likely to quit, and also resulted in customers becoming 11 per cent happier. Greater engagement came from employees simply feeling that other people at work knew who they really were.

But this is really about the environment that we enable as leaders and the type of leadership that allows for more personalized approaches. It's impossible for change to happen if we don't bring our staff on the journey with us. It's impossible to bring our staff on the journey if they're not engaged in their work and the direction that we're taking. Transformation cannot happen without it. It's time that we paid far greater attention to how we can truly change those Gallup figures. The future of your business depends on it.

Valuing curiosity in business

Curiosity is one of those qualities in business that most of us recognize as having value, yet few businesses actually do anything to recognize or support. Many organizations are in fact very efficient curiosity-killers, developing policies and ways of working that actively squash any inclination by their staff to explore. No one is given any time to dedicate to it; few have serious strategies in place to support it; the prioritization of the business acts against it. Author John Hagel has described how curiosity fundamentally conflicts with the scalable efficiency model that characterizes many large organizations yet will be key in enabling the shift towards scalable learning that I discussed earlier in the book.[16]

Research conducted by behavioural scientist and Harvard Business School Professor Francesca Gino showed that out of 3,000 employees surveyed from a wide range of industries, only 24 per cent reported feeling curious in their jobs on a regular basis.[17] Moreover, 70 per cent of respondents said that they face barriers to asking more questions at work.

And yet there is a solid business case for the value of curiosity. Francesca Gino's research has also shown that greater curiosity results in fewer decision-making errors (we're more likely to think deeper about decisions and be less susceptible to confirmation bias or stereotyping) and more innovative approaches. Other research by her has indicated that when evaluating staff, natural curiosity in employees was associated by bosses with better job performance, and that curiosity helped people to be less defensive, to increase open communication and empathy, reduce group conflict and improve team performance. Work by Spencer Harrison, Associate Professor of Organizational Behaviour at INSEAD, has demonstrated that curiosity boosts creativity, even in relatively structured roles such as those in a call centre.[18] In Francesco Gino's 3,000 person survey 92 per cent of respondents regarded curiosity as a catalyst for motivation, job satisfaction, high performance and innovation.

Yet it's clear that the attitudes of leaders and employees often diverge. A large study by Spencer Harrison in collaboration with SurveyMonkey, which surveyed more than 23,000 people (including 16,000 employees and 1,500 C-Suite leaders), found that whilst 83 per cent of senior leaders said that curiosity is encouraged in their company 'a great deal' or 'a good amount', only 52 per cent of employees felt the same.[19] An amazing 81 per cent of lower-level staff believed that curiosity made no material difference in their compensation.

Clearly senior leaders in many organizations believe that they are supporting and encouraging this attribute when the reality is very different. It's easy to talk about simplistic fixes like 'be more curious' and 'give employees more time to explore', but the answer needs to be more systematic than that.

So that we might understand how to build systems and behaviour that can support and amplify curiosity we need to better understand the behaviour itself. Specifically, it is worth appreciating the different types of curiosity. Psychologist Daniel Berlyne (1954) famously distinguished between the different types of curiosity using two dimensions:[20]

- **diversive** (seeking stimulation from any source to avoid boredom, for example) versus **specific** (where we might be looking for a particular piece of information);
- **perceptual** (our liking for novel or new things) versus **epistemic** (our desire to grow our knowledge).

We might represent these dimensions (along with some examples of each type) on the matrix in Figure 7.6.

Since perceptual curiosity speaks to our desire for novelty it may well diminish the more we are exposed to the same stimuli but can help really motivate exploratory behaviour. Berlyne described epistemic curiosity as a drive aimed: 'not only at obtaining access to information-bearing stimulation, capable of dispelling uncertainties of the moment, but also at acquiring knowledge'.[21]

This is our relentless appetite to understand and grow our knowledge. On the other dimension, we have the degree of information specificity where we might have a more general desire for mental stimulation or be after a particular piece of information. Our desire for information and understanding comes from how useful both these things can be to us, whether in the

FIGURE 7.6 Dimensions of curiosity

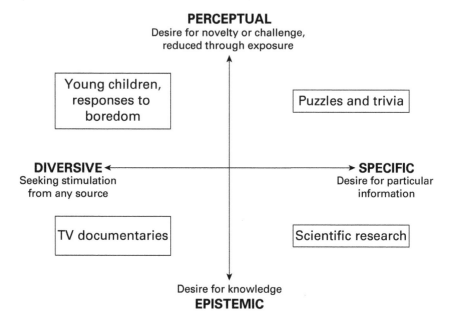

present or at some point in the future, and so curiosity is commonly thought of in terms of motivating learning. If there is a gap in our information knowledge, we therefore have a desire to fill it. US academic George Loewenstein described curiosity as: 'a cognitive induced deprivation that arises from the perception of a gap in knowledge and understanding'.[22]

The information gap (Figure 7.7) means that if we have a small amount of information about something we are motivated to find out more than if we know nothing or think we know a lot or everything. Information gaps exist between the knowledge that we currently have, and that which we want to have or think we need, effectively create a feeling of deprivation, which in turn motivates us to learn.

Information gap theory is supported by a 2009 study conducted by Caltech researchers Min Jeong Kang and Colin Camerer who used fMRI (functional magnetic resonance imaging) to identify the neural pathways of curiosity.[23] They scanned 19 people whilst they were being presented with 40 trivia questions that had been selected to provide a diverse mixture of high and low specific/epistemic curiosity, and found that people were least curious when they had no idea about the answer or if they were extremely confident in their knowledge, and most curious when they had some idea

FIGURE 7.7 The information gap

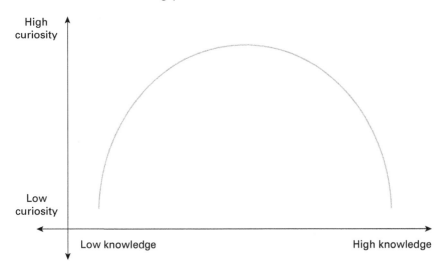

about the idea but lacked confidence. This latter situation created a signifi-cant compulsion to want to know the answer.

Curiosity is critical to intrinsically motivated learning, key to the devel-opment of capability and influential in how we make decisions. And as we discussed earlier, systematic learning at scale is essential to the agile, forward-thinking business. So, building on this understanding of how curiosity works, we can define a set of leadership behaviours that can embed this critical trait into team and organizational culture.

Let's start with the importance of questions, and how those that leaders ask of their teams and staff can be key in stimulating greater curiosity. In the rush to deliver, execute and solve problems, for example, do we ever really pause to ask whether we're actually asking the right questions? Rather than spending all our time thinking hard about answers, perhaps we should spend more time thinking harder about the question that we are actually asking. Have we framed the problem in the right way? Are we solving the right problem? It has never been truer to say that great leaders ask great questions. Kevin Kelly, in his book *The Inevitable* has described how good questions cannot be answered immediately, challenge existing answers, create new territory of thinking, are the seed of innovation: 'A good question cannot be predicted. A good question will be the sign of an educated mind. A good question is one that generates many other good questions. A good question may be the last job a machine will learn to do. A good question is what humans are for.'[24]

And how do we respond when we get asked the questions by the team? If we think we know the answer or have an opinion on the subject a leader's typical response is always to just hand the answer down and move on. But is the team member learning anything in that process? What happens if we ask a question back or challenge them to find the answer themselves? Children have been found to ask an average of 73 questions a day.[25] They have natural curiosity that peaks around the age of four. Studies have shown that children use questioning as a way to explore gaps or inconsistencies in knowledge.[26] Yet it has also been shown that parents can foster ongoing curiosity in their children by modelling a love of learning, trying new things and responding to their offspring's questions with more questions that encourage exploration. It is therefore important that leaders model the right learning behaviours, and create a culture of exploration by asking follow-up questions and build questions. Leaders shouldn't always feel that they have to answer every question brought to them in the interests of expediency. Why not ask the employees in return how they are proposing to find the answer themselves and challenge them with another relevant, follow-on question.

If the information gap tells us that people are more curious when they have partial knowledge about something, then leaders can support curiosity by encouraging the team to learn at the edges of their domains of expertise. To explore at the edges of what they know. Simple techniques such as involving people in projects that are stretching and put them outside of their core comfort zone can help this. Novel experiences, or conflicting or ambiguous information can all stimulate more curiosity so create situations where team members can learn from unusual or non-typical sources.

In her work around experience design, researcher Shih-Mei Lee has described how we develop the desire to understand and explore in ways that are sociable, embodied and playful.[27] In other words, sociability curiosity allows us to create social bonds through naturally learning from others. Embodied curiosity speaks to how we learn through our senses. And playfulness can support self-directed exploration by lowering the fear of failure. Leaders can proactively create situations that enable the opportunity for employees to learn from others through group learning and exploration sessions. They can support regular defined times in the week when team members can explore and work, play with ideas and experiment (like the Andrei Geim and Kostya Novoselov graphene example that we mentioned earlier in the book). Spencer Harrison's work has shown the value of encouraging individuals to bring their interests with them into the workplace and share them. It creates a sense of identity but also prompts others to explore more.[28] Leaders that create environments that naturally enable people to be themselves and do their best work, but also give them space to explore, can truly amplify curiosity in their teams.

As well as demonstrating the information gap and that specific epistemic curiosity is linked to seeing information and the resolving of that gap as a reward, Min Jeong Kang and Colin Camerer's study also showed that memory formation was stronger if people were curious but hadn't necessarily got the answer right the first time. Exploration and experimentation therefore enhance the potential for real learning, so leaders should encourage more of it, and support learning from both successes and failures.

And finally, one of the most effective ways of successfully embedding learning is to teach others what we know. US theoretical physicist Richard Feynman originated a technique for learning that involved teaching a concept that you want to understand more to others (he actually suggested children were the best audience), reviewing the gaps in the knowledge that you become aware of, going back to the source material, organizing and simplifying it, and perhaps even teaching it again.[29] The ability to convey a concept to other people is a good test of your knowledge of that concept. As US philosopher Mortimer Adler once said: 'The person who says he knows what he thinks but cannot express it usually does not know what he thinks.'

Curiosity is not a luxury, it is essential.

What? So what? Now what?

Imagine a scenario where every team in your business had robust decision-making processes founded in good situational awareness, a great understanding of the context around decisions, and good alignment on next actions once a decision has been taken. Now imagine a scenario where continuous learning was baked into the operating model for how every team in the business worked. This is the vision for a truly agile business. Yet developing a real culture of continuous improvement and the kind of scalable learning that was discussed in Chapter 3 requires a multi-dimensional approach to the building of organizational and team knowledge, experience and practice.

The medical profession has long understood the value of more involved and multi-faceted learning. Trainee surgeons are often taught their craft using a 'See One, Do One, Teach One' methodology (originated by American Surgeon William Stewart Halsted[30]) which involves learning first by observation, and watching a more experienced practitioner perform the procedure. The trainees then undertake the procedure themselves whilst being supervised and are then expected to teach it to another trainee. Combining multiple forms of observation with practising the procedure combines visual and experiential learning. Teaching the procedure serves to further cement a deeper level of understanding. The Nobel Prize-winning physicist Richard Feynman famously developed a process for intensifying learning (the Feynman Technique) by asking practitioners to pretend that they were explaining a concept to a young student that had not come across it before. The ability to simplify and articulate the concept in a way that enables it to be successfully taught can only come from having a deep understanding of the topic. So teaching something well means that you really know it.

This multi-dimensionality is also reflected in the well-established 70/20/10 learning and development model which posits that 70 per cent of development comes from on-the-job experiences (solving problems, completing tasks, innovating, overcoming challenges, reflecting), 20 per cent from feedback and interaction (coaching, learning from networks and conversation), and 10 per cent from formal training interventions and reading (courses, e-learning workshops).[31]

Rapid learning through data and feedback loops is critical in agile organizations and teams, but so is learning through experience and practice. Learning consultant Charles Jennings has made the point that the proportions in the 70/20/10 model may change in different situations and contexts, but also that learning is likely to be most effective when it is closer to the point of use, meaning that learning should be integrated into the flow of work.[32] By far the greatest proportion of learning in the 70/20/10 model comes from active participation, challenging experiences and opportunities to practice. This means setting expectations for agile teams around continuous learning, scaling this expectation outside of innovation and project teams to run right across the organization, and going beyond training programmes and formal interventions.

As Jennings notes, one of the best ways to augment this kind of experiential learning is to complement it with conversations and time for reflection.[33] In their paper on reflective practice Professor Gary Rolfe and colleagues have expounded the value of experiential knowledge alongside more evidence-based decision-making and learning.[34] Their framework for reflection (originally developed for nursing education) helps teams to understand problems, evaluate a shared experience, and determine solutions or ways to improve. It involves asking and reflecting on three questions:

- **What?** This helps the team to develop a common understanding of the event or the challenge.
- **So What?** Reflecting on this helps a team to comprehend implications, consequences, contexts, potential routes or options.
- **Now What?** This aligns the team around a course of action, next steps, a positive direction or a solution.

The simplicity of this model belies its power in embedding an ongoing cycle of reflection into working practice in a way that can really amplify experiential and on-the-job learning

In the modern business environment, competitive advantage is inseparable from the organization's ability to rapidly acquire and apply knowledge, and to do it at scale. Learning should be constant, and it should be integrated. Designing multi-dimensionality into company-wide learning is the only way to truly bake continuous improvement into the organizational DNA.

The relevance paradox

In the modern business environment, it is surely more valuable than ever to encourage and look for inputs from as broad a range of sources as possible. It's very easy to get stuck in a focus that seeks answers and examples from contexts that are very close to the ones we know – solutions or best practice from inside our own sector or industry, for example. Yet there is huge value in applying a bit more imagination – looking for solutions that may seem unrelated or far outside of our known territory, but which have similar contexts and so can reveal truly innovative answers.

When NASA scientists were developing the first space suits, they began in the obvious way by adapting the high-altitude pressure suits that had been worn by aircraft pilots. As the space programme matured and the requirements of the suits became more sophisticated, however, NASA realized that it needed to develop something altogether more bespoke. A particular challenge was presented in the Apollo programme by the need to be able to walk on the moon. Having a fully enclosed suit whilst still enabling maximum mobility proved to be a tricky challenge. NASA engineers spent a fortune trying unsuccessfully to develop complex knee joints in the suits that would enable smooth movement whilst still being fully enclosed and structurally strong.

Eventually, in 1962 one of the companies working on this technical challenge, Garrett AiResearch, was directed by the New York Metropolitan Museum to the Tower of London. The Met had pointed out that a suit of tournament armour made for Henry VIII to use in 1520 at the Field of the Cloth of Gold had been designed specifically for foot combat rather than horseback, and so might provide the answer that they were looking for. When the Tower of London sent pictures of the suit of armour to the Garrett AiResearch and NASA teams, they saw that the joint was made from seamlessly overlapping plates of steel that left no gaps but allowed freedom of movement. The suit of armour provided the key inspiration for critical parts of the space suit that would allow Neil Armstrong to take his first steps on the moon.

One NASA engineer reportedly commented that it would have saved them a lot of time and investment had they looked at the armour earlier, but the team fell victim to a common problem – the relevance paradox. This occurs simply when individuals or groups are unaware of critical information that would help them make better decisions but in being unaware of it they don't see its relevance and so carry on in ignorance. We usually only seek advice or information that we think we need to solve a problem and fail to question whether we have as full an appreciation of that information as we should. Once again, taking the broadest inputs, applying imagination and being open to challenge is key to solving problems in an agile business well. This means opening the business up to fresh perspectives, similar contexts from other industries, and the challenge that can come from new employees who question existing entrenched practices or habits.

Democratising knowledge access

In the agile business employees are empowered not only through access to powerful tools but also access to knowledge. In economics the concepts of stock and flow describe different but interdependent types of capital or economic variables. Stock refers to a variable which is measured at a given point in time and may have accumulated in the past (examples may include savings, bank deposits, the value of assets). Flow is more dynamic and relates to variables which are measured over a period of time (examples might include income, investment, interest). They are heavily intertwined. Stocks can only be changed by flows (increased by inflows, depleted by outflows). In economics a greater quantity of stock capital will increase the flow of services, and a greater flow of money supply results in increases in the quantity of money.

In their book *The Power of Pull*, the authors John Hagel, John Seely Brown and Lang Davison describe the interdependent nature of stocks and flows of organizational knowledge. Networked organizations with externally facing, connected employees can not only rely on existing stocks of knowledge that may be held within the boundaries of the business but more easily accumulate new ones. A continuous flow of fresh perspectives into and within a business (which they describe as a 'porous enterprise') can catalyse progress and innovation.

How does access to knowledge impact organizational learning and innovation? For the answer to this question, we can look at the legacy of one of most famous and richest industrialists and philanthropists of the 19th century, Andrew Carnegie. Carnegie was a complex character who rose from being a poor Scottish Immigrant to the US to building a steel empire that he sold for almost half a billion dollars to JP Morgan. Along the way he presided over one of the most bitter labour disputes in history, the Homestead strike, but he was also a believer in the power of knowledge and philanthropy as instruments of change. Once he had acquired his fortune, he went on to give most of it away, writing in his famous 1889 essay 'The Gospel of Wealth' that 'the man who dies thus rich dies disgraced' and that 'in bestowing charity the main consideration should be to help those who help themselves'.[35] Carnegie donated $60 million to fund a network of 1,689 public libraries across the country which were open to everyone and which hugely democratized the access to knowledge in the towns and cities where a Carnegie library was built. A study by Enrico Berkes of Ohio State University and Peter Nencka of Miami University of Ohio looked at the effect that these libraries had on innovation by comparing city-level patent rates between those cities which had built a Carnegie library and those which had applied to be part of the programme but ultimately didn't start construction.[36] The study found that patenting in Carnegie library towns and cities increased by 7–11 per cent in the 20 years following the construction of the library, with innovation rates being catalysed by both 'access to scientific knowledge and opportunities to interact with follow patrons'. Figure 7.8 shows the difference in patents per year between the cities that built Carnegie libraries and those that didn't.

Democratizing access to knowledge means empowering employees to innovate and get the answers they need when they need them. Shared resources, knowledge management tools and repositories can be useful but in the age of artificial intelligence the opportunity is to use technology to

FIGURE 7.8 Patents per city-year in cities that did and did not build libraries after grants

SOURCE Berkes, Enrico and Nencka, Peter, Knowledge Access: The Effects of Carnegie Libraries on Innovation[37]

help staff find the information they need and enact solutions faster and easier. As an example, the Unilever human resources team created an AI-driven chatbot called Una which was capable of conversing with staff in 106 countries and 32 languages and which employees could use to find information relating to a wide range of benefits and support actions such as selling shares or claiming for healthcare.[38] The company has also built an online talent marketplace, powered by AI, which staff can use to create a profile of their current skills and the areas that they are looking to upskill in, and then find new projects and opportunities from around the business.[39] A 2022 paper by Mohammad Hossein Jarrahi, David Askay, Ali Eshraghi and Preston Smith which looked at the application of artificial intelligence to knowledge management defined four key potential applications:[40]

- **Knowledge creation:** including the ability to recognize unseen patterns, make predictions, discover new relationships in organizational data, and generate new declarative information (or stocks of knowledge).
- **Knowledge storage and retrieval:** this may involve classifying, analysing, organizing and harvesting explicit knowledge, perhaps from across multiple

channels of communication, and even knowledge reuse by teams. An example might be a team that is able to easily retrieve dispersed pieces of knowledge that relate to a particular challenge.

- **Knowledge sharing:** including creating a comprehensive view of knowledge sources and inefficiencies in the flow of information, connecting systems of coordination across organizational silos, and connecting people working on the same issues.

- **Knowledge application:** examples here may include preparing relevant knowledge sources, enabling more intuitive interaction with sources (for example through voice-based assistants), and enabling a more democratized approach to the access of knowledge removed from the kinds of internal politics which may hamper good information flow.

The great promise of AI when applied internally within the organization is not only that it will vastly improve the efficiency of knowledge access but also that it will enable a new level of automation which can free up employee time to focus on higher value-adding work. Shai Wininger, Co-founder, President and COO of disruptive insurance startup Lemonade Insurance (mentioned in Chapter 5) has written about his vision for an 'autonomous organization' in which AI is relied upon to take care of routine and repetitive tasks but also increasingly complex assignments.[41] This shift, says Wininger, will fundamentally change organizational governance, hierarchy and structures. As an example, Lemonade's internal automation brain Cooper has been applied to a wide variety of automation tasks including preparing testing environments, automating the engineering workflow, running thousands of tests and actioning improvements, and assigning specific tasks. This has then been extended even wider to encompass answering knowledge-based questions, tracking KPIs, setting up IT, supporting the onboarding process and improving customer acquisition, and even creating modular legal documents. Cooper also helps Lemonade staff to make smarter decisions through data analysis, alerts, and notifications, for example by analysing data drawn from NASA satellite imagery to create an early warning system for catastrophic events such as fires and storms around the world.[42] Cooper also connects useful data points to identify patterns that may be useful to inform decision-making. In an interview with Dave Lee, Lemonade CEO Daniel Schreiber describes the example of the customer that called up customer service to confirm that he could be covered for his scuba equipment being stolen from his car.[43] Having confirmed that this would be covered, two weeks after the call the claims department received a claim for stolen scuba gear from the same customer. Cooper was able to make the connection in the internal data so raise a warning flag for the claims team.

Yet the answer is not only about technology. Encouraging staff to build informal networks with other staff and with useful external sources of inspiration and perspective can help build connections to knowledge and stimulus.

Communities of practice

In the 70/20/10 blended learning model that was mentioned in the previous section, communities of practice (CoP) can play a critical role in enabling learning through networks, conversation and interaction (the 20 per cent). The concept was defined originally by Etienne and Beverly Wenger-Trayner as 'groups of people who share a concern or a passion for something they do and learn how to do it better as they interact regularly'.[44] Communities of practice can come together around specific objectives, shared interests, problems or domains of knowledge with a purpose to progress learning, improvements or solutions. In a post-pandemic world, the growth in virtual tools and remote working has catalysed the potential for geographically disparate groups of people to come together with a common purpose in mind.

Such informal networks which operate outside of formal hierarchies can be hugely valuable in enabling the level of knowledge sharing, organizational learning and high performance which is required for true business agility. There are some specific benefits which communities of practice bring which go beyond more formal structures of information sources and sharing. Molly Wasko and Samer Faraj from the Department of Decision and Information Technologies at the University of Maryland have studied how online communities share information and defined three distinct types of knowledge: knowledge as object (much like the 'stocks' of knowledge mentioned earlier this can be stored, reused, transferred), knowledge that is embedded within individuals, and knowledge that is embedded within a community. Communities of practice can be hugely valuable in enabling a free flow of knowledge held by individuals and within communities, or what we might call the tacit knowledge that is not explicitly codified but instead implicitly understood and learned through experience, which can in turn support deeper and wider learning, and better problem solving. They can help 'raise the floor' by ensuring a good baseline of expertise, catalyse the learning for new staff, and better coordinate effort or reduce duplication. Yet they can also 'raise the ceiling' by enhancing domain expertise, enable the exploration of new knowledge territories, and the development and harvesting of new ideas.[45] With their Eureka project, Xerox created one of the early examples of a deliberately formed community of practice when they brought together 14,000 support centre staff and service technicians to share helpful information around fixing office equipment. The community grew out of the informal conversations that reps would have over working breakfasts and lunches but went on to save the company an estimated $100 million.[46]

As agile scales across a business, communities of practice can create the informal connections which enable the efficient sharing of learned experience, domain expertise and ideas. Communities can be established around specific disciplines to bring together dispersed functional expertise, or areas of business focus to support cross-disciplinary objectives, or even specific challenge areas to support problem solving and progress.

CASE STUDY
Arup shared learning at scale

Engineering business Arup has around 16,000 people working across 140 countries and a huge wealth of knowledge embedded in that workforce. Seeking to unlock access to conversation and community-based learning the company created a whole series of global skills networks for a wide variety of disciplines and knowledge domains. Forty-five skills networks have been established across a range of disciplines including transport planning, mechanical engineering, acoustics and architecture.[47] Each network has a leader who determines what skills development is required in that specific discipline to ensure that staff are at the cutting edge of expertise on the topic, and an online forum where members can post questions and get input and answers from other experts.

As an example, Andrew Trickett, Associate Global Rail Knowledge and Information Manager, describes how Arup's rail business has a dedicated skills community comprising 1,200 members across all five Arup regions that enables staff to tap into the collective global knowledge bank around that topic.[48] A culture of never leaving a question unanswered has been developed to ensure timely responses and that the forum remains useful for its members, and discussions around lessons learned or different experiences have led to the origination of new ideas. Both Arup and the members see the community as 'a place where new concepts or innovative ideas can be discussed in a safe, supportive, and sustaining space.'

Arup's skills networks have been long established. As an example of their utility, when Arup were asked to build the equestrian centre for the 2008 Beijing Olympics, they soon realized that they had a significant challenge in understanding how much waste all the highly strung horses that had arrived on flights from all over the world would produce. No engineer that was working on the project had had to solve a problem like this before. A traditional approach in a different company may have involved spending countless hours speaking to vets and generating estimates from a whole series of complex spreadsheets. Instead, the engineers working on the equestrian centre posted their challenge up onto a relevant Arup skills network and within hours had had a response from another Arup employee from halfway around the world who had happened to design the Jockey Club building in New York. The engineers were able to get an informed answer to their question and save themselves many hours of research.

Communities of practice will likely develop through several stages of maturity but can be supported by establishing a regular frequency and rhythm to updates and gatherings, finding ways to routinely celebrate the benefit that comes from community sharing or initiatives, and encouraging active engagement whilst recognizing that there will likely be varying levels of participation.[49]

Agile practitioner Emily Webber has developed a useful maturity model for CoPs that defines four key stages:[50]

- **Potential:** At the earliest stage the potential for a CoP to add value and be formed is identified. There needs to be a clear reason behind the creation of the community, a plan for who may join, and a few initial members that are enthusiastic enough to make the time to work on establishing it.

- **Forming:** When forming the CoP it's important to establish the right foundation and conditions for success, including having a clear purpose for the community which members can articulate, criteria for membership, regular gatherings, a core group of enthusiastic organizers, and support from the wider organization. A supportive network can be created by generating a safe space for members to share contributions and having agreed values and ways of communicating. Learning and knowledge sharing can be facilitated through members connecting with people they haven't had the chance to before, adopting common approaches and standards, and agreeing the use of specific tools.

- **Maturing:** As the community matures, leadership is likely shared amongst a wider group of members, community interaction becomes more varied and the working of the community is adapted and improved. External knowledge is now regularly brought into the group and members actively seek out help and advice from other members. The community and its outputs become demonstrable and visible to the rest of the organization, and it plays an increasingly vital role in the professional development of its members.

- **Self-sustaining:** The ultimate goal is to ensure that the community has a momentum which is not reliant on a few members, that it becomes a recognized part of members' routines, has an explicit role in building capability, and that people outside of the community advocate for it.

FIGURE 7.9 The Tacit Community of Practice maturity model

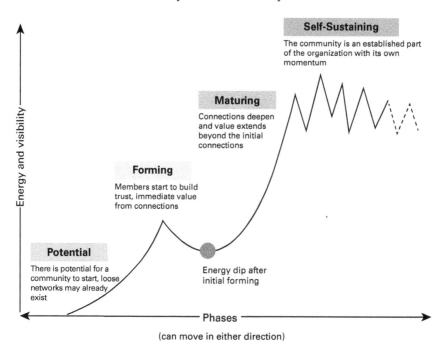

SOURCE Tacit's Community of Practice Maturity Model[51]

Communities of practice can play a critical role in establishing the kind of informal networks that can catalyse knowledge sharing, learning, capability building, innovation and agility.

Building momentum through progress

Sprint working can be a powerful driver of both rapid organizational learning and strategic adaptability but done right it can not only create new value and be applied in the creation of new products and services but can also support far wider organizational change and be used to find a way through key business challenges, and reorient the business towards heightened levels of experimentation. As we've discussed earlier, learning and continuous improvement are embedded in the fabric of this working methodology, not least in the regular retrospectives that are conducted at the end of each sprint. Flexibility and adaptation are too, in the regular reprioritization of the backlog of jobs to be done. As continuous learning generates improved ways of getting stuff done and achieving key goals, sprint working can support growing organizational momentum towards an overarching vision or objective.

But there is something else about sprint working, another way in which it can contribute to building momentum for change, that is less often discussed – it's role as an inclusive, motivating, energy-generating way of working. There are a number of reasons for this but a particularly powerful one is that this way of working can make the value that the team is delivering very visible and very tangible and making progress tangible is a key principle of building momentum for organizational agility and change.

Teresa Amabile, Professor in the Entrepreneurial Management Unit at Harvard Business School, has described this as the 'progress principle'.[52] At the heart of this concept is a simple, but very compelling idea – the power of progress: 'Of all the things that can boost emotions, motivation, and perceptions during a workday, the single most important is making progress in meaningful work. And the more frequently people experience that sense of progress, the more likely they are to be creatively productive in the long run.'[53]

Amabile's extensive workplace research based on thousands of daily surveys has shown that above more visible and extrinsic rewards and incentives, a key driver of creative and productive performance is the quality of what she calls a person's 'inner work life', or that mix of emotions, motivations and perceptions experienced over the course of a work day: 'how happy workers feel; how motivated they are by an intrinsic interest in the work; how positively they view their organization, their management, their team, their work, and themselves.'[54]

A positive inner work life, characterized by these qualities, is fundamental in enabling higher levels of achievement, commitment and even collaboration. When the researchers looked at the triggers that shaped how positive this inner work life was on any given day, it was meaningful progress (however large or small) made by the individual or team that was the key determinant. Setbacks against progress created a negative inner work life. Surrounding this were 'catalysts' (those actions that directly support work) and 'nourishers' (including encouragement, respect or recognition) that contributed towards positive emotions. 'Inhibitors' (things that negate progress) and 'toxins' (things that discourage or undermine) had the opposite effect.

This makes intuitive sense, and yet so much in the workplace seems designed to inhibit or discourage. Waterfall processes can often involve lengthy time periods where work is done but with limited visible signs of value (particularly value for the end-users) being generated. It is often characterized by large project teams that become unwieldy and difficult to move forwards at pace. How often have we stepped away from a project and returned later only to find that nothing has really moved on from where we left it? Sprint working is not a panacea, but the point about it is that it is designed around tangible, visible progress. Releasing early and often. Tracking velocity against goals. Reprioritizing based on learning.

At the simplest level, workflow visualization tools such as Kanban boards are an example of making work velocity and progress visible. Designed to optimize the flow of a team's work, they enable everyone in the team to immediately see what work is underway, and also to see progress being made in value and outputs as elements of the backlog move across to the right (Figure 7.10).

It's easy to dismiss these tools as tactics that belong in technology or product teams but there are important principles at work here. It is key that we find better ways for everyone in the business to see the progress that they, the team, and the organization are making. It's easy when we spend our days in meetings and e-mail to lose sight of the forward trajectory that we're actually on. It's very demotivating to get to the end of a busy week and feel as though we've not actually accomplished much at all. This requires leadership to find more tangible ways of communicating progress towards well-understood goals, but also tools to be made available to support the visibility of team progress.

FIGURE 7.10 Example Kanban board

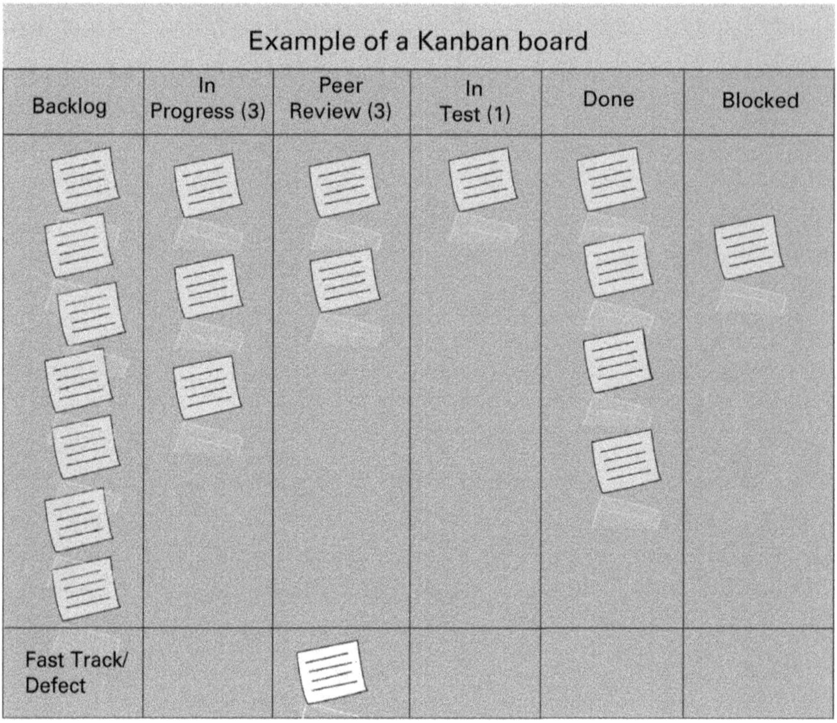

Backlog	In Progress (3)	Peer Review (3)	In Test (1)	Done	Blocked
Example of a Kanban board					

SOURCE Created by Dr Ian Mitchell and available under Creative Commons Attribution-ShareAlike 2.5 Generic (CC BY-SA 2.5) https://commons.wikimedia.org/w/index.php?curid=20245783

Building on this and as I discussed earlier, it is important for leaders to find more tangible ways of connecting staff to the impact that they are making. Author and academic Adam Grant conducted a well-known study focused on just this point.[55] He studied a group of telemarketing fundraisers who were raising money to provide student scholarships. The annual turnover rate in the call centre where the fundraisers worked was 400 per cent.

Grant brought in a student who had been a recipient of one of the scholarships to talk to the workers about how much the scholarship had changed his life and how grateful he was for the work that the fundraisers did. After that meeting the average amount of money that the call centre workers raised rose by 142 per cent and the average number of minutes that they spent on the phone went up by 171 per cent. In a similar vein, when Grant positioned a picture of the patient alongside an X-ray for radiologists, diagnostic accuracy went up by 43 per cent.

The principle at play here is the power of connecting people with the impact of the work that they are doing. As Grant says: 'Very often we do work that matters to some group of people, but we're really left disconnected from knowing what is the real consequence.'[56]

Connecting staff with impact increases not only motivation but also engagement and resilience, and so it remains an undervalued yet powerful tool for leaders. Simple ways to deliver this include getting more staff in front of customers, enabling employees to be part of customer feedback processes, connecting work to the impact on progress towards goals, and making the results of customer/supplier/partner impact or feedback far more visible. We have to find better ways to make progress more tangible and to connect employees to the consequences of the work that they are doing. Such a positive sense of progress can be a powerful catalyst to generating momentum.

Ownership and when to let go

In an agile business situational leadership is important. Understanding when a leader needs to step in more directly and set the pace, when a leader needs to support and coach a team to find the solutions, and when a leader needs to let go to enable a competent team to move fast can be the difference between agility and rigidity, and success and failure.

This requires leaders to have greater self-awareness of their own leadership style to ensure that one approach is not overly dominant and that their leadership style can be adapted as necessary. It also requires leaders to have good situational awareness to recognize when new approaches are needed and to relate different leadership styles appropriately to what is needed in that moment in time. A high level of self-awareness combined with a low level of situational awareness can mean that leaders are adaptable in their style but they don't know which style is needed at specific times. Conversely a high level of contextual or situational awareness combined with a low level of self-awareness can mean that leaders understand what needs to happen but lack the ability to adapt their leadership style as required to ensure the best outcomes.

It is this combination of self-awareness and situational awareness that enables true agility in leading teams to find the best solutions. It can be tempting to apply more directive leadership when there is significant pressure within a situation such as when a big deadline is approaching, yet this is not always the optimal approach. More directive styles of leadership can

FIGURE 7.11 Leadership self-awareness and situational awareness

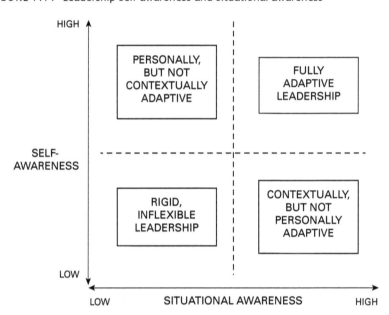

make it harder for team members to take ownership of resolving problems. When teams or team members are more mature, or when their levels of competency and confidence are high, it can make more sense to allow the team more freedom and autonomy in decision-making. This combination of confidence and competence can provide a good guide for helping leaders to understand how to apply different styles of leadership to enable teams to get the best outcomes.

Leadership coach and consultant Alice Chapman frames how this combination can lead to not only more effective leadership but also a more consistent approach to applying different leadership styles at the appropriate times. Teams that are high in confidence but low in competence are likely to need support to improve capability or maturity (for example through training). Teams that are high in competence but low in confidence, however, need a leader who can coach and enable in ways that build assurance and morale.

High levels of both confidence and competence in a team can mean that it is better for a leader to get out of the way and allow a greater degree of autonomy and empowerment in the team to make decisions. This will help the team to move faster but also to feel more engaged and motivated.

Confidence and competence are of course related. The more competent a team are the more confident they feel in tackling challenging situations. Yet these attributes can come from a variety of different sources including the

FIGURE 7.12 Situational leadership

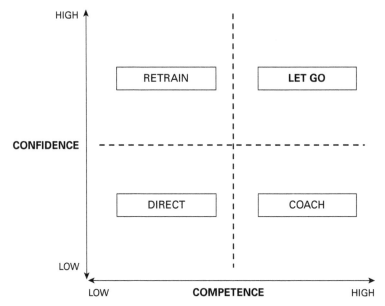

SOURCE Alice Chapman[57]

knowledge levels held by the team around a particular context or domain, previous experiences that the team have had in solving similar problems, team personalities, the confidence that senior leaders have and demonstrate that they have in the team.

What is often called the Dunning-Kruger Effect is a cognitive bias which can lead to people with a relatively limited level of expertise overestimating their knowledge or ability in a certain domain. Knowing a little about a topic can result in people believing that they know more than they actually do, resulting in them being overly confident in making decisions in that area relative to their actual level of knowledge. Often, the more we explore a topic (particularly complex subjects) the more we realize how little we actually know about it, and so confidence can actually decline as we gain knowledge. It is only when we regard ourselves as genuine experts in a topic that our confidence peaks again.

The Dunning-Kruger Effect can also mean that experts in a topic can make assumptions about how simple tasks are for everyone and consequently underestimate the ability that people have to complete those tasks.

Leaders that flip between different leadership styles unpredictably but also in ways that lack any context or reasoning risk creating disquiet and

FIGURE 7.13 The Dunning-Kruger Effect

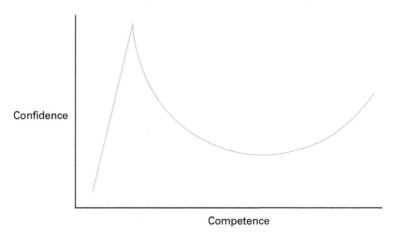

agitation in their teams. However, leaders that apply good self and situational awareness to adapting their leadership style to different contexts can be far more effective at getting the best out of the teams that they lead.

A team's willingness to take ownership can also support greater autonomy and moving fast since it encourages more pro-active approaches and the ability to take responsibility for actions and outcomes. Ownership may relate not only to tasks and activities, but also to knowledge building and learning. Since an agile environment is characterized by continuous learning, taking responsibility for building knowledge, finding the answers and removing barriers is essential. Greater ownership in a team can not only lead to better problem solving but also to higher levels of resilience and more creative solutions to complex problems.

Building on Alice Chapman's combination of confidence and competence, we can also understand how leaders can create an environment in which ownership can thrive. Agile practitioner Peter Koning (in his book *Agile Leadership Toolkit: Learning to thrive with self-managing teams*[58]) defines a useful model for team ownership which balances the freedom or autonomy that the team have in making decisions with the maturity and experience that they have on achieving goals.

Situations where a team has low levels of maturity or experience but in which they are also given a large degree of flexibility and autonomy can result in chaos. Whereas a team can feel trapped or restricted when they are mature and competent but are not given the freedom to make decisions. The

FIGURE 7.14 Freedom and maturity ownership model

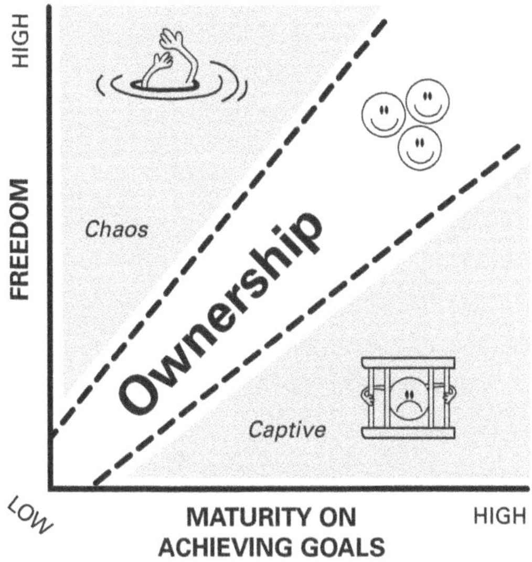

SOURCE Peter Koning

sweet spot for ownership sits between these two extremes. People are more likely to take ownership of their actions and of finding solutions when they are empowered with both the knowledge and understanding that they require to make good decisions and the autonomy to actually make them. Any upset in this balance will require the intervention of leaders to rectify it, but greater ownership should go hand-in-hand with the willingness of leaders to let go when the balance is right.

Getting things done in large organizations

It is amazing in large organizations, in spite of all the talent, will and intelligence surrounding us, how difficult it can be to get (new) initiatives off the ground. Sometimes it almost feels as though the company is set up to thwart people who want to create something new and different.

In 1944 the predecessor to the CIA, the Office of Strategic Services (OSS) created a 32-page *Simple Sabotage Field Manual* for use by its agents and citizen-saboteurs in the Second World War.[59] Alongside recommendations around physical interventions, the manual included a series of suggestions for more indirect but no less damaging sabotage through means such as poor decision-making in organizations and obstructing progress through overburdensome bureaucracy. This list of sabotage tactics (paraphrased here) that might be deployed in meetings and elsewhere, unfortunately reads like a list of what can so easily happen every day in large organizations:

- Insist on doing everything through 'channels'.
- Make 'speeches'. Talk as frequently as possible and at great length. Illustrate your 'points' by long anecdotes and accounts of personal experiences.
- When possible, refer all matters to committees, for 'further study and consideration'. Attempt to make the committees as large as possible – never fewer than five.
- Bring up irrelevant issues as frequently as possible.
- Haggle over precise workings of communications, minutes or resolutions.
- Refer back to matters decided upon at the last meeting and attempt to reopen the question of the advisability of that decision.
- Advocate 'caution'. Be 'reasonable' and urge your fellow conferees to be 'reasonable' and avoid haste, which might result in embarrassments or difficulties later on.
- Be worried about the propriety of any decision – raise the question of whether such action as is contemplated lies within the jurisdiction of the group or whether it might conflict with the policy of some higher echelon.[60]

In contrast, Thomas Kalil, who was Deputy Director for Policy in the White House Office of Science and Technology Policy during the Obama administration, wrote an excellent paper on getting things done in large organizations.[61] He emphasized strategies including having an agenda rather than reacting to the agenda of others, making it easy for people to help you, working from the top-down and bottom-up, finding and recruiting allies, asking interesting questions to help solicit ideas or help, using standing meetings effectively, and thinking of the end at the beginning to ensure good outcomes. To help onboard new members of the team, he created a 'Team Kalil whiteboard', which carried a succinct list of principles that condenses these broader strategies into a punchy and useful checklist.

The list also included points relating to ownership:

- Steer; don't row.
- Have an opinion.
- If you had 15 minutes to pitch POTUS, what is on your list and are you working on it?
- Strong relationships are built on trust, mutual understanding and reciprocity.

It included missives focused on action and productivity:

- Hours you contribute/hours overall.
- Entrepreneur = someone not limited by the resources directly under his or her control.
- Find your doers.
- Better to light a single candle than cry out in the darkness.
- Don't be a bottleneck.

And missives relating to direction, organization and collaboration:

- Write it down. Make it happen.
- Schedule is your friend.
- Think of the end at the beginning.
- If you want people to do something, make it easy.
- You can get more done if you don't care who gets the credit.[62]

There are some clear themes from this simple checklist that speak well to overcoming some of the common obstacles to getting things done in complex environments: the importance of ownership; starting small and making progress however limited; being resilient; the power of influence; direction and governance.

CASE STUDY
ANZ Bank

ANZ Bank is a great example of combining the need to change leadership mindset with a new, scaled approach to agile structures. Motivated by a need to increase the speed with which it creates measurable customer value, to break down silos and inefficient functional hand-offs, and a desire to reinvent itself as a great place to work and be competitive in the battle for talent, ANZ Bank's agile transformation has focused on two key strands of work, which the organization has called New Ways of Leading (NWOL) and New Ways of Working (NWOW).[63] The former has focused on five key leadership behaviours:

- **Be curious** – curiosity is seen as a fundamentally powerful tool in the information era.
- **Create shared clarity** – each team member should be able to explain simply the collective purpose of the team.
- **Empower people** – working through others as well as yourself.
- **Connect with empathy** – human bonding and empathy as a motivator to do better work.
- **Grow people selflessly** – sharing power and developing people to do their best work.

Alongside new leadership behaviours ANZ implemented a programme to transform ways of working. The business asked 9,000 people, from the senior leadership team down, to reapply for their jobs, as a signal that the business was serious about change but also a chance to deliberately select people that reflected the new behaviours for a new agile organization. The business made significant cuts to staffing as part of the transformation but to support transparency in the process it ran the programme from a glass room called 'the fishbowl', which anyone could enter and look at what was happening, and ran twice weekly pizza sessions with 70 people at a time to give updates and answer questions. Not only does ANZ now have more than 9,000 people working in agile teams but, according to General Manager of Omnichannel Christian Venter, is accomplishing the same amount of work with 20 to 30 per cent less people. Small, multidisciplinary teams or Squads are tightly focused on specific customer objectives, and 20 to 30 Squads are grouped together into Tribes, which are focused on proposition areas. Some specific functions, such as compliance, for example, had a dedicated person for each Tribe rather than one in every Squad.

The transformation has not come without difficulties and new emergent challenges. New ways of working soon began to clash with old ways of funding projects, for example. Traditional methods of budgeting, which worked on annual cycles and/or a project basis, struggled to absorb the cost of change needed with iterative, agile working.

The UK Government faced a similar challenge in its transformation. Traditional approaches to project funding involve writing a business case and fixing the time period for investment.[64] This kind of upfront specification very quickly creates problems when working iteratively on complicated and potentially unpredictable development projects resulting in friction between the teams doing the work and those that are agreeing the budgets, which simply slows everything down. Linear funding models assume nothing or little will change and so ensure that the cost of adaptation is high.

In addition, the costs in establishing a new team or stepping down an existing one is rarely taken into account in funding proposals. Difficulties in adapting to changing circumstances mean that senior stakeholders and approvals boards end up making decisions about even relatively minor changes to funding or development. Giving the teams that are doing the work greater autonomy to make product or development decisions keeps those decisions with the people who are closest to the work (and often the customer), but also frees-up senior time to focus on broader strategic aspects and governance.

Taking approaches that are more aligned to the innovation accounting approach from Lean Startup that I mentioned earlier in the book allows for greater flexibility and adaptability and can effectively enable investment in teams and progress along a pipeline of work rather than inflexible investment in individual projects.

Agile meetings

As well as challenging the defaults around operating norms such as meetings, we can actively work to make gatherings shorter and smarter to not only create space and move quicker but also to improve the working environment (and perhaps protect the sanity of our employees whilst we're at it).

Meetings are a necessary tool to help any business run effectively, but they can also be a demotivating time suck. When salary data business Salary.com surveyed more than 3,200 people in 2012, the biggest waste of time in the workplace was perceived to be too many meetings (this was named by 47 per cent of respondents and was followed by dealing with office politics, which was cited by 43 per cent).[65]

A 2018 study of 19 million meetings conducted by scheduling service Doodle (which also involved 6,500 employee interviews) found that the most irritating waste of time, identified by 89 per cent of participants, was ineffective or poorly organized meetings.[66] More than two-thirds of those surveyed said that they lost time every week due to unnecessary or cancelled meetings. The cost of those poorly organized meetings was estimated to be almost US $400 billion in the United States alone.

Dr Steven Rogelberg, Professor at the University of North Carolina (and the author of *The Surprising Science of Meetings: How you can lead your team to peak performance*[67]), has conducted extensive research into meetings over 15 years and thousands of employees in different companies, demonstrating the significant upside of improving how meetings are run both for the business and the employee. His research has shown, for example, that meetings are better if they are kept small and not subject to 'meeting bloat'. Having people attend who do not contribute or are unnecessary observers is counterproductive. A 2010 Bain & Company study, for example, showed that for each additional person over seven members in a decision-making group, decision effectiveness is reduced by approximately 10 per cent. The rule is simple – no hangers on.

Typically, says Rogelberg, the leader of the meeting is the one who ends up leaving it happiest, so he suggests rotating meeting leads as a way to maintain and improve effectiveness over time, and to challenge the 'manager's schedule' of hour-long blocks of meeting time. He suggests reducing an hour to a nominal length like 45 minutes as a way to introduce a slight urgency to the meeting to get decisions made.

Perhaps an even more powerful way to challenge the defaults is to adopt Percolate's 'meetings should be 15 minutes by default' rule that we discussed earlier in the book as a way to really break long-established habits. More regular short 'huddles', like a daily standup that an agile team might run, can often achieve as much as an hour-long status update meeting. A study recounted in the *Journal of Applied Psychology* in 1999 found that sit-down meetings last 35 per cent longer than those held standing up, with no gains in effectiveness.[68]

Rogelberg stresses the benefits of having clear outputs required of the gathering, securing agenda inputs in advance and assigning ownership, and doing a pre-mortem to identify anything that might get in the way of good outcomes. It is notable just how many meetings spend disproportionate amounts of time on trivial items. Cyril Northcote Parkinson, who originated the law about work expanding to fill the time assigned for its completion, also created the 'Law of Triviality': 'The time spent on any item of the agenda will be in inverse proportion to the sum (of money) involved.'

Parkinson's Law of Triviality can be explained by what has been termed the 'bike-shed effect' or 'bikeshedding' – the tendency for significant amounts of time to be wasted in corporate meetings by focusing on trivial issues that attendees know more about. Parkinson gives the fictional example of a committee charged with approving plans for a nuclear power plant spending the majority of their time discussing easier-to-grasp issues such as the materials to use for the staff bike shed. Since they know much less about nuclear power stations they talk about it briefly and then just approve the recommendation that has been put in front of them.

We've all been in meetings where too much time is spent discussing trivial issues that people may know more about at the expense of time spent on more complex but important subjects. The term 'bikeshedding' is used most notably amongst the software engineering community but it describes a widespread phenomenon. As strategist Russell Davies has said: 'The difference is that software people have identified and named the pattern. That naming is an organizational hack that allows them to break out of it and get on with something more useful.'[69]

Momentum for change (3): data and decision-making

Efficacious agile transformation depends heavily on adaptive strategy and resourcing. It's no good moving fast if we're moving fast in the wrong direction, so continual reappraisal is needed to achieve the vision that has been set. A critical element in effective adaptation is making smarter decisions through data and avoiding the common pitfalls and bias that can misdirect us.

Using adaptive strategy and resourcing to keep fast and focused

Earlier in this part of the book I discussed the value of sprint working in embedding learning (notably through regular review and retrospective) and adaptation (through reprioritizing of the backlog and sprint planning) into the fabric of how the organization is working. This can only have real value at an organizational level rather than just a team level if learning and prioritization is fed back up and taken into account to evolve wider product and business strategy. Just as a team uses a reprioritized backlog to reflect latest contexts, so the organization should use feedback loops to be more responsive to shifting dynamics. To do this well we need to get good at structuring, organizing, interpreting and actioning what data can tell us, but also be aware of some of the common biases that can easily skew interpretation and recognize the value of human-centred approaches such as getting in front of actual customers, the value of empathy, intuition and creativity. The point is that moving fast can build momentum only if we build-in regular adaptation to evolve the strategy of *how* we are achieving our vision.

This response to shifting dynamics may be adaptive strategy but in order to truly capitalize on adaptive opportunity the agile business needs to manage resourcing in more fluid ways. It may, for example, need to spin up new small, multidisciplinary team/s to focus quickly on an emerging opportunity or explore a new strategic challenge. Operating at larger scale in small teams or Squads makes it easier to swap team members in and out of teams as required, but also to explore a new or challenging area at speed. Remember, small teams can drive big change, and rather than respond to perceived opportunity by immediately generating a large new business initiative there is the opportunity for a small agile team to work more quickly to begin creating some answers. In order to do this well we need to be prepared to allocate talent right across the explore, execute, extend and exploit spectrum.

Being data-driven AND data-informed

Data are, of course, of fundamental and existential value to businesses in the modern era. And yet so many organizations still seem to struggle to derive exceptional value from the copious data that they already have. Many futurists, conference speakers and commentators before now have used the phrase 'data are the new oil' as a way to express the heightened worth of data yet this suggests that data are something simply to mine and exploit in mechanical ways. Far better to acknowledge how we can not only be more data-driven in our decision-making but also *data-informed*.

As something of an expert in extracting value from data Clive Humby, the founder of customer science business Dunnhumby, has spoken of how data are like oil in the sense that their true value is only realized when we refine the data, and change them into valuable entities that can drive profitable activity.[70] If we fail to do this well, data can lead to wasteful or damaging courses of action or be subject to misreading through bias or inexperience. In other words, data may well be the new oil, but in the sense that they are toxic unless you refine them.

The Data, Information, Knowledge, Wisdom (or DIKW) pyramid, long part of the language of information science, provides a useful strategic approach to not only understanding a hierarchy of value from data, but also the fundamental underlying capabilities that a truly agile business needs in order to thrive in a data-rich world (Figure 7.15).

FIGURE 7.15 The DIKW pyramid

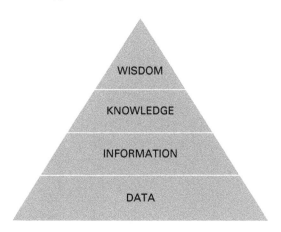

SOURCE Created by Longlivetheux and available under Creative Commons Attribution-ShareAlike 4.0
International (CC BY-SA 4.0) https://commons.wikimedia.org/w/index.php?curid=37705247

At the bottom of the pyramid, raw data are like the raw material – they have little or no value until we do something with them. Jennifer Rowley of Bangor Business School, in her 2007 study of DIKW definitions given in a wide range of textbooks, has characterized data as being: 'discrete, objective facts or observations, which are unorganized and unprocessed and therefore have no meaning or value because of lack of context and interpretation.'[71]

Still, it remains critical here to be collecting the right kind of data and gathering them in a way that ensures that they are usable. Innovations are, of course, far more useful to those who have copious amounts of raw material to work from. Thomas Newcomen, one of the pioneers of the Industrial Revolution, invented the first steam engine in 1712. He lived in the South West of England working as an ironmonger, and some of his biggest customers were the early tin mines that proliferated across the region. These tin mines had a significant problem with flooding as the mines became progressively deeper and the traditional methods of removing the water using manual pumping or horses were slow and expensive.

Newcomen's new steam engine pumped water using a vacuum and was far more efficient at dealing with flooding in mines, enabling them to reach greater depths than had been previously possible. Yet the steam engine was powered by coal and so was rather more useful to those who had a lot of coal to hand. It was good, but not beneficial enough to warrant buying lots of coal and transporting it to the South West. So rather than the first steam engine being built in a Devon tin mine, it was actually installed at a coal mine at Dudley Castle in Staffordshire.

So it is with data. We need to ensure that we have sufficient quantities of usable, relevant, quality data in order to derive true value. We therefore need to ask whether we are asking the right questions, acquiring data that might be useful in driving business outcomes, and ensuring compliance with necessary regulation.

The first key step in generating value from that data is to organize and structure the data and make them accessible in ways that make sense. Structured data is information, and information is more useful than raw data in its ability to answer basic who, what, where, when questions. This relates to the need to structure systems in ways that mean they can interact with others and share data, and to architect data in ways that can enable us to join them up, interrogate or segment. A 'single customer view', for example, or the ability to attribute behaviour and interaction back to one customer, is foundational to enabling true omnichannel customer experience, which puts the customer at the centre and supports joined-up, seamless journeys and interaction.

After that, we then need to apply meaning to that structured data – to identify patterns, draw conclusions, understand relationships and connections. This enables us to create knowledge, which can answer the how and why questions. Knowledge is more valuable than information since it gives us understanding beyond simple questions and enables us to look for patterns that can inform responses.

At the top of the pyramid, wisdom comes from the smart application of knowledge, relating to our ability to establish processes and feedback loops that can put insight into action, learn over time and improve, and derive advantage through experience, efficiency, and effectiveness, for example through algorithmic personalization, machine learning and automation.

A good data strategy and implementation joins up these levels in seamless ways that can enable real and continuous improvement as well as creative leaps forward. Much of this value will come from the application of machine-driven forms of architecting, optimizing and learning, but at every stage there is human intervention necessary to capitalize on the value that comes from the application of data science, interpretation, creativity and intuition. There is huge benefit in the wider application of data-driven decision-making, for example in enabling responsiveness through real-time data dashboards, but there is also significant advantage that can come from the ability to interpret patterns, to predict, envisage and imagine future scenarios and possibilities and be able to realize them through strategy and action.

Data-driven decision-making is more automatic, mechanical, rules based and more governed by evidence and causality. We identify what the data are telling us and we know what to do in response. Data-informed is more about the human ability to interpret identified patterns in the data and use intuition or creativity to imagine and create different possibilities, outcomes or goals. Human ingenuity, creative intelligence, empathy, originality and resourcefulness might all be used to be data-informed.

But we need both. The businesses that will succeed in the data-rich world in which we live now will be those that combine human and machine capability in the most adept ways.

On being data-informed

Data-driven decision-making suggests more mechanical processes to optimize, improve and execute, and so is more likely to be governed by rules, precedents and guidelines. The much greater level of human intervention involved with data-informed decision-making on the other hand, means that we need to be aware of both the brilliance that humans can bring to solving problems, and the potential flaws and vulnerabilities that this can open us up to.

It's all too easy, for example, for human interpretation to be subject to bias and misdirection and to ignore the importance of intuition and sense making. When the Brodie helmet, designed by John Leopold Brodie in 1915, was introduced to the British army in the First World War it was intended to protect the soldiers from flying shrapnel. Until 1915 soldiers went into battle wearing cloth, felt or leather headgear but it soon became apparent from the huge number of fatal head wounds from modern artillery weapons that something more was needed. After the French army first introduced tin helmets, the British army swiftly followed suit.

Following the introduction of tin helmets, however, when the War Office personnel recorded the number of head injuries per battalion, they were astounded to discover that instead of the total number declining, it had actually gone up by a significant percentage. The intensity of the fighting was no different so they might easily have concluded that tin helmets were no better or were actually worse than cloth caps in protecting the soldiers. But fortunately they realized that what was actually happening was that fewer soldiers were dying on the spot of their head injuries and that more of them were surviving. In other words, the number of recorded head injuries increased but the number of deaths decreased as the helmets did a better job at protecting the troops. It was more likely after helmets were introduced that fragments of shrapnel would cause injury rather than death.

The Brodie helmet represented a masterpiece of simple design and became the inspiration and forerunner of many more modern, technologically advanced combat helmets. By the end of the war, some 7.5 million Brodie helmets had been produced. And yet it might so easily have been dismissed and thousands, perhaps hundreds of thousands, of soldiers might never have survived. Rapid conclusion and action from data without thought and intuition can easily lead to misinterpretation and poor outcomes.

Using data to challenge and to pivot

Smart, agile businesses use evidence-based decision-making combined with human creativity and intuition to create exceptional advantage. But sometimes even data-supported arguments can struggle to overcome entrenched views or approaches.

Freeman Dyson, a renowned British-born theoretical physicist, worked in the Operational Research Section (ORS) of the British Royal Air Force's Bomber Command during the Second World War. The original ORS, a mixture of civil servants and academics, was established to advise the Royal Navy on such critical challenges as verifying the destruction of German U-boats and was led by the highly respected experimental physicist Patrick Blackett who had been a naval officer in the First World War. Blackett's academic standing and naval experience meant that his advice was respected by the admirals and the ORS was extremely effective in its contribution to winning the war against the U-boats in the Atlantic.

Bomber Command was led by the extremely forthright Sir Arthur 'Bomber' Harris. The leader of the ORS attached to Bomber Command was Basil Dickins, a career civil servant, whose influence was less direct meaning that the ORS struggled to really challenge the tactics and strategies being championed by Sir Arthur. There were significant challenges in statistically identifying the reasons why so many British bombers were being lost over Germany during the war. Focus was put on how the planes could fly on missions in order to avoid anti-aircraft fire, interceptions from German night fighters, and collisions with other bombers on the raid. The German night-fighter force was tiny in comparison with Bomber Command and was hardly ever shot down by the guns on the bombers, but unknown to the British they had developed a firing system called Schräge Musik ('crooked music') which enabled them to fly unseen underneath the bombers and fire upwards against a bomber clearly silhouetted against the night sky. It is estimated that this system efficiently shot down thousands of bombers, but it was only discovered too late for Bomber Command to find anything to counter it.

Perhaps many more bombers would have been saved, however, if Freeman Dyson's ideas at Bomber Command ORS had not fallen on deaf ears. The planes and their gunners rarely saw the fighters that shot them down. Dyson had suggested that a clear way to reduce the catastrophic losses that Bomber Command was suffering in the Battle of Berlin was to remove two gun turrets from the RAF Lancaster bombers. This would leave them unable to fire on the enemy but would also mean that the planes would be much lighter, faster and more manoeuvrable. Dyson's work had shown that this would not only make it easier for the Lancasters to evade German fighters, but it would also mean that they were in reach of the fighters for a much shorter amount of time and that each plane could carry five airmen instead of seven. Losses might therefore have been significantly reduced.

Yet as Dyson recounts, the RAF commanders did not like the idea of removing firepower, and his advice ran against prevailing beliefs: 'our proposal to rip out the turrets went against the official mythology of the gallant gunners defending their crewmates. Dickins never had the courage to push the issue seriously in his conversations with Harris. If he had, Harris might even have listened, and thousands of crewmen might have been saved.'[72]

This story demonstrates how challenging it can be, even with the support of statistical evidence, to challenge mythologies, beliefs and convictions that can become widely embedded in businesses. If the prevailing stories and traditions that have grown up with the business are challenged by new evidence, it can be very difficult to change course. In order to be genuinely adaptive and build real momentum for change we have to be more willing to hold strong views lightly. To believe with conviction but be willing to change that belief when data tell us that another course of action is necessary.

Navigating with data

If we are to navigate well with data-driven and data-informed decision-making we need to recognize the potential but also the limitations of both. Key to this is the need to balance optimization and iteration with vision.

Silicon Valley venture capitalist and startup advisor Andrew Chen has described how metrics are typically reflective of a current strategy, position or audience since they are based on existing or past circumstances.[73] For this reason, they may help you to iterate towards what he calls the 'local maximum' – the point at which you may reach the limit of the current design, structure or customer foundation. It's as good as it can get given the existing foundation.

In mathematics, functions can have local maximums which are high points that can be reached within a given range or context, but they can also have global maximums which are the highest points that you can reach over the entire domain or function (Figure 7.16).

Evidence-based decision-making is still hugely under-utilized in most businesses, but there is a limit to the gains that we can derive from optimization and it can be tempting to take this too far, de-prioritizing the bigger picture, the broader aspects of a problem or the potential bigger solution. Data are often systematically biased and require intelligent human intervention to design and interpret systems that not only optimize around existing scenarios but open up new possibilities. The kind of data, for example, that are easiest to collect and interrogate are often not the kind that will show us what's truly possible or where our end-vision could be.

So whilst data-driven decision-making may help us to navigate to local maximums, it is data-informed decision-making that can help us to set a visionary new course towards a new global maximum. In setting that new course, it is likely that we won't have all the data that we might need right now to complete the journey (since it is, after all, new), so we need to break down the work into smaller pieces and use data to help validate hypotheses and navigate towards the realization of that new end-goal.

Not everything is an optimization problem and whilst there is exceptional value to be had in continual incremental improvement, now and then we need to take a leap forwards in our thinking and set a bigger goal or new course, and entirely new parameters for success.

FIGURE 7.16 Local and global maximums

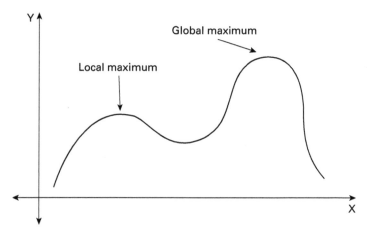

Learning effectively from data

As we've discussed earlier in the book, scaled learning is key to agile transformation. When we take continuous organizational learning to a new level, it is critical that we do this in ways that avoid poor use of data, poor decision-making and the potential limitations or pitfalls in human intervention.

Let's take target setting as an example. Goodhart's Law, named after Charles Goodhart, a chief economic advisor to the Bank of England, states that: 'When a measure becomes a target, it ceases to be a good measure'. It is the principle that once we have set a specific target people will have a tendency to optimize behaviour to that single goal, regardless of whether that is at the expense of other important objectives. Oversimplified target setting can encourage behaviour that might superficially deliver one goal, but not the overarching objective.

Famous examples of Goodhart's Law are the Soviet factories that, when given targets around numbers of nails, manufactured many hundreds of thousands of tiny, useless nails and, when given targets on the basis of weight, produced a few, very large nails. Or the French colonialists in 1902 Hanoi who, when faced with a potential outbreak of bubonic plague, offered payments to anyone who handed in rats' tails. Only to find that whilst the total rat population failed to decline, the numbers of tailless rats in the city ballooned.

Goodhart's Law can mean that in setting targets for complex scenarios we can easily lose sight of any information that qualifies something as a valid measure in the first place, and can result in a misalignment of behaviour through incentives. This means that we are often in danger of pursuing short-term impacts with digital metrics since they can be easier to measure.

Instead, an approach that balances both short-term measures with longer-term impact gives a more rounded view of performance and direction. As Richard Shotton (author of *The Choice Factory: 25 behavioural biases that influence what we buy*) has observed, tracking data is reductive in that it takes a complex, messy reality and converts it into easily manageable numbers but at a potential cost: 'This process involves a trade-off: a loss of representativeness in return for simplicity... Problems arise when the trade-off is forgotten and tracking data is treated with reverence, as if it was the definitive answer rather than mere evidence.'[74]

When we're tracking individual metrics it's all too easy to get caught up in incremental optimization of those metrics and lose sight of the bigger picture. The fetishization of data can mean that we undervalue the benefit that can come from getting out and speaking to real customers. Richard Shotton references the experience of Terry Leahy who, whilst leading marketing at Tesco, was analysing the performance of their gluten-free range of products. The sales data indicated that people who bought these products were not spending much on them each shopping trip and appeared to show that the products were underperforming. Yet rather than just de-list them right away, Leahy interviewed gluten-free shoppers and discovered that their desire to shop in places that had good availability of these products was a determining factor in their choice of supermarket. So rather than stop selling gluten-free products he went the other way and introduced Tesco's 'Free From' range long before the competition and it became highly successful.

In a similar fashion, it is important that we balance our use of more traditional market research, which is often based on claimed behaviour, with our use of analytics and customer data, which may well be based on real behaviour. The former can be subject to misrepresentation and misinterpretation. A large study by data-driven online dating site OKCupid in 2010, for example, found that people on the site almost universally added a couple of inches to their actual height on their OKCupid profiles.[75] People also exaggerated their salaries, resulting in there being almost four times the number of people who said that they were making US $100,000 a year than there should be. Not only that, but when analysing the technical details of profile photos uploaded to the site they found that, whilst most of the pictures were of recent vintage (with a median age of just 92 days), older people tended to upload older photos of themselves.

Combining claimed behaviour with real behaviour can give us a more three-dimensional view of our customers, for example, by defining personas through not only demographics, age, motivations, needs and frustrations but also real behaviour and interaction. Traditional market research may be great at identifying big picture market or customer changes, views or even opportunity but real behaviour offers different value in some crucial respects. When it comes to prototyping, fast customer feedback loops and iterative development, for example, real behaviour trumps claimed behaviour every time.

One of the vulnerabilities around the human interventions involved with learning from data and data-informed decision-making are the cognitive biases that we are all subject to. Earlier in this section we discussed (with the story of the Bomber Command ORS in the Second World War) how hard it can be to overturn powerfully held opinions, even with data that support a different point of view. Confirmation bias, or the tendency that we have to look for information that confirms our pre-existing beliefs or hypotheses, can be a powerful blocker to change, organizational learning and adaptability. Economist John Kay (also the author of *Obliquity: Why our goals are best achieved indirectly*[76]) has written about how in his early career he believed that his work constructing economic arguments and building models for corporate clients was about helping them to make better decisions when in reality it was often about justifying conclusions that had already been arrived at. This he describes as 'Franklin's Gambit' in reference to Benjamin Franklin's approach to decision-making, which is: 'the process of finding a weighty and carefully analysed rationale for a decision that has already been made'.[77]

Whilst there is often an appearance of setting-out objectives, and a process for proper evaluation of evidence and options, the objectives might well be dictated by the conclusions, the options presented in ways that make the preferred course of action look most beneficial, and the data selected to demonstrate the desired result.

Confirmation bias can be particularly powerful when it comes to negative views of change, where people are against a certain course of action and actively look for things that might justify their position or thinking. The best course of action in this context is to build wider support for the course of action using both evidence and the visible support of key people surrounding the detractors. People have a tendency to overrate their own capabilities and intelligence and so find reasons not to believe contradictory opinions. So enabling detractors to undertake their own journey and find their own reasons why the preferred course of action is a good one helps to support real, lasting change.

One of the most important biases to be aware of, particularly when it comes to agile transformation, is survivorship bias – the tendency we all have to prefer to learn from successful instances and examples rather than those that have failed. One of my favourite stories about this phenomenon is another more widely known story from the Second World War involving bomber planes. Abraham Wald, a renowned mathematician and statistician, was asked by the United States Air Force (USAF) in 1943 to be part of a group that was looking at how the US bombers that were flying daytime raids over Germany might be reinforced to prevent the heavy losses that they were suffering at the time. The USAF was proposing to put armour

FIGURE 7.17 Example damage to a Second World War bomber plane

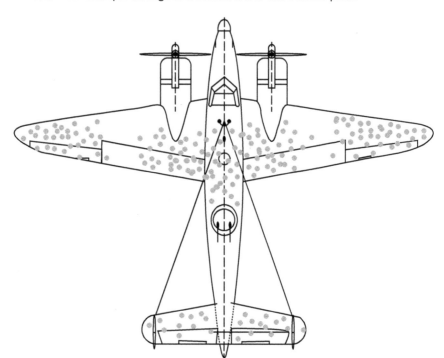

SOURCE Created by McGeddon and available under Attribution-ShareAlike 4.0 International (CC BY-SA 4.0) https://commons.wikimedia.org/wiki/File:Survivorship-bias.png

plating on the planes, but could do this only to a limited degree or the bombers would be too heavy to fly. The research that the military had conducted into damage that planes returning from missions had suffered revealed that bullet holes on the bomber planes often clustered notably around the wings, the centre of the fuselage and around the tail gunner (Figure 7.17). As a result the USAF proposed to reinforce these exact areas where the most damage could be seen.

Wald, however, recognized that this was a big mistake and told the USAF that it should in fact do the opposite. He knew that the bullet hole clusters were actually showing where a plane could be hit and still make it back to base. The organization actually needed to be placed in the areas where the surviving planes looked relatively unscathed, since the planes that were hit in these areas never returned. Wald's resultant calculations about the vulnerability of particular parts of planes no doubt saved many lives and are still used today.

Survivorship bias in business typically shows itself in a greater willingness and enthusiasm to learn from successful initiatives or examples in and outside of the company, and in the undervaluing of the learning we can gain from what has been unsuccessful. This can not only lead to false conclusions but can also reinforce behaviours that avoid risk and potential failure. A great culture of learning in the organization needs to support and encourage learning from both successes and failures.

Avoiding complexity bias

The modern business operates in arenas of heightened complexity which often requires emergent approaches to successfully navigate them. Yet sometimes the answer is right in front of us. Alongside the need to test and learn to solve complex problems, we need to simplify. Complexity bias is a well-recognized cognitive bias which describes the tendency to make things seem more complicated than they really are or to look for solutions that are more complex than they need to be, particularly when we are confused about how to solve a problem. When problems seem difficult our tendency is often to believe that the solution must be complex, even when it may be staring us in the face.

Complexity bias can be compounded by teams or team members who wish to demonstrate how intelligent they are or how hard they have had to work to solve a problem. The practice of organization domains of knowledge can sometimes add unnecessary layers of complexity rather than simplify communication and understanding. Consultants can over-complicate recommendations in order to try and justify higher fees. Product teams can easily build in features which are surplus to customer requirements in the belief that more features will lead to greater customer satisfaction.

One example of this bias in action relates to Australia's most famous observatory, the Parkes radio telescope. The team that ran the observatory were baffled for 17 years by strange radio signals that were appearing on their equipment. It was in 1998 that scientists stationed at the telescope first detected what are known as 'perytons', fleeting bursts of radio signals which were interfering with the main mission that the astronomers had. Another set of fast radio bursts with potentially extragalactic origins had earlier been identified but they had proved elusive. The perytons were getting in the way of the search for the original radio signals but the astronomers couldn't work out where they were coming from. They seemed to originate from a local source but were strangely intermittent and seemed to happen during the day and when the telescope pointed in a certain direction, contradicting the initial theory that the signals were coming from lightning strikes in the atmosphere.

It took the scientists years to finally identify where the curious radio bursts were actually coming from. The source was a microwave oven that was in the break room of the observatory. The telescope was being operated remotely which meant that the astronomers were mainly offsite, but there was a small crew of maintenance staff that stayed on-site. When one of the maintenance crew was heating something up in the microwave oven and opened the door of the appliance (perhaps to check on how their lunch was doing) it emitted signals that were being picked up by the huge radio telescope when it was pointed in the general direction. The answer was right there for the scientists to discover but a natural tendency to look for complicated solutions meant that it took years for anyone to discover where the signals were really coming from – a maintenance worker heating up their ready meal.[78]

The lesson here is for teams to always consider if there may be a simpler explanation for what they may be observing, and to avoid the temptation to look for over-complicated solutions or answers. Getting an outside perspective can be particularly valuable in challenging team assumptions and stripping away unnecessary complexity.

The power of data flow and access

We tend to think of the significant role that data can play in organizational decision-making as a relatively recent phenomenon. Yet the modern enthusiasm for enabling greater autonomy through data-driven decision-making has a fascinating precedent from history.

The first modern organization chart ever created was originated by Daniel McCallum, who in 1854 took charge of running operations at the New York and Erie Railroad. Running operations at the railroad meant overseeing almost 500 miles of track, with the added complexity of trains running on single tracks meaning that a single problem could lead to significant service disruption and even accidents. In the previous couple of decades, the invention of the telegraph had begun to revolutionize long-distance communication but for McCallum it created the unusual problem of a surfeit of near real-time data about mechanical problems, broken equipment, and train delays. With so much data coming in, it was a challenge for him to organize it in a way that could enable greater efficiency and informed

FIGURE 7.18   Organizational diagram of the New York and Erie railroad, 1855

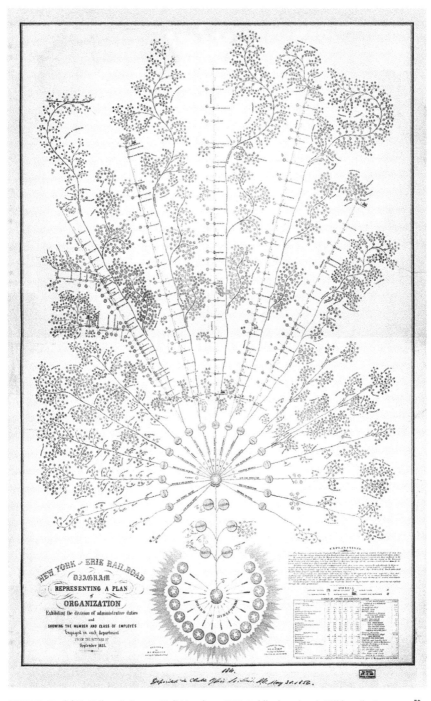

SOURCE Daniel McCallum & George Holt Henshaw, 1855, Public domain, via Wikimedia Commons[79]

decision-making. So McCallum created the world's first organizational chart as a way of showing how decision-making, empowered by operational data, could be distributed more widely through the organization. Rather than the traditional hierarchical pyramid that is so familiar today, the chart was a beautiful design modelled on a tree.

In McCallum's dazzling design the hierarchy was reversed so that the board of directors were at the roots of the tree, the chief officers the trunk and the railroad's divisions and departments the branches. Importantly, the model showed how authority for day-to-day scheduling and operations could be distributed more widely to empower the divisional superintendents who oversaw branches of the railroad and this, as Caitlin Rosenthal from McKinsey notes, was done because *they possessed the best operating data, were closer to the action, and thus were best placed to manage the line's persistent inefficiencies.*[80] The chart helped to empower the people that were closer to the data but also that had the ability to take more localized action to identify and solve problems quicker, leading to a much more efficient system. The role of senior leaders evolved to focus less on directing and more on supporting and guiding. A system of targeted metrics was set up flowing from the branches to the roots of the tree where useful aggregate measures such as cost-per-ton-mile and average load per car could enable informed centralized and more strategic decisions.

There are some strong parallels in McCallum's model with the need for modern, agile businesses to empower more distributed decision-making through access to data and tools. Yet this needs to run alongside an approach to leadership which enables and supports rather than directs and micro-manages. As Rosenthal notes in her piece McCallum gained control by giving up control. The opportunity is to align flows of data in ways that enable greater autonomy for front-line and other staff whilst also giving senior leadership the metrics that can inform oversight and more strategic decisions.

Empowering agile teams through metrics

Data dashboards and deciding which metrics to track can play a critical role in empowering more widely distributed but also informed decision-making through the business. Yet there are some notable pitfalls in defining metrics to track and establishing dashboards to track them which businesses often fall into.

One of the most common mistakes is to measure the wrong thing. Most dashboards, for example, are set up to measure lagging indicators, or what has happened. This may be a way to track progress towards an end goal of some kind but does not provide any real insight into drivers of success. Instead, dashboards and other tracking of metrics should include both lagging *and* leading measures or in other words metrics that relate to not only the outputs (the results of actions) but to inputs (the actions themselves). In an agile environment a team will need to use data and feedback to continually adjust, adapt and occasionally pivot. Including both forms of metrics enables teams to understand progress much better, but also the impact of specific activity in relation to that progress.

As an example of this, metrics at Amazon are divided into two main types: what they call 'controllable input metrics' (leading indicators) and output metrics (lagging indicators). More attention is paid to input metrics, notably ones that are controllable. In their book *Working Backwards: Insights, stories and secrets from inside Amazon.*[81] authors Colin Bryar and Bill Carr detail how Amazon go through a rapid test and learn process to define and adapt metrics until they can find the ones that specifically relate to the inputs which most directly impact the outcome. This process is set out in a method captured in the acronym DMAIC, which stands for Define, Measure, Analyse, Improve, and Control.

- **Define:** this is a process of testing and debating in order to get to the right metrics which are related to the inputs that matter. The Amazon 'flywheel' is a positive reinforcing loop that has remained at the heart of the company's strategy to build momentum and growth. Author Brad Stone in his book *The Everything Store: Jeff Bezos and the age of Amazon*[82] describes the flywheel as: 'Lower prices led to more customer visits. More customers increased the volume of sales and attracted more commission-paying third-party sellers to the site. That allowed Amazon to get more out of fixed costs like the fulfillment centers and the servers needed to run the website. This greater efficiency then enabled it to lower prices further.' This reinforcing loop that Jeff Bezos reportedly once sketched onto a napkin forms the basis of their growth strategy.[83] Feeding any part of this flywheel could accelerate the entire loop. Almost every metric that senior leadership and teams track in the company falls into one of these elements. This creates alignment and a way to coordinate metrics that matter right across the business. Identifying the right metrics involves a process of testing and learning to get to the right set of controllable input metrics which will have the maximum impact on outcomes and growth. Whilst it takes time and resource to arrive at the correct measures, this is clearly worth it since it sets the teams up for success.

- **Measure:** having identified the right measures, this stage is about setting up the systems and tools that will enable the team to closely monitor them in ways that can avoid human bias. This is important to ensure that teams and leaders are not bringing cognitive bias into decision-making with data but also to avoid them selecting and tracking measures that will make the team look good rather than show a true picture of how the business can drive growth. Instrumentation to enable ease of monitoring is required, and teams are encouraged to regularly audit their metrics to ensure that they are still measuring what they should be measuring.

- **Analyse:** having established the right metrics and the best way to monitor them, teams should then understand the essential underlying drivers that sit behind these measures. The objective here should be to reduce variance in the metrics and to understand how the team can best control them. Ultimately the team is aiming for predictability in the relationship between key actions and the measures that they are tracking.

- **Improve:** having created a good understanding of both the right metrics to track to drive growth and the levers which can be pulled to push these measures in the right direction a team is now set up to begin the work of improvement. The objective here is to focus the team effort on the elements that will have maximum impact. Agility is not only about moving fast, but about ensuring that teams are always focused on the highest-value work.

- **Control:** this last stage of the process is there to ensure that teams are controlling metrics efficiently over longer periods of time and that there is no gradual degrading of performance or drift away from the metrics that really drive growth. It may be, for example, that automation of tracking and actions can support greater efficiencies, but this might take a lengthy period of developing a deeper understanding of the relationship between different measures to make this happen. As an example, Amazon's purchasing and forecasting is now completely automated.

Amazon ensures focus by attributing ownership of metrics to individuals who can track them daily and develop a greater comprehension of the patterns and variances that may occur. As Bryar and Carr describe, metrics are brought together and presented at Weekly Business Review meetings

(WBRs) which are a way of joining up metrics and activity across the company. So every department and operational team runs a WBR, and the senior leadership team run one which brings together all the key metrics from across the company into one visually based document. Charts and measures are formatted in familiar ways to ensure consistency and ease of understanding, the meetings focus on variances to make best use of time, and their weekly cadence mean that emerging problems can be tackled immediately.

This process drives alignment, consistency, ownership, continuous improvement, and maximizes the impact of team activity. Whilst output metrics can show results over time, controllable input metrics inform how the team can drive activity which will improve these outputs. It is the combination of these leading and lagging indicators that provides an organization with the information and direction that it needs to drive true agility.

Agile governance

During the shift to more adaptive, agile ways of working, and particularly as agile scales beyond the technology team towards a much broader application across multiple functions, questions often arise around governance and control. Concerns can be raised about alignment, control of costs and direction. People often feel uncomfortable moving away from the apparent comfort of a detailed, forecasted end-point, and leaders shy away from the apparent inherent risks.

The irony of this situation, of course, is that many traditional approaches are built on false certainty anyway. Plans and forecasts become outdated as soon as they're inked. Predicted outcomes quickly become obsolete and in need of updating. Managers spend their time justifying why they've moved away from forecast numbers rather than getting on and doing the work.

Yet *doing* agile does not mean that there is poor quality control involved in the work. *Being* agile is not an excuse for sloppiness. If by governance we essentially mean doing the right things in the right way, then agile, iterative working should actually enable this more than rigid linear thinking and working since it allows you to bring more flexibility to how you can change direction and not go too far down a path that is wasteful or even potentially damaging. Agile governance done right means mitigating risk rather than compounding it. The ability to be more adaptive means that we never get too far before we can switch course; the practice of working closely with end-user input and feedback; continuous testing and delivery.

Jamie Arnold, the Head of Agile Delivery at UK retailing and banking group the Co-op, has highlighted eight key components for how to do governance well in an agile context, which are worth paraphrasing and highlighting in this context:[84]

1 **Outcomes are better than deliverables:** the importance of orienting the team around what the product or service actually does, aligning that with the wider vision, easily measurable mid- or long-term goals, space to learn what works rather than specifying the solution upfront.

2 **Measure the right things at the right time:** measure a few quantitative things, make the measures visible, independently verifiable, review often. The right measures can motivate, focus and build confidence.

3 **Teams are the units of delivery:** small, multidisciplinary, non-hierarchical teams focused on momentum and given enough autonomy to plan, prioritize and do the work in the order that works for them.

4 **Network of teams beats hierarchy:** networks of small, self-directed teams with minimal interdependencies using data to plan and prioritize.

5 **Quality is everyone's responsibility:** common agreement around what quality means, how to measure it, user feedback validating the delivery of business value, continuous quality assurance.

6 **Assure as you go:** improvement is continuous and supported by regular, short, challenging forums, minimal stop–start but instead the flow of value delivery.

7 **Behaviours matter more than documents:** less long-term documentation, more user research logs, weeknotes, verified metrics. Focus on how the team collaborates, responds to feedback, is part of a network of teams, involves stakeholders, removes blockers.

8 **See delivery for yourself:** not just talk, but regularly showing work in progress.

These principles for how to do agile governance well have application beyond just the teams in a business that might be using Agile methodologies. They speak to wider opportunity to follow principles that can ensure a balance that allows for greater adaptation whilst not sacrificing the need for proper quality control, testing and governance.

Supporting self-awareness and trust

It is important that we close this penultimate section by acknowledging again the importance of leadership in supporting agile transformation. Great leadership has always been about great communication, exceptional collaboration skills, and the ability to get the very best out of people and teams, but this has never been more important in this highly changeable age.

It is very difficult to work in effective, fast, cross-disciplinary ways if there are not high levels of trust in the business. Leaders who can create an environment that not only enables people to do their best work, but one that enables people to do their best work as part of a highly functioning team, can add disproportionate value. This requires high levels of self-awareness.

The Johari window[85] is a useful heuristic technique that can help leaders of all kinds to understand how they might improve group dynamics, inter-group relationships and team development but also their own communication, self-awareness and working relationships. Developed by psychologists Joseph Luft and Harrington Ingham in 1955, the window is one of the few tools that focuses on so-called 'soft skills', and it supports better self-awareness of how well we know ourselves, how others perceive us, how we interact with others and how we present ourselves.

The framework is simple but powerful and is based on considering what we know about ourselves and what we don't, and what others might know about us and what they don't.

In Figure 7.19, the four panes of the window look equal, but the idea is that the 'openness' of each panel depends on how well we know ourselves, how much we share about ourselves with others, and how well others know us:

- **Open self or arena** (top left): information about you that both you and others know.

- **Blind self** (top right): information about yourself that you don't know but others do.

- **Hidden self or façade** (bottom left): information about yourself that you know but others don't.

- **Unknown self** (bottom right): information about you that neither you nor others know.

One way of using the Johari window is to have subjects choose from a predefined list of adjectives (which may be possible descriptions of the

FIGURE 7.19 The Johari window

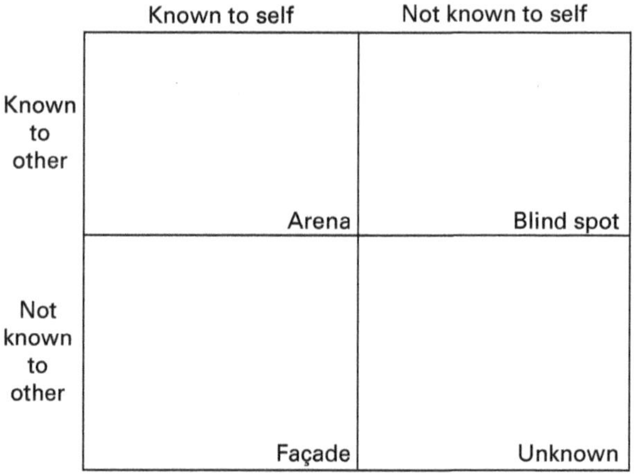

	Known to self	Not known to self
Known to other	Arena	Blind spot
Not known to other	Façade	Unknown

SOURCE Created by Simon Shek and available in the public domain at https://en.wikipedia.org/wiki/File:Johari_Window.PNG

participant) a selection of those which they feel best describe their personality, and then have their peers do the same with an equal number of adjectives.[86]

Positioning the adjectives into the two-by-two grid enables subjects to focus on how they might work towards opening their personal open windowpanes and closing their blind or hidden ones. Someone who has high self-awareness and high trust will have windows that are bigger on the left-hand side. Someone who has low self-awareness and low trust will have windows that are bigger on the right-hand side. As we become more intentional with our self-awareness and as we trust other team members more, the more we expand the open windows. Doing this for each team member enables better communication, improved trust and transparency, openness and honesty, and so increases productive and effective working. These kinds of attributes may seem nice to have but are increasingly critical in enabling teams to move fast and collaborate horizontally in ways that can create disproportionate advantage and performance.

Leading teams through change and uncertainty

Change is always emotive. So leading teams effectively through transformation helps us to appreciate the emotions that might be involved with significant change. The Kübler-Ross Grief Cycle is a relatively well-known way of thinking about the more emotive responses to high levels of change and unpredictability.[87] Although the model was originated in the context of responses to grief, it is useful in supporting an appreciation of the emotional aspects of broader, significant change. The model features five key stages:

1 Our initial response may well be founded in shock and even denial that the change is even happening. The leadership response to this should be founded in clear messaging and signals about the reality of the need to change.

2 We then may react with anger and frustration, which calls for understanding but also communication and information.

3 We may then attempt to find meaning in the change and reach out to others but still struggle initially to understand it fully. Emotional support is key.

4 Some may feel overwhelmed by change, and even slightly lost, in which case coaching and guidance will help.

5 The importance of storytelling, shared experiences, guidance and direction to help people to find their own meaning in the change and eventually to accept and move on.

It is a great way of thinking about the stages of change but, of course, the reality of the transformation that many organizations are undergoing is less of transition from A to B and more of a journey to become a business that in itself is characterized by continuous change. So the point that many miss is that leaders trying to navigate this process will likely find that they need to deal with these reactions from many different sources and all at once.

The real skill in leading through times of high uncertainty is being highly tuned to the emotive context of our surroundings: to have empathy. Sure, we need clear direction, continuous communication, shared learning, accountability, openness and transparency, and a bias towards action, but we also need the emotional intelligence to understand the support that people really need to come on the journey with us.

References

1 Kniberg, Henrik and Ivarsson, Anders [accessed 10 April 2019] Scaling Agile @ Spotify, with Tribes, Squads, Chapters & Guilds [Online] https://blog.crisp. se/wp-content/uploads/2012/11/SpotifyScaling.pdf (archived at https://perma. cc/Q5PT-R2XM)

2   McKinsey and Company [accessed 10 April 2019] ING's Agile Transformation, *McKinsey Quarterly* [Online] https://www.mckinsey.com/industries/financial-services/our-insights/ings-agile-transformation (archived at https://perma.cc/6Q8Q-MM8Z)

3   McKinsey and Company [accessed 10 April 2019] ING's Agile Transformation, *McKinsey Quarterly* [Online] https://www.mckinsey.com/industries/financial-services/our-insights/ings-agile-transformation (archived at https://perma.cc/6Q8Q-MM8Z)

4   McKinsey and Company [accessed 10 April 2019] ING's Agile Transformation, *McKinsey Quarterly* [Online] https://www.mckinsey.com/industries/financial-services/our-insights/ings-agile-transformation (archived at https://perma.cc/6Q8Q-MM8Z)

5   Carroll, L (2015) *Through the Looking-Glass*, Macmillan Children's Books

6   Drucker, Peter F [accessed 30 May 2019] Managing for Business Effectiveness, *Harvard Business Review*, Harvard Business Publishing [Online] https://hbr.org/1963/05/managing-for-business-effectiveness (archived at https://perma.cc/SEA4-3TLC)

7   UK Government [accessed 10 April 2019] Digital Service Standard and Service Manual [Online] https://www.gov.uk/service-manual/service-standard (archived at https://perma.cc/5MGK-AVES) and https://www.gov.uk/service-manual (archived at https://perma.cc/9LTN-78PP)

8   Read, Tom [accessed 10 April 2019] Technology At Least As Good As People Have At Home, *Cabinet Office Technology*, November 2013 [Online] https://cabinetofficetechnology.blog.gov.uk/2013/11/13/technology-at-least-as-good-as-people-have-at-home/ (archived at https://perma.cc/CZ2H-QF3N)

9   UK Government [accessed 10 April 2019] Digital Performance Dashboards [Online] https://www.gov.uk/performance (archived at https://perma.cc/SS8G-RNS8)

10 Spotify Labs [accessed 13 March 2019] Spotify Engineering Culture Part 1 [Online] https://labs.spotify.com/2014/03/27/spotify-engineering-culture-part-1/ (archived at https://perma.cc/8JC8-Q54G)

11 Gallup [accessed 15 April 2019] The Engaged Workplace [Online] https://www.gallup.com/services/190118/engaged-workplace.aspx (archived at https://perma.cc/3QPY-QDG5)

12 Cable, D (2018) *Alive at Work: The neuroscience of helping your people love what they do*, Harvard Business Review Press

13 Gallup [accessed 14 April 2019] The Strengths Revolution [Online] https://news.gallup.com/businessjournal/547/strengths-revolution.aspx (archived at https://perma.cc/SFN4-4DDZ)

14 EatSleepWorkRepeat podcast [accessed 14 April 2019] Alive At Work – Dan Cable [Online] https://play.acast.com/s/eatsleepworkrepeat/aliveatwork-dancable (archived at https://perma.cc/G9ED-55AV)

15 EatSleepWorkRepeat podcast [accessed 14 April 2019] Alive At Work – Dan Cable [Online] https://play.acast.com/s/eatsleepworkrepeat/aliveatwork-dancable (archived at https://perma.cc/G9ED-55AV)

16 Hagel, John and Seely Brown, John [accessed 13 March 2019] Institutional Innovation, *Deloitte Insights* [Online] https://www2.deloitte.com/insights/us/en/topics/innovation/institutional-innovation.html (archived at https://perma.cc/U2HJ-WURZ)

17 Gino, Francesca [accessed 13 March 2019] The Business Case for Curiosity, *Harvard Business Review* [Online] https://hbr.org/2018/09/curiosity#the-business-case-for-curiosity (archived at https://perma.cc/DXY4-XV3H)

18 Harrison, Spencer and Cohen, Jon [accessed 13 March 2019] Curiosity Is Your Super Power, *TEDxLosGatos* [Online] https://www.youtube.com/watch?v=xZJwMYeE9Ak (archived at https://perma.cc/V75K-BAWB)

19 Harrison, Spencer, Pinkus, Erin and Cohen, Jon [accessed 13 March 2019] Research: 83% of Executives Say They Encourage Curiosity. Just 52% of Employees Agree, *Harvard Business Review* [Online] https://hbr.org/2018/09/research-83-of-executives-say-they-encourage-curiosity-just-52-of-employees-agree (archived at https://perma.cc/93XK-UG9F)

20 Berlyne, DE [accessed 13 March 2019] A Theory of Human Curiosity, *British Journal of Psychology*, 45 (3), pp 180–91, First published August 1954, Wiley Online Library [Online] https://onlinelibrary.wiley.com/doi/abs/10.1111/j.2044-8295.1954.tb01243.x (archived at https://perma.cc/85CS-BLZ9)

21 Kidd, Celeste and Hayden, Benjamin [accessed 13 March 2019] The Psychology and Neuroscience of Curiosity, *Neuron*, 88 (3), pp 449–60, ScienceDirect [Online] https://www.sciencedirect.com/science/article/pii/S0896627315007679 (archived at https://perma.cc/ZYX6-AQJ8)

22 Loewenstein, G [accessed 8 August 2019] The psychology of curiosity: A review and reinterpretation, 1994, *Psychological Bulletin*, 116, pp 75–98, [Online] https://psycnet.apa.org/record/1994-41058-00122 (archived at https://perma.cc/D4UR-DE9S)

23 Kang, MJ *et al* (2009) The wick in the candle of learning: epistemic curiosity activates reward circuitry and enhances memory, *Psychological Science*, 20 (8), pp 963–73, Sage Journals

24 Kelly, K (2017) *The Inevitable: Understanding the 12 technological forces that will shape our future*, Penguin Books

25 Elsworthy, Emma [accessed 13 March 2019] Curious Children Ask 73 Questions Each Day – Many of Which Parents Can't Answer, Says Study, *The Independent* [Online] https://www.independent.co.uk/news/uk/home-news/curious-children-questions-parenting-mum-dad-google-answers-inquisitive-argos-toddlers-chad-valley-a8089821.html (archived at https://perma.cc/R85R-RVNB)

26 Chouinard, MM [accessed 13 March 2019] Children's Questions: A mechanism for cognitive development, *NCBI* [Online] https://www.ncbi.nlm. nih.gov/pubmed/17394580 (archived at https://perma.cc/VZ9E-VZNF)

27 Lee, Shih-Mei [accessed 13 March 2019] Curiosity and Experience Design: Developing the desire to know and explore in ways that are sociable, embodied and playful, *Era* [Online] https://www.era.lib.ed.ac.uk/ handle/1842/20977 (archived at https://perma.cc/UC8X-CVV4)

28 Harrison, Spencer, Pinkus, Erin and Cohen, Jon [accessed 13 March 2019] Research: 83% of Executives Say They Encourage Curiosity. Just 52% of Employees Agree, *Harvard Business Review* [Online] https://hbr.org/2018/09/ research-83-of-executives-say-they-encourage-curiosity-just-52-of-employees-agree (archived at https://perma.cc/93XK-UG9F)

29 Parrish, Shane [accessed 13 March 2019] The Feynman Technique: The best way to learn anything, *Farnam Street*, April 2014 [Online] https://fs.blog/2012/04/ feynman-technique/ (archived at https://perma.cc/4RYE-8N5A)

30 Kotsis, Sandra V and Chung, Kevin C [accessed 20 August 2022] Application of See One, Do One, Teach One Concept in Surgical Training, National Library of Medicine, March 2016 [Online] https://www.ncbi.nlm.nih.gov/pmc/ articles/PMC4785880/ (archived at https://perma.cc/W2C9-SD5M)

31 Lombardo, Michael M and Eichinger, Robert W (2000) *Career Architect Development Planner*, 3rd Edition, Lominger Limited

32 Jennings, Charles [accessed 20 August 2022] The 70:20:10 Institute, Integrate Learning into the Workflow [Online] https://702010institute.com/702010-model/ (archived at https://perma.cc/TAP7-YDHS)

33 Jennings, Charles [accessed 20 August 2022] The Four Ways Adults Learn: Learning Technologies 2013 [Online] https://www.youtube.com/ watch?v=Y0ItF1s9O9Y (archived at https://perma.cc/2ESA-ZEW7)

34 NursingAnswers.net [accessed 9 January 2023] Rolfe's reflective model, November 2018 [Online] https://nursinganswers.net/reflective-guides/rolfe-reflective-cycle.php?vref=1 (archived at https://perma.cc/U7KW-JBU6)

35 Carnegie, Andrew [accessed 20 August 2022] The Gospel of Wealth, 1889, The Carnegie Corporation of New York [Online] https://www.carnegie.org/ about/our-history/gospelofwealth/ (archived at https://perma.cc/EHX7-9QUJ)

36 Berkes, Enrico, and Nencka, Peter [accessed 24 August 2022] Knowledge Access: The Effects of Carnegie Libraries on Innovation, December 2021 [Online] https://ssrn.com/abstract=3629299 (archived at https://perma.cc/ SN2E-NS5U)

37 Berkes, Enrico, and Nencka, Peter [accessed 24 August 2022] Knowledge Access: The Effects of Carnegie Libraries on Innovation, December 2021 [Online] https://ssrn.com/abstract=3629299 (archived at https://perma. cc/2K9W-U25D)

38 Hildebrands, John [accessed 10 August 2022] A workplace chatbot might soon be one of your new best friends, Insight, March 2019 [Online] https://workplaceinsight.net/an-office-chatbot-might-soon-be-one-of-your-new-best-friends-in-the-workplace/ (archived at https://perma.cc/JE2J-9Y6Q)

39 Fleming, Molly [accessed 8 August 2022] How Unilever is using AI to 'democratise' upskilling and future-proof its employees, Marketing Week, June 2019 [Online] https://www.marketingweek.com/how-unilever-is-using-ai-to-democratise-upskilling-and-future-proof-its-employees/ (archived at https://perma.cc/EQU2-4GDA)

40 Jarrahi, Mohammad Hossein, Askay, David, Eshraghi, Ali and Smith, Preston [accessed 6 August 2022] Artificial intelligence and knowledge management: A partnership between human and AI, March 2022 [Online] https://www.sciencedirect.com/science/article/pii/S0007681322000222 (archived at https://perma.cc/R9KC-2CP2)

41 Wininger, Shai [accessed 8 August 2022] The Rise of the Autonomous Organisation, December 2017 [Online] https://www.lemonade.com/blog/rise-autonomous-organization/ (archived at https://perma.cc/CQX2-2UW4)

42 Hsieh, Nelson [accessed 4 August 2022] Lemonade's Project Watchtower: Protecting customers from fires and storms, Volt Equity, March 2021 [Online] https://www.voltequity.com/post/lemonades-project-watchtower-protecting-customers-from-fires-storms (archived at https://perma.cc/3C4C-WLSX)

43 DaveLee on Investing [accessed 6 August 2022] Lemonade CEO Daniel Schreiber: How we're reinventing insurance (CEO Interview, Ep 188) [Online] https://www.youtube.com/watch?v=5l8lfCFRf04 (archived at https://perma.cc/55FY-BDX3)

44 Wenger-Trayner, E and B [accessed 5 August 2022] Introduction to Communities of Practice [Online] https://wenger-trayner.com/introduction-to-communities-of-practice/ (archived at https://perma.cc/G62K-YUVG)

45 Lesser, E L and Storck, J [accessed 6 August 2022] Communities of Practice and Organisational Performance [Online] https://web.archive.org/web/20110409160937/http://www.providersedge.com/docs/km_articles/CoP_and_Organizational_Performance.pdf (archived at https://perma.cc/8P5T-BW7D)

46 Brown, John Seely and Duguid, Paul [accessed 6 August 2022] Balancing act: How to capture knowledge without killing it, *HBR*, 2000 [Online] http://lymabe.edublogs.org/files/2007/04/balancing-act.doc (archived at https://perma.cc/FZJ3-FNA6)

47 Arup's Quarterly Review of Innovation [accessed 6 August 2022] Design and Ideas [Online] https://www.arup.com/-/media/arup/files/publications/a/4issue13final.pdf (archived at https://perma.cc/TS2S-V5QW)

48   Trickett, Andrew [accessed 5 August 2022] Skills Networks – We All Need a COP Sometimes, January 2021, LinkedIn [Online] https://www.linkedin.com/pulse/skills-networks-we-all-need-cop-sometimes-andrew-trickett/ (archived at https://perma.cc/VY9Q-ZUM8)

49   Webber, Emily [accessed 15 August 2022] Building Successful Communities of Practice [Online] https://hellotacit.com/building-successful-communities-of-practice/ (archived at https://perma.cc/A3AT-ABJZ)

50   Webber, Emily [accessed 15 August 2022] Building Successful Communities of Practice [Online] https://hellotacit.com/building-successful-communities-of-practice/ (archived at https://perma.cc/FX8B-FJHX)

51   Webber, Emily [accessed 15 August 2022] Building Successful Communities of Practice [Online] https://hellotacit.com/building-successful-communities-of-practice/ (archived at https://perma.cc/V8KM-US72)

52   Amabile, T (2011) *The Progress Principle: Using small wins to ignite joy, engagement, and creativity at work*, Harvard Business Review Press [accessed 9 March 2019] [Online] http://progressprinciple.com/books/single/the_progress_principle (archived at https://perma.cc/M874-AT9N)

53   Amabile, Theresa [accessed 9 March 2019] The Power of Small Wins, *Harvard Business Review*, May 2011 [Online] https://hbr.org/2011/05/the-power-of-small-wins (archived at https://perma.cc/2QA7-CN3B)

54   Amabile, Theresa [accessed 9 March 2019] The Power of Small Wins, *Harvard Business Review*, May 2011 [Online] https://hbr.org/2011/05/the-power-of-small-wins (archived at https://perma.cc/2QA7-CN3B)

55   Grant, A (2013) *Give and Take: Why helping others drives our success*, Viking [accessed 9 March 2019] [Online] https://www.adamgrant.net/give-and-take (archived at https://perma.cc/2Y88-D755)

56   Clifford, Catherine [accessed 9 March 2019] Adam Grant: Resilience Is the Secret to Success. Here Are 2 Ways to Improve Yours, *CNBC Make It* [Online] https://www.cnbc.com/2017/06/06/adam-grant-how-to-improve-resilience.html (archived at https://perma.cc/2CLA-EN22)

57   Chapman, Alice [accessed 26 August 2022] Situational Leadership [Online] https://myddelton.substack.com/p/16-situational-leadership-three-adverts (archived at https://perma.cc/N5RC-5U5W)

58   Koning, Peter (2019) *Agile Leadership Toolkit: Learning to thrive with self-managing teams*, Pearson

59   OSS/CIA [accessed 30 March 2019] Simple Sabotage Field Manual, 1944 [Online] https://www.cia.gov/news-information/featured-story-archive/2012-featured-story-archive/CleanedUOSSSimpleSabotage_sm.pdf (archived at https://perma.cc/LB6J-G8DG)

60   OSS/CIA [accessed 30 March 2019] Simple Sabotage Field Manual, 1944 [Online] https://www.cia.gov/news-information/featured-story-archive/2012-featured-story-archive/CleanedUOSSSimpleSabotage_sm.pdf (archived at https://perma.cc/LB6J-G8DG)

61 Kalil, Thomas [accessed 10 March 2019] Policy Entrepreneurship at the White House: Getting Things Done in Large Organizations, *MIT Press Journals* [Online] https://www.mitpressjournals.org/doi/pdf/10.1162/inov_a_00253 (archived at https://perma.cc/KMM2-9UDP)

62 Kalil, Thomas [accessed 10 March 2019] Policy Entrepreneurship at the White House: Getting Things Done in Large Organizations, *MIT Press Journals* [Online] https://www.mitpressjournals.org/doi/pdf/10.1162/inov_a_00253 (archived at https://perma.cc/KMM2-9UDP)

63 Crozier, Ry [accessed 19 March 2019] ANZ Reveals the Good and Bad of its Agile Transformation, *IT News* [Online] https://www.itnews.com.au/news/anz-reveals-the-good-and-bad-of-its-agile-transformation-523277 (archived at https://perma.cc/LYG3-8SNS)

64 Thomas, David [accessed 19 March 2019] Let's Fund Teams Not Projects, *Defra Digital Blog* [Online] https://defradigital.blog.gov.uk/2017/09/19/lets-fund-teams-not-projects/ (archived at https://perma.cc/FPQ5-AGD3)

65 Salary.com [accessed 17 February 2019] Why & How Your Employees are Wasting Time at Work [Online] https://www.salary.com/articles/why-how-your-employees-are-wasting-time-at-work/ (archived at https://perma.cc/KE4D-T3UX)

66 Doodle [accessed 17 February 2019] State of Meetings Report 2019 [Online] https://meeting-report.com/ (archived at https://perma.cc/BXD9-WT4C)

67 Rogelberg, S (2019) *The Surprising Science of Meetings: How you can lead your team to peak performance*, Oxford University Press

68 Bluedorn, Allen C, Turban, Daniel B and Love, Mary Sue [accessed 15 February 2019] The Effects of Stand-Up and Sit-Down Meeting Formats on Meeting Outcomes, *Journal of Applied Psychology*, **84** (2), pp 277–85, University of Missouri [Online] https://business.missouri.edu/sites/default/files/bluedorn_turban_love_1999_jap.pdf (archived at https://perma.cc/79WM-3QSV)

69 Davies, Russell [accessed 18 February 2019] Four Things About Creative Productivity, *Marketing Society* [Online] https://www.marketingsociety.com/the-gym/four-things-about-creative-productivity#pYTQxzVlVhbyBoCV.97 (archived at https://perma.cc/3WJP-W7CR)

70 Palmer, Michael [accessed 5 January 2019] Data is the New Oil, *ANA Marketing Maestros* [Online] http://ana.blogs.com/maestros/2006/11/data_is_the_new.html (archived at https://perma.cc/8MNT-HJFK)

71 Rowley, Jennifer [accessed 6 January 2019] The Wisdom Hierarchy: Representations of the DIKW Hierarchy, *Journal of Information Science* [Online] https://journals.sagepub.com/doi/abs/10.1177/0165551506070706 (archived at https://perma.cc/7Z3F-J48Z)

72 Dyson, Freeman [accessed 5 January 2019] A Failure of Intelligence, *MIT Technology Review* [Online] https://www.technologyreview.com/s/406789/a-failure-of-intelligence/ (archived at https://perma.cc/EEQ2-SUR8)

73 Chen, Andrew [accessed 2 January 2019] Know the Difference Between Data-Driven and Versus Data-Informed, *@andrewchen* [Online] https://andrewchen.co/know-the-difference-between-data-informed-and-versus-data-driven/ (archived at https://perma.cc/EHX4-WA8M)

74 Shotton, R (2018) *The Choice Factory: 25 behavioural biases that influence what we buy*, Harriman House [accessed 2 February 2019] [Online] https://www.harriman-house.com/choicefactory (archived at https://perma.cc/MN56-7CBJ)

75 OkCupid [accessed 2 February 2019] The Big Lies People Tell in Online Dating [Online] https://theblog.okcupid.com/the-big-lies-people-tell-in-online-dating-a9e3990d6ae2 (archived at https://perma.cc/Z93R-3RVF)

76 Kay, J (2011) *Obliquity: Why our goals are best achieved indirectly*, Profile Books

77 Kay, John [accessed 28 March 2019] Beware of Franklin's Gambit in Making Decisions, *Financial Times* [Online] https://www.ft.com/content/f442a1cc-87e0-11e1-b1ea-00144feab49a (archived at https://perma.cc/HPE5-3W9K)

78 Tan, Monica [accessed 28 August 2022] Microwave oven to blame for mystery signal that left astronomers stumped, *The Guardian*, May 2015 [Online] https://www.theguardian.com/science/2015/may/05/microwave-oven-caused-mystery-signal-plaguing-radio-telescope-for-17-years (archived at https://perma.cc/2Z2T-7XJE)

79 McCallum, Daniel and Henshaw, George Holt [accessed 15 August 2022] 1855, Wikimedia Commons [Online] https://commons.wikimedia.org/wiki/File:Organizational_diagram_of_the_New_York_and_Erie_Railroad,_1855.jpg (archived at https://perma.cc/JRL7-VVQS)

80 Rosenthal, Caitlin [accessed 16 August 2022] Big Data in the Age of the Telegraph, *McKinsey Quarterly*, March 2013 [Online] https://www.mckinsey.com/capabilities/people-and-organizational-performance/our-insights/big-data-in-the-age-of-the-telegraph (archived at https://perma.cc/6REB-AUEW)

81 Bryar, Colin and Carr, Bill (2021) *Working Backwards: Insights, stories and secrets from inside Amazon*, Macmillan 2021

82 Stone, Brad (2014) *The Everything Store: Jeff Bezos and the age of Amazon*, Corgi, ISBN-10:0552167835

83 About Amazon [accessed 24 August 2022] [Online] https://www.amazon.jobs/en-gb/landing_pages/about-amazon (archived at https://perma.cc/FW3L-M32K)

84 Arnold, Jamie [accessed 28 March 2019] Building What's Useful: Governance and Agile Delivery, *Co-op Digital Blog* [Online] https://digitalblog.coop.co.uk/2017/02/08/building-whats-useful-governance-and-agile-delivery/ (archived at https://perma.cc/4FYG-KNPT)

85 Luft, J and Ingham, H (1955) The Johari window, a graphic model of interpersonal awareness, Proceedings of the western training laboratory in group development, University of California, Los Angeles

86 Kevan.org [accessed 10 March 2019] Johari Window [Online] https://kevan. org/johari (archived at https://perma.cc/BW2D-JWFK)

87 Gregory, Christina [accessed 10 March 2019] The Five Stages of Grief, *Psycom* [Online] https://www.psycom.net/depression.central.grief.html (archived at https://perma.cc/5C62-G3QT)

08

Reinventing the organization

Designing your new agile operating system

This book has set out why we need a new type of organization for a new age, and an approach to transforming businesses to become fit for purpose for both the present and the future. Agile transformation is not a journey from A to B. We don't reach a point when we can sit back and say we are now fully transformed and congratulate ourselves on a job well done. Instead, it is the transition to a different type of company that in itself is characterized by continuous change.

Agile transformation is never a strictly linear process, but the critical stages and tasks can be distilled into an effective model for change that follows the organizing principle of 'think big, start small, scale fast'.

Think big

Recognizing the need and context for change; developing the compelling vision that can set the direction; investing in fundamental technology, people and culture enablers that can establish the foundation to enable change to happen.

CRITICAL TASKS

Vision and urgency: expressing why the world has changed, and why that creates an existential challenge for an organization that doesn't change; creating a positive sense of urgency through visualizing the potential and bringing it to life with effective storytelling; communicating the vision repeatedly through words and action.

Foundational enablers: developing a technology and data architecture that enables agility, data-driven and informed decision-making, and experimentation; identifying and investing in core systems infrastructure that is flexible but scalable; proficient and efficient application of automation and machine learning to augment human capability; awareness of the critical barriers to change; empowering high-velocity decision-making and a culture and leadership mindset to support agile approaches; scaled learning about agile principles and their appropriate application; supporting an environment and expectation that is not afraid to challenge convention; enabling velocity through an adept balance of alignment and autonomy; establishing governance and a vision to create the space for change.

Context mapping: understanding where your organization is on the S-curve and the positioning from which to drive directional change; developing situational awareness and effective problem exploration; understanding the different contexts/problem environments across the business, and where to DO Agile and where to BE agile.

ESSENTIAL CONSIDERATIONS

- Does your organization have a point of view on the future? Does it have a strong, directional and well-understood vision? Do employees understand the need for change, and are they excited about future potential?

- Does the leadership team and organization have good situational awareness that can inform a roadmap for achieving the vision?

- Do you have the right technology and data infrastructure to support genuine agility, and the right approach to future-proof through adaptation?

- How can the organization think beyond incremental change and avoid looking at the new through the lens of the old? Are you thinking boldly enough?

- Is there a broad understanding of the potential of applying agile principles proficiently and at scale?

Start small

Taking a focused approach to developing new ways of working and new value creation; piloting new approaches and learning rapidly in order to create informed scalability.

Focus: selecting the critical challenges, initiatives or areas in which to develop new ways of working; aligning small, multidisciplinary teams or Squads as the engines of change to catalyse new approaches; creating and socializing early quick wins to signal the potential of the new.

Setting up the teams for success: creating the environment and space to enable the teams to thrive; taking steps to mitigate process and culture tensions between new and old ways of working; populating the teams with people rich in the right skills and attitudes; support with training and coaching.

Mindset: avoiding drift and the suffocation of new approaches by developing broader understanding to key mindset shifts involved in starting small; creating the right learning mindset to enable informed rapid scaling.

ESSENTIAL CONSIDERATIONS

- How can the initiatives selected signal intent whilst iterating around key areas of change?
- How can the leadership of the organization generate enough space to enable the new to survive whilst still keeping strong connection back to the rest of the business?
- Are you defining the key problems to solve in the right way?
- Are you genuinely allowing a new culture to emerge and evolve around agility and manoeuvrability?

Scale fast

Building on early successes; creating genuine momentum for transformation through adaptive change and bringing our people on the journey with us; scaling agile teams; rapidly expanding the understanding of new ways of working; learning fast at scale to enable a truly ambidextrous organization.

CRITICAL TASKS

Building momentum for scaled change: enabling rapid growth in new approaches through standards, spend controls, and linking strategy to execution; enabling speed through high-velocity decision-making and the right balance between alignment and autonomy.

Scaling agile structures: growing the number of agile teams, creating a genuinely ambidextrous business; understanding the key stages of growth.

Adaptive change: rapid learning at scale; continuous assessment and reprioritization; continuous experimentation and innovation; navigating effectively with data; data-driven and data-informed; avoiding key pitfalls and bias; agile governance.

Embedding the new: a growth leadership mindset that enables a culture of collaboration and learning; focus on behaviours that support agility.

ESSENTIAL CONSIDERATIONS

- How can you establish controls and standards that set clear expectation without suffocating different thinking and innovation?
- What are the ways in which the wider leadership team can adopt a mindset that supports agility and change?
- What are the new expectations of leaders?
- How can the organization effectively flex the balance between the hierarchical and networked elements?
- How can the business ensure a tight connection is never lost between these two components and that they are complementary, not antagonistic?
- What is the best approach to moving staff between the different elements in the business?
- How can you build a network of advocates to champion new approaches?
- Are you ensuring a tight connection between business strategy/objectives and customer needs/problems?
- Does the business value curiosity in its employees? Does it enable the space for a continual inflow of fresh perspectives?

What now?

Just start.

INDEX

Page numbers in *italic* indicate figures or tables